CW01021463

# MARTIAL'S ROME

This provocative book is a major contribution to our understanding of Martial's poetics, his vision of the relationship between art and reality, and his role in formulating modern perceptions of Rome. The study shows how, on every scale from the microscopic to the cosmic, Martial displays epigram's ambition to enact the sociality of urban life, but also to make Rome rise out of epigram's architecture and gestures. Martial's distinctive aesthetic, grounded in paradox and inconsistency, ensures that the humblest, most throwaway poetic form is best poised to capture first-century empire in all its dazzling complexity. As well as investigating many of Martial's central themes – monumentality, economics, death, carnival, exile – this book also questions what kind of a mascot Martial is for classics today in our own advanced, multicultural world. It will be an invaluable guide for scholars and students of classical literature and Roman history.

VICTORIA RIMELL is Associate Professor of Latin Literature in the Department of Greek and Latin Philology, Sapienza, University of Rome.

# MARTIAL'S ROME

*Empire and the Ideology of Epigram*

VICTORIA RIMELL

CAMBRIDGE
UNIVERSITY PRESS

# CAMBRIDGE
## UNIVERSITY PRESS

University Printing House, Cambridge CB2 8BS, United Kingdom

Published in the United States of America by Cambridge University Press, New York

Cambridge University Press is part of the University of Cambridge.

It furthers the University's mission by disseminating knowledge in the pursuit of education, learning and research at the highest international levels of excellence.

www.cambridge.org
Information on this title: www.cambridge.org/9780521828222

© Victoria Rimell 2008

This publication is in copyright. Subject to statutory exception and to the provisions of relevant collective licensing agreements, no reproduction of any part may take place without the written permission of Cambridge University Press.

First published 2008

*A catalogue record for this publication is available from the British Library*

*Library of Congress Cataloguing in Publication data*
Rimell, Victoria.
Martial's Rome : empire and the ideology of epigram / Victoria Rimell.
p.   cm.
Includes bibliographical references and index.
ISBN 978-0-521-82822-2 (hardback)
1. Martial. Epigrammata.   2. Epigrams, Latin – History and criticism.   3. Rome – In literature.
I. Title.
PA6507.R56   2009
878'.0102 – dc22      2008033471

ISBN 978-0-521-82822-2 Hardback

Cambridge University Press has no responsibility for the persistence or accuracy of URLs for external or third-party internet websites referred to in this publication, and does not guarantee that any content on such websites is, or will remain, accurate or appropriate.

*For Lottie and Emily*

Flentibus Heliadum ramis dum vipera repit
    fluxit in opstantem sucina gemma feram:
quae dum miratur pingui se rore teneri,
    concreto riguit vincta repente gelu.
ne tibi regali placeas, Cleopatra, sepulchro,
    vipera si tumulo nobiliore iacet

*Ep.* 4.59

# Contents

# *Acknowledgements*

I am enormously indebted to John Henderson, Philip Hardie, Kirk Freudenberg and the several anonymous readers at the Press who pointed me down the right roads and gave such helpful and generous criticism. I would like to thank Alessandro Schiesaro for all the love, encouragement, advice and inimitable multitasking that allowed this *liber* to grow and made its future *domus*. And I could not have done without Jill Rimell and Marisa Scorcucchi, who gave me all those jewels of time and showed me how each moment counts.

# Getting to know Martial

*tu causa es, lector amice, mihi,*
*qui legis et tota cantas mea carmina Roma.*[1]
*Ep.* 5.16.2–3

Think back. It's the mid-nineties. We are on the brink of a new century, and are living and breathing the 'New Age' people have been preaching about since the eighties. Thanks to more efficient communication, and the regularising machine of empire, the world seems to have got smaller, and more and more provincials are gravitating towards the sprawling, crowded metropolis, all manically networking to win the same few jobs (they all want to be 'socialites', or 'artists'). Many of us are richer and more mobile than ever, but arguably have less freedom. Modern life is a struggle, it seems – it's dog eat dog in the urban jungle, and those who can't keep up the pace soon become victims (actually, being a 'victim' is the in thing). 'Reality' is the hottest show in town: we're done with drama and fantasy, as amateur theatrics and seeing people actually suffer is such a blast (as well as being a really 'ironic' creative experiment). This is a culture that has long realised Warhol's prophecy, where everyone wants their bite of the fame cherry, but where fame itself is a dirty shadow of what it used to be.[2] The young recall nothing but peace, yet fierce wars still bristle at the world's edges, and even as the concrete keeps rising, a smog of instability and malaise lingers.

A cynical, middle-class sketch of 1990s Manhattan or London, or a summary of Martial's Rome at the peak of his career under Domitian? While in real terms, Flavian Rome may have little in common with the capitals of the most recent Western empire, it's also true that the vision of

---

[1] I have used Lindsay's Oxford Classical Text of Martial throughout. All translations to follow are my own.
[2] American artist Andy Warhol famously predicted in 1968 that in the future everyone would be world-famous for fifteen minutes.

high urbanity that we find in Martial's *Epigrams* looks more 'contemporary' than ever. Martial's wicked commentary on literary fame, for example, the major obsession of Augustan success-stories like Vergil and Horace, is a fascinating one in a world where identikit pop-idols reach their sell-by dates in months and celeb-rags vie to dethrone and replace yesterday's heroes with today's. His ultra-commodified culture, where even poetry is reduced to *thing*, where books mean profits, writers must cater to Attention Deficit Disorder, and where the city appears as a live web of ideas and interactions, can feel very familiar to an on-line, iPod generation – the children of an urbanised, post-modern West.

Romanisation can find its parallels in globalisation, and at the beginning of the third millennium we are as obsessed as Martial is about conceptualising urban space and empire as (evolving) ideas. So too, in an intellectual climate in which rubbish can be high art, and soap operas are studied alongside Shakespeare, we are almost bound to warm to the wry, populist cheek of Martial's project, which sets up throwaway, bargain-basement epigram as the new (alternative to) epic. And just as the boom in Ovidian criticism in the 1980s and 1990s coincided, not entirely by accident, with the popular digesting of post-structuralist and post-modernist thought in the humanities, so Martial seems to suit an academe grappling with what comes *after* the post-modern. For (if we simplify things for a second), Martial sells himself not just as a virtuoso post-Ovidian trickster, but as an anti-Ovid looking back on a past era, giving us the real, the succinct, the deadpan, where Ovid offered illusion, make-believe and luscious description. This is poetry about *getting real*, even though it often presents 'the real' as more fantastic than your wildest dreams.

So is Martial, as Fitzgerald puts it, 'a poet of our time'[3] – a time defined by the soundbite, the headline, the paparazzi shot, by surfing, browsing, shuffling and fast food? Well yes, for sure. It's certainly curious that it is now, in the first decade of the third millennium, that Martial is again being rehabilitated – bearing in mind that he had already almost single-handedly defined epigram for the Western tradition. By the second century AD, the emperor Hadrian's adoptive son Aelius Verus was calling him his 'Vergil'; the persistence of epigram-writing in the Middle Ages and Renaissance was largely due to him, and he reached dizzying heights of fame between the sixteenth and nineteenth century in Europe, imitated by a long list of important poets and wits, including Donne, Ben Jonson, Pope and

---

[3] Fitzgerald (2007) 1.

Goethe. *Ep.* 10.47, for example, his poem on friendship and the Happy Life, is 'perhaps the most frequently translated poem in English literature'.[4] But after a long period of relative obscurity[5] (he is probably the last of the post-Augustan poets to remain 'trash'), the last few years have seen a rush of new commentaries, translations, books and articles.[6] As scholars (a bit like Martial himself) move to grab the few remaining undervalued genres and authors for themselves, branding Martial as seductively 'modern' is a predictable move, reflecting a more general pressure on Classics to pronounce its relevance, to be more about sex, gladiators and Russell Crowe than dusty books, 'dead' languages and philological queries.[7]

Yet it is not just this that leads us to draw comparisons between Martial's world and our own. The question 'why Martial *now*?' is one I have found myself asking throughout the writing of this book, in part because the *Epigrams* demand we recognise how historically specific and how personal our perspectives on the world (always, *our* world) really are. Of all classical authors, Martial makes us most aware of what kind of readers we are, or want to be. What's more, he stresses that *we* are the ones that make this poetry – it lives on in us, and changes shape according to our moods and preferences: 'if anything is not to your taste, just pass it by', he reassures us at the beginning of the *Xenia*, for example, his pick-and-mix collection for the Saturnalia, and instructions at the start of Book 10 read: 'Make me as short for yourself as you like.' In fantasising about what different kinds of consumers want and experience, Martial actively invites intimacy, imagining well-thumbed codex copies of his books held in avid hands, and developing the kind of love affair or (often) love–hate relationship with his audience that Roman elegists enjoyed with their favourite mistresses. (Incidentally, this might be the *only* romance you find in Martial.) He writes for our pleasure: 'you're my inspiration, *lector amice*,' he flutters at poem 16 of Book 5, a naughtily chaste book dedicated to housewives, boys and virgins, 'you who read and sing my verses all over Rome'. If it wasn't for us, the easily bored, sophisticated but tabloid-hungry masses, he'd be a

---

[4] Sullivan and Boyle (1996) xvii.

[5] Despite this, a few poets have continued to translate and get inspiration from Martial throughout the twentieth century. See e.g. the work of Tony Harrison and Fiona Pitt-Kethley collected in Sullivan and Boyle (1996).

[6] Most recently, for example, Lorenz (2002), Galán Vioque (2002), Hennig (2003), C. Williams (2004), K. Coleman (2006), Fitzgerald (2007), Hinds (2007).

[7] Although critics still feel the need to apologise for how 'boring' and 'repetitive' Martial looks: see e.g. Watson and Watson (2003) 20 ('it must be said that there is a good deal of justice in the poet's assessment of his work as uneven in quality. Many of M.'s epigrams will strike the reader as feeble, forced, frigid, or downright tedious'); cf. Fitzgerald (2007) 1.

serious bard making a decent living. But one has to suffer for love (*amor*, 5.16.4). The Flavian metropolis, his darling *mea Roma*, adores its favourite poet. As he tells us at 6.60, 'I am in every pocket, every hand.' And for every fan that *laudat, amat, cantat* ('praises, loves, sings') these epigrams, there is one who blushes, turns pale, yawns, is stunned, or just disgusted. Much to Martial's delight (6.60.3–4).

Like one of his first-century groupies, I've often carried Martial around today's Rome, which thanks to Domitian is mostly a Flavian, not an Augustan, capital. You feel you can see, hear and smell the city in Martial – he is, and has been, brilliant fodder for all those 'everyday life' books about ancient Rome, helping us imagine what really went on in dark taverns, in brothels, baths, theatres and public lavs, among prostitutes and pickpockets, lawyers and gladiators, undertakers, artists and cooks. But more than that, to read Martial is to plunge into a new world, the fractured, tightly sprung and metamorphic universe of epigram. After a while (and his surviving corpus is huge, bigger than it first appears), his ongoing, mock-affectionate dialogue with readers seems almost to become a metaphor for just how much epigram's Weltanschauung *gets to you*. For one thing, at a time when classics like Vergil's *Aeneid* and Horace's *Odes* have become school texts and are on sale in multiple copies in Rome's many bookshops, the *Epigrams* sum up and rework what seems like the whole of ancient literary history, especially Augustan poetry. So much so that when you get into Martial's cosmos, Latin literature will never be the same again. And you'll both love and hate him (back) for it.

## SUMMING UP MARTIAL

'Realist' Martial fixates on facts and figures, so that when critics size him up, they're almost bound to do so on his terms. Later in this book (chapter 3) I'll be showing just how much this poet counts on (us) counting, but for the moment, here are the basics:

Marcus Valerius Martialis was born in the Spanish hill-town of Bilbilis in northern Aragon[8] between AD 38 and 41. He is only one of a handful of well-known Roman authors who were Spanish in origin – including Seneca the Younger, his nephew Lucan, Quintilian and Columella, the first-century writer on agriculture. As a young man, Martial followed the

---

[8] About four kilometres north-east of the modern Calatayud, an area now known as El cerro de Bámbola on the River Jalón in Aragon. The population of the Roman *municipium*, known officially as Augusta Bilbilis, has been estimated at 50,000.

usual path of the son of well-to-do parents, and headed for the capital in 64 to complete his education: he was quickly taken under the wing of the most conspicuous Spanish family in Rome, that of Seneca. We don't know much about his early writing, but it's clear he had already established a reputation when he published the first anthology of poems we have, the *Liber de Spectaculis*, written (most think) to inaugurate Titus' games in the amazing new Colosseum in AD 80.[9] His surviving oeuvre includes over 1,500 epigrams, adding up to around 10,000 verses (the poems vary quite a lot in length, from a single couplet or even a single verse to thirty or forty lines). Although the *Xenia* ('guest gifts') and *Apophoreta* ('take-aways') are now numbered Books 13 and 14, they were published first, between 81 and 86. Martial himself numbered the collections that followed, Books 1–12, and turned out roughly one book per year from AD 86 onwards. As we hear at the end of Book 10 (which, as we have it, is presented as a second edition after the death and *damnatio memoriae* of Domitian), he retired to Spain in 98, and died at Bilbilis around AD 104.

The main body of work, then, is made up of the twelve numbered books which are each around 100 epigrams long, written with a few exceptions in three metres – the elegiac couplet, the Phalaecean hendecasyllable, and the scazon, or limping iambic. The *Xenia* and *Apophoreta* have 127 and 223 poems respectively, all of which are single elegiac couplets, while the *De Spectaculis* survives in a mutilated and probably much truncated form: only 35 or 36 poems are left, again all written in elegiacs. Each collection has its own distinct character which is made more or less explicit in opening poems or prose prefaces (beginning Books 1, 2, 8, 9 and 12), and most books also end with obviously closural pieces which give a sense of overall structure. For example, Book 1 is presented as a theatrical show for the kind of audience that enjoys the *Ludi Florales,* the annual spring games which included obscene mimes; Book 11's 'theme' is the new liberty to be enjoyed under Nerva – the setting is the Saturnalia, the December carnival which is also the stage for books 4, 5, 7, 13 and 14, as I discuss in chapter 5; Book 12 (after Book 3, written from Gaul) is (half-)Spanish, exploring what it is for urbano-centric epigram to extend its reach and view the city from a distance, as I investigate in chapter 6; Book 8, addressed directly to Domitian, is uncharacteristically restrained (Martial reassures the emperor: 'I have not allowed these epigrams to talk as wantonly as usual', Pref. 13–14), while Book 3 is split into two, the first 68 poems

---

[9] On the notion that the book may have been written for Domitian, see K. Coleman (2006).

designed to please the chaste *matrona*, and the remaining 32 letting loose
to cater for randy young men and 'easy' girls (69.3–5). Within the depths
of each long-short book, as I discuss throughout but especially in chapter 1,
what is traditionally described as Martial's exemplary display of two basic
principles of poetic arrangement – *variatio* ('variation') and juxtaposition –
is immensely colourful and intricate. In terms of subject matter, we might,
within the space of a few codex pages, move from philosophies on life and
death and reflections on what it is to be a poor client-poet in Rome, to
poems about money, physical deformities, adultery, plagiarism, friendship,
real estate, retirement, murder, architectural wonders, military victories,
gardening or travel.

   Thanks to Martial, 'epigram', for us, means a short, usually satirical poem
with a punchy ending. Yet although famous Hellenistic epigrammatists
(among them Asclepiades, Posidippus and Callimachus) used the term
*epigramma* and discussed it as a genre in its own right, the term is still
quite vague in first-century Rome. Sitting at the bottom of the literary
hierarchy, it covers all kinds of occasional verse, especially the sort that
lubricated relationships between Greek poet-clients and Roman patrons.[10]
Suetonius' *Lives of the Caesars* is full of anonymous epigrams or references
to epigrams directed at the emperors, and we know that Augustus himself
dabbled in the form (see *Ep.* 11.20). Following on the heels of Neronian
Lucillius who (we gather from the 150 or so of his poems that survive[11])
wrote satirical, spiky epigrams, Martial has big ambitions to lay claim to
epigram and give it a brand-new, Roman identity. Although he is much
influenced by a long Greek history of epigram writing, which we know
about mainly through the tenth-century *Palatine Anthology*,[12] Martial is

---

[10] As Fitzgerald puts it (2007, 27), 'by the time of Philip's *Garland*, Greek epigram and epigrammatists
were firmly embedded in the world of client and patron at Rome, with important mutual effects.' As
we see in Martial, epigrams were often composed to accompany, or to function as, social invitations,
gifts, requests, celebrations of birthdays, weddings, deaths, etc. Well-known Greek epigrammatists
in the Roman court include Crinagoras, a client of Octavia, and Leonidas of Alexandria, who wrote
for Nero and Vespasian.

[11] Nearly all Lucillius' epigrams, collected in Book 11 of the Greek Anthology, are satiric. As Watson
and Watson (2003, 32–3) summarise, scoptic epigram becomes a recognised sub-category of the
genre for the first time with Lucillius, and 'some 17 of Martial's epigrams trace their parentage to a
Lucillian model' (see Burnikel 1980). The most obvious way in which Lucillius anticipates Martial
is in the way he attacks satiric types instead of individuals, often with a touch of surreal hyperbole.
Watson and Watson (2002) 33 find Lucillius 'less emotionally engaged', 'less mordant' and 'a great
deal less amusing' than Martial.

[12] Also known as the Greek Anthology, put together by Cephalas in the early tenth century. This
includes earlier anthologies, most significantly the Garland of Meleager, put together about 100 BC,
and arranged according to four categories (erotic, epitaphic, dedicatory and epideictic or descriptive),
and the Garland of Philip of Thessalonica, presented to the consul Camillus during Nero's reign,
around 150 years later, which collected together writers of epigram active after 100 BC. Since the

largely silent about the Greeks, while engaging in close and obvious ways with his Roman predecessors. So, as I explore at length in chapter 2, although the *Epigrams* play on the idea that *epigramma* means 'inscription' ('epigrams', in this sense, survive on objects and monuments from as early as the archiac period), and on epitaphic formulae often used in Hellenistic epigram, Martial is most interested in how Flavian epigram can comment on the trope of monumentality in Latin literature – from Ennius to Horace, Ovid to Petronius. Martial wants to be 'second to' Callimachus at *Ep.* 4.23, yet in the Preface to Book 1, he likens himself to the Roman writers Catullus, (Domitius) Marsus, (Albinovanus) Pedo and (Cn. Cornelius Lentulus) Gaetulicus (Pref. 11). For us, the last two are little more than names, but we know that Marsus produced a collection of apparently satirical epigrams called *Cicuta* ('Hemlock') and a prose work, 'On wit' (*De Urbanitate*), a sentence from which is preserved in Quintilian (*Inst.* 6.3.104). Catullus, meanwhile (along with Ovid), has the most visible presence in the *Epigrams* of any poet, and at points throughout this book, I'll be looking closely at where Martial's multiple echoes and parodies of his poems take us.[13] In Book 14 (the *Apophoreta*), where from 183 to 196 Martial flaunts his penchant for distilling and dumbing down the whole of classical literature, we read two couplets on Homer (182, 183), and one on Menander's first comedy (187), mixed in with all the Roman greats – Vergil, Cicero, Propertius, Livy, Sallust, Ovid, Tibullus, Lucan and Catullus. We'll be seeing in the course of this book how deeply indebted Martial is to the Roman satiric tradition, to Roman epic and pastoral, to Petronius' novel, Statius' court poetry, and perhaps most overtly, to the erotic elegiac tradition leading up to Ovid's *Metamorphoses* and letters from exile. The cheap labels at *Apophoreta* 183–96 come to exemplify the *Epigrams*' push to cram *everything* in, to chop up, reduce and remake Rome as and through its literary production.

## THE WHOLE WORLD IN OUR HANDS

Martial makes epigram define and perform a Zeitgeist: his poetry *is* Rome, both the city itself (a mass of streets, buildings, monuments and people)

---

discovery of the Milan papyrus, a third-century manuscript containing 100 epigrams of Posidippus, we have evidence that Hellenistic poets published books of epigrams before the Garland of Meleager (see Austin and Bastianini 2002, and Gutzwiller 2005); Gutzwiller (1998) argues that other poets from as early as 300 BC also composed their own collections. For lengthier discussion of the history of ancient epigram and Martial's place in it, see e.g. Sullivan (1991) 78–114, Laurens (1965, 1989).

[13] On Catullus' influence on Martial see Paukstadt (1876), Ferguson (1963), Newman (1990) Swann (1994), with Batstone (1998), Fitzgerald (2007) 167–86.

and Rome as concept and dream – the epicentre and embodiment of a vast, complex empire. All 'reality' is in here, and nothing is left out. In an era most famous for the long-haul, ornate epics of Statius, Valerius Flaccus and Silius Italicus, Martial elects, in a contrary, almost surreal career move, to devote his entire life to the most humble and little of poetic forms. Yet, as he is fond of stressing, many tiny poems can make a big book, and the main, twelve-book corpus is a post-Callimachean, daedalean feat par excellence, rivalling the *Aeneid*, and Ovid's fabulous *Metamorphoses*.[14] In the wake of the great Roman epics, whose claims to totality are far more strident than anything in the Greek tradition,[15] Martial's feat marks, in a twisted way, the boldest kind of poetic expansionism yet. Through the *Epigrams*, even more than through Pliny's *Natural History* or Tacitus' *Agricola*, we visualise the Roman empire as a known and summarisable entity that spins around and is synthesized in the glitzy microcosm of Rome. Martial's writing life, from the late 70s to the beginning of the second century AD, itself spans the entire Flavian dynasty, as well as Domitian's *damnatio memoriae* after his death in 96, followed by the rise to power of senator Nerva and then his adopted son Trajan; spatially, too, we see epigram conquering the globe, a consciously *Roman* kind of colonisation. These *libelli* are thumbed by Roman soldiers in what was the wilderness of Ovidian exile, and in the once mysterious realms of northern Britain, exported by tourists and carried in travellers' pockets to all four corners of the world. In an empire as successful, far-reaching and evolved as this one, Martial imagines, the Ovidian opposition in the *Tristia* and *Ex Ponto* between Rome and not-Rome, between the civilised and barbarous, centre and margin, is outdated. Epigram's world is both inconceivably immense, diverse, fractured, and at the same time unified, collapsible, homogeneous. In the right company, Martial jokes at 10.13, even the deserts of Carthage or the hamlets of Scythia can be Rome, while the city itself is a multicultural giant drawing wannabes and consumers not only from the provinces, but from the furthest reaches of the globe. You can almost feel 'in exile' without going anywhere, just as today we can visit Chinatown or Little Italy in New York, or eat out Philippino, Algerian or Iraqi in London. This idea is probably captured best in poem 3 of the *De Spectaculis*, where the inaugural games at the microcosmic Colosseum attract Arabs, Egyptians, the wild Sarmatian 'fed on draughts of horses' blood', even the Northern Britons and afro-haired Ethiopians:

---

[14] The *Aeneid* is 12 books, Ovid's *Metamorphoses* 15 books (Martial published twelve books numbered 1–12, but 15 in all if you count the *De Spectaculis*, *Xenia* and *Apophoreta*).
[15] As P. Hardie (1993, 2) puts it of the *Aeneid*.

'what race is so remote, so barbarous', Martial asks, 'that no spectator from
it is in your city? . . . the crowd rings with different languages, and yet it
is one' (3.1–2, 11–12).

Martial's epigram doesn't just represent the city, it creates it. Rome arises
*out of* it. Reading the *Epigrams* is a crash course in living in Rome, but
also vice versa: in understanding the nuances of poetic interaction, we get
to grips with social and political manoeuvring, as well as the other way
around. Throughout this book, I will be exploring different perspectives
on Martial's radical vision of the relationship between poet, art, language,
and the 'outside' world. What Martial does with this relationship, I shall
stress, is fascinating and unprecedented, and goes far beyond what has
traditionally been perceived as 'realism', or as Sullivan puts it, 'a denigration
of the real'.[16] At the heart of his project, as I discuss in depth in chapter
5, is an exciting reconceptualisation of space, a rethink of poetry's (and
poet's) place and scope. Martial sees epigram as historically apt, his only
option in a literary culture sucked dry of *otium* and nostalgic for the
idealised patronage of figures like Maecenas, who supported and protected
the Augustan greats. It is the absence of a single rich patron, and hence the
chronic lack of separation, of a protective intermediary figure between poet
and world, and between poet and emperor, that provides the impulse, as
Martial envisages it, for his project in merging poetry with world. Without
a 'Maecenas', the poet and his personified book are immersed in a cruel
and unforgiving landscape, in which physical integrity and originality are
threatened. They face plagiarism, are hounded by soiled fingers and sweaty,
contagious bodies, and menaced by the sharp noses of merciless critics.
The *libellus*-as-slave, as scholars have noted, is a key ongoing metaphor for
poetry's/poet's penetrability and lack of autonomy, jarring with the more
confident imagery of book as cocksure bully and hardened survivor.[17] It all
happens on the streets in Martial, and even inside spaces (echoing Horace's
*angulus* and *recessus*, or Persius' intense, dark study) are turned inside-
out in the mind: at 12.57, for example, Martial can't sleep in his town
apartment, complaining, 'the laughter of the passing crowd awakes me,
and Rome is at my bedside, *ad cubile est Roma*' (26–7). Conversely, outside
spaces and rural havens are swallowed up by the city, especially by Titus'
microcosm, the arena of the Colosseum: who needs to write an epic about
travelling to the ends of the world and cosmos, when it's all here in Rome
itself?

[16] See Sullivan (1991) 73, 236.    [17] See e.g. Fitzgerald (2007) 97–105 and C. Williams (2002b).

Cleverly, Martial turns what he sees as the death of poetic independence
and seclusion to his own ends. The social determination and 'cheapening' of
literary activity inspires a new, comic take on neo-Callimachean aesthetics,
so that smallness is motivated by pragmatic concerns, poverty is harsh and
real, not a lifestyle choice, and tiny, intricate poems are not necessarily
perfect and polished.[18] While Domitian (whose reign spans a large chunk
of Martial's career) styles himself, after Augustus, as avant-garde imperial
architect, so Martial presents himself as writing in the shadow of, and over,
his predecessors – along with dozens of other frost-bitten clients claiming
to be 'the next Ovid', 'the new Vergil' (see 3.38). Yet at the same time
his project aggressively rejects an aesthetic, and a set of moral ideals, that
belong to a lost era, and hacks out new poetic territory in a changed world.
In Martial, ambition and insecurity, the big-time and the small-time, go
hand in hand. As we will be seeing in each chapter, he exploits an energising
tension between the imperialistic, terrain-gobbling aspect of his project,
which allows this tiny form to puff up arrogantly and take over the globe,
and the painful constraints germane to full immersion: the epigrams strain
against their own limits, aware of never quite escaping (a dependency on)
the claustrophobia and dirt of urban life.

Indeed, one of the most interesting and difficult features of Martial's
poetry is its reliance on paradox. The epigrams constantly manipulate
and distort space and scale, twist hierarchies, and build up edifices only
to make them splinter. Martial draws on all the tropes and ironies of
neo-Callimacheanism and Roman satire, as well as the complex history
of epigram as a poetic form, to rebrand epigram for posterity as a jigsaw
of contrasts and contradictions – a product, he imagines, of a literary
and social world neurotic about its relationship with the past and highly
conscious of its identity in the present. As critics have emphasised, epigram
is vaunted as simultaneously speech and writing, conversation and text, as
humble, occasional poetry that is at the same time monumental, a guarantor
of fame and immortality; it is both free and closeted, autonomous and
dependent, chaste and obscene, both spectacular and repressed, raucous
and silent, or silenced; at once a genre of established, fixed qualities, and
a chameleonic form out to expose the ignorance of anyone who tries to
pin it down.[19] So Martial is a populist writing for 'all of Rome', yet he also
requires a discerning *studiosus lector*. It may be easy to write one epigram,

---

[18] On this see especially Roman (2001).
[19] On the importance of contradiction to Martial's aesthetic see especially Fowler (1995), Roman
(2001), and Fitzgerald (2007) 2–4.

but to write a whole book is a serious challenge (7.85), and we are warned at 4.49: 'anyone who calls these poems frivolities and jests doesn't know what epigrams are, believe me.' Thus despite the fact that, as Sullivan argues, we can see in this poetry a 'constrained and constraining social vision' dominated by a conservative, hierarchical social and political ideology,[20] the *Epigrams* are also extravagant in fracturing or upturning different kinds of orders and hierarchies, in part through this living, multifaceted relationship with readers, who (are imagined to) experience the poems in many different forms and contexts – via the codex, papyrus roll or inscription, at recitations and performances, amid the banter and gossip of dinner parties, street markets and public baths.

The form of the epigram book, containing around a hundred poems at a time, becomes fertile ground for performing these creative contradictions, which can be felt on every scale, from the microscopic to the cosmic. For example, an important marker of Martial's aesthetic is the repetition of a few key words within the same book, often but not always between poems that are obviously linked in some way, in different contexts and to different effect, so that the word might mean something else entirely from what it started out meaning. In this way, epigrammatic miscellany and fragmentation are held and focused in a single signifier, itself split by repetition and repositioning – a defining shrinking down or concentration. Or, in a blast of hyperallusivity, one word will contain multiple puns, and single lines a kaleidoscope of references. In a myriad of instances, we are reminded again of the trick of *Apophoreta* 183–96, in which single couplets tag and sum up vast literary works like Livy's Histories, or Cicero's entire oeuvre. Most characteristic is how one word is seen to condense not just a multitude of associations, but entire realms of activity – typically, the political, social, sexual and literary. So, to give some of the simpler examples I touch upon in individual chapters, *monumentum* (like *opus*) refers to both physical monument and monumental poem, the *turba* ('crowd') is also a gathering of epigrams in a book, the verb *tangere* ('to touch') is used in parallel of sexual touching, physical aggression, and of readers' various kinds of contact with the epigrams, *furta* in Book 1 means sexual tricks, a plagiarist's thefts, and a drunk's deceptions, and both the city and Martial's female patron are *dominae* ('mistresses'). Repeatedly, forces of separation and merging, dissection and unification are held in tension.

---

[20] See Sullivan (1991) xxv *et passim*, with Boyle (1995).

On a larger scale, this ability to expand and contract (often simultaneously) is mirrored in the visualisation of empire as cosmos, amphitheatre
arena as Rome, or as universe, in the distilling of *urbs* into epigram. The
architecture of the book, as we see especially in chapter 1, is an essential
vehicle for this concertina effect: each poem operates both as individual
entity and as a cog in the book's social machine; epigrammatic closure is
in constant competition with open-endedness and fluidity. Moreover, as
I stress in particular in chapter 1, the distinctive ordered disorder of the
epigram book in Martial is not just generated by variation, contrast or
surprising juxtaposition: the *turba* ('crowd'), a metonym for and epigrammatic entombing of *urbs*, is a stimulating metaphor for poetic gatherings
because of the way it gets us thinking about how each epigram not only sits
alongside others, but moves, jostles, sucks up to, mates with, sticks its fingers into neighbouring poems like the urban being it is. Whilst critics have
explored the 'imperfect' structures of Martial's books, usually vis-à-vis the
objective 'ideal' of a Horace's *Odes* or a Propertian monobiblos, in terms of
patterns of opposition or complementarity, unifying themes and independent 'cycles' of poems,[21] I emphasise how such patterns are complicated by
a rather more messy, and much more radical, intermingling or infection.
We are constantly reminded that as well as resembling epitaphs and still
monuments (*epigramma* literally means 'inscription'), Martial's poems and
books are also fleshy bodies, wisps of gossip, 'soaked' manuscripts about
to be erased. The figure of metamorphosis that runs through the corpus is
much inspired by Ovid, I argue, as well as by the metaphors that dominate
Neronian literature (we think especially of Petronius, Persius and Seneca).
It accompanies Martial's unstable and nervy perception of the world, but
also becomes epigram's most ambitious feature: materiality marks the epigrams as *nihil*, 'nothing', yet also enables them to live on and on, survive
in any environment, slip through any net.

Each book, we will be seeing, pressures various kinds of boundary-
policing and collapse. As I discuss in chapter 3, the *Epigrams* explore how
basic ways of understanding the world (e.g. counting) are germane to
many different fields of activity, linking the plotting of poetic metre to
political machinations, business transactions, the mapping of time and

[21] Sullivan (1991) 221: 'for all Martial's efforts, the critic has to admit that the structure of each of
the books is, in various ways, imperfect, at least by comparison with Horace's *Odes* or Propertius'
*monobiblos.*' On epigrammatic cycles and thematic structuring devices see e.g. Barwick (1958),
Sullivan (1991) 218–19, Watson and Watson (2003) 29, C. Williams (2004) 10–11, Lorenz (2004)
with fuller references in chapter 1. The most nuanced work on juxtaposition in Martial is to be
found in Fitzgerald (2007).

space, and banal street vending. This poetry presents a constant challenge to classicists' tendency to do *either* texts *or* history, either 'intertextuality' or cultural poetics. At the core of Martial's poetry is the (both banalising and wildly imaginative) point that social and literary activity/interaction overlap and infiltrate one another, so that we must talk about the sociality of the poetic book, and the poetics of the textual city. The move to aestheticise (so redolent in many ways of post-modern virtual realities, of the Derridean idea that there is no outside-text[22]) tugs against the forces of materialisation: epigram sees the city as text, but it also flaunts poetry as social tool and common day job; poetic tricks can substitute, not just depict, real-life imperial entertainments, yet are also dependent on and inseparable from them.[23] Liberty too, as I discuss especially in chapters 4 and 5, is ever at stake in epigram's consistently paradoxical poetics. Do you have to be free and able to retreat from the city in order to write real literature? Is to embrace and compact everything also to erode any space for the imagination, for any proper fun? What does the ambitious Flavian poet have to sacrifice, especially vis-à-vis his predecessors? What is it to live in the shadow of Augustus' mausoleum (5.64), in the 'afterlife' of Flavian Rome?

The contradictions at the core of Martial's aesthetic and world view also become crucial to the way the poet negotiates his position politically. Much has been made of the 'problem' of Martial's apparent sycophancy and hypocrisy, especially under (and after) 'monster' Domitian.[24] Critics have largely either tied themselves in knots 'rescuing' the poet by offering a more generous image of Domitian and thus defending Martial's sincerity,[25] or have emphasised the subversive potential of certain poems, and especially certain combinations of poems: Garthwaite alone proves this is not a difficult thing to do.[26] There is a discomforting tendency in both camps for the post-war critic to play moral policeman, either to justify, or self-consciously not to justify, their own political identifications. There are no easy answers, nor should there be, to the questions of what Martial really thought, or meant readers to think he thought, about the several emperors

---

[22] See e.g. Fitzgerald's use of Baudrillard (2007, 34–67).
[23] In this sense, Baudrillard's nihilistic theory of hyperreality in a post-modern age offers an interesting but limited model for understanding Martial's reconceptualisation of the real.
[24] See summary in Watson and Watson (2003) 9–12: 'M.'s flattery of Domitian has always offered cause for concern' (9).
[25] See e.g. Watson and Watson (2003) 9–12, with Waters (1964) on the image of Domitian.
[26] See especially Garthwaite (1990, 1993), and also Szelest (1974), Holzberg (1988), W. B. Jones (1992) 106–7.

he writes for. As the more nuanced discussions in the reductive debate about 'pro-' and 'anti-'Augustanism have shown, we can't pin down intricate poetic texts so that they function as captions for figurative or ideological pictures.[27] What I do stress at points throughout this book, however, is how Martial's brave play with paradox and inconsistency within the frame of the *libellus* entertains by sustaining a tightrope-walking sense of political risk and transformability. Complex, multiple interactions between poems, so many that the critic is never really satisfied he or she has 'read' a book, create an environment of split perspectives and theatrical posing, while Martial's emphasis that it is readers (and there are many different kinds of readers) who make this poetry is the ultimate device for sliding loose of incrimination. This is a context designed to make it very difficult to judge when encomium is double-edged, when a spiky joke is or isn't harmless, even flattering, when we (or other readers) might be foolish to get offended, or foolish not to be. As I discuss at several points, Martial chooses subtle ways, often via the model of Ovidian licence and exile, to evoke the perils and unpredictability of the poet's relationship with the emperor, and the vulnerability of the poet to malicious interpretation. But he is also a suave operator who makes political advantage, and a political game, out of an aesthetic of insubstantiality and incoherence. As he sees it, there *is* no other way to survive in Flavian Rome.

*

In different ways, all the chapters in this book explore how we might see the economies of epigram, and of Martial's Rome, in constant interaction and symbiosis. I am interested in the fundamental question of why exactly Martial chose to write epigram, and (apparently) epigram alone. How does epigram become a tool for thinking about what it is to write poetry under the Flavians, especially as opposed to under the Julio-Claudian dynasty? Why is this 'epigram's time'? What do classical poetry, and the world of late first-century Rome, look like through Martial's strange and all-consuming eye? What is 'revolutionary', as Sullivan puts it, about his poetic programme?[28]

   In my attempt to do justice to how Martial engages us in analysing interactions between poems and books, in understanding a creative play-off between openness and closure, contagion and isolation, sociability and autonomy, I am all too aware of having to do much in a small space. Any lengthy study of Martial is both overly ambitious and out to underachieve.

---

[27] I paraphrase Barchiesi (1997) 6. Cf. Fitzgerald on Martial (2007, 112).     [28] Sullivan (1988) 179.

I aim to give a broad sense of what is distinctive and invigorating about Martial's poetics that appeals to the reader coming to these poems for the first time as much as to academics who already have 'their' Martial in mind. In doing this I take up the poet's invitation to read the corpus as a whole, and tune into his all-encompassing vision of epigram, while exploring how this vision also divides, mutates and adapts, both to keep up with the times and to keep us on our toes. As I stress throughout, and as I want to communicate vividly in my readings, there is often the sense of epigrammatic miscellany, the epigrammatic imagination, as an unstoppable engine which allows lines, poems and books to grow the more they are handled by readers. This is partly our prejudice – it can seem surprising, so often have we been led to believe that the *Epigrams* are stale, repetitive, mostly dull poems, apart from the really rude ones. But it is also how this poetry operates, how Martial elaborates his perspective on the imperial world. Epigrams can *become* epic(s) within the vortex of the book, and in a *cumulatio* of reading encounters.

I start at the 'beginning', the layered tour de force that is *Epigrams* 1 – the first numbered book, albeit not the first to be published. For *my* Martial, this is the best launch pad, as the book makes an unmissable show out of how social lubrication, mixing and infection enact an extreme experiment in poetic *variatio*, and vice versa. After exploring how the image and poetics of epigram blur into the dirty crowds of Martial's Rome throughout the corpus, I discuss the precocious way Book 1 lures us into the textuality of the city, and see Martial as carving out a crucial role for Roman epigram in the history of the poetry book. In chapter 2, I expand on what I have said about the modernising and comic forces of transformability in *Epigrams* 1 to look in detail at a specific aspect of Martial's poetics: his development of the paradoxical rhetoric of monumentality that has long been a feature of imperial Latin literature. I discuss epigram's capacity to solidify into/as its urban environment – a scarred, palimpsestic Rome that is all the time being remapped and rebuilt, especially under Domitian – and explore how the entire corpus works over the issue of how poetry and poets can cheat death in what is imagined as a culture of ephemerality and decay. After Horace's *carpe diem* ('seize the day'), *vive hodie* ('live today') is Martial's motto, and looking mortality squarely in the eye is part and parcel of his pioneering aesthetic and bid to make it now, or never. Yet he continues to manipulate the tropes of monumental fame that have already been twisted by Horace, Ovid and Petronius in particular. I stop to pore over the intriguing patchwork or bricolage that is Book 10 (second edition), and pinpoint the amber miniatures of Book 4 within their watery frame as exemplary studies of this poetry's obsession with sticky endings, before stepping back into Book 1 to survey the model eco-grave that is 1.88.

Chapter 3 tackles another hallmark of the epigrams – Martial's use of figures and sums. Numbers are fascinating epigrammatic signifiers, condensing in staccato rhythms both the denial and celebration of poetic language and erotic deferral (both death and eternity), experiences both social and literary, real and fantastic, trite and world-changing. Counting in Martial, I suggest, is engrossing and catching, another way of ensuring that to read the *Epigrams* is to get drawn into a world, to have to make sense of poetry-as-world. The second half of the chapter studies the programmatic addings up and subtractions of the *De Spectaculis*, noting in particular how they frame epigram's quasi-imperialistic ambitions. I then take large bites out of *Epigrams* 2, which leads us through a fun, multifarious introduction to the management of facts and figures in epigram's Rome.

Chapters 4 and 5 are where we see Martial's poetics of full immersion, the source of such great entertainment and partner to readerly licence at points throughout the corpus, being pushed to its limits and put to the test. Chapter 4 concentrates on Martial's exploitation of the Roman carnival, the Saturnalia – still a pretty understudied, though crucial, aspect of Latin satiric literature. I look both at the 'Saturnalian' books (that is, books presented explicitly as accompaniments to the festival), especially Book 13 (the *Xenia*) and Book 11, but also at how the *mundus inversus* ('world upside-down') of carnival penetrates and becomes core to Martial's poetics more generally. In the Saturnalia, we are seeing epigram's distinctive contrariness or paradoxicality writ large, 'officially' sanctioned. Yet this is also a compelling forum for illustrating epigram's tense and nostalgic relationship with the past (December's partying is a revisiting of golden ages, mythic, political and literary), for thinking through the possibilities for creative freedom and poetic autonomy which are both evoked and cancelled out in the oxymoron of imperial Saturnalia.

Finally, chapter 5 brings together strands from previous discussions to investigate in detail how Martial imagines and redetermines space, grounding Roman epigram as a response to and culmination of the late first-century evolution of capital and empire. The *Epigrams* re-map space, while also striving to transcend geography (are both objects embedded in tangible contexts, and winged, fluid beings that never stop moving). I trace the motif of mobile poetry and of the travelling poet/emperor through the *Epigrams,* focusing in particular on how Martial remoulds the Ovidian trope of exile – from the model of personified poem winding its way through Roman streets in Books 1, 5, 10 and 11, and the sending off of books to Germany and Gaul in Books 7, 8 and 5, to collections composed in foreign lands (Book 3 in Gaul, and Book 12 in Bilbilis). At the heart of Martial's imperial vision is the idea that epigram splits and twists, extends and shrinks down the relationship or journey between Rome and outside Rome: this is felt not only in the books that announce being written from or sent abroad, but throughout the corpus. In the second half of this chapter, I discuss Martial's difficult 'retirement' book, *Epigrams* 12, in detail, and argue that this odd, culturally hybrid anthology might be read as an advanced exercise in spanning and distorting space that expresses Martial's empire in terms of epigram's ingenious poetics, and vice versa. The elastic spatiality on show in Book 12 sends us zigzagging back to Titus' packed Colosseum via the bloody shows scattered through Books 1, 2, 3 and 8, and via the many poems that mix up or swap around the categories of town and country, centre and margin, in Books 1, 3, 7, 8, 10 and 11. Along the way, we take in views, *Apophoreta*-like flashes, of Roman pastoral, and are pushed to think about the significance of space to poetic production in a new world nostalgic for the writer's *otium*, privacy and seclusion. On every level, epigram's exciting new turf is veined with frustrated longing, with a sense of loss as well as triumph.

There is an undisguisable and inevitable randomness about the thematic approach of chapters in this book. I attempt to cover a great deal of the corpus, to map how the ever-expanding empire throbs through it. I also pursue 'themes' that Martial explicitly promotes as such, and often uses to structure an entire book (as is the case, for example, with 'Ovidian exile' or 'Catullan counting'). Yet reading Martial, one can't help being ultra-conscious of one's own selection, neglect and rejigging. My attempt to pursue the domino effect of reading a single Martial epigram within its book, and within its corpus, must also expose what I leave out: a sense of dissatisfaction or impotence must always be, I think, in constant tension with the image Martial offers us of fragmentation and desultory reading as carnivalesque liberation. As we see in close-up in chapter 3, less is more where this poetry is concerned, but equally, more is more, too. Pile them up high, Martial tells us, and you'll reach the stars: every little brick counts. Yet the chocolate-box approach is so much more fun . . . On the other hand . . . This to-ing and fro-ing is integral to the dialogue Martial imagines with his readers, an exchange in which our expectations, desires and cynicisms are often held up for inspection and (we suspect) satirised. As he quips in the final poem to Book 11: 'Dear reader, anyone'd think you'd be full after so long a little book, and yet you beg me for a few more couplets. But Lupus demands his interest and the boys want feeding. Pay up, dear

reader. You say nothing and fake deafness? Good-bye.' One of the things
I strive to emphasize, then, is the extent to which reading Martial in cut-
and-paste anthologies is always a *guilty* pleasure. Biting off more than we
can chew is an equally insistent model for reading (and writing) epigram
which becomes central to Martial's poetic identity. As I summarise in the
epilogue, if we read these texts *through* (*perlegitur*, Book 1, Pref. 12), there is
always the sense – one that blurs conviction into suspicion into paranoia –
that there can be no escape from the empire of Martial's small-scale,
epigrammatic world.

# CHAPTER I

# Contagion and copyright:
# the city as text

*rimas per omnis basiator intrabit.*
*Ep.* 11.98.13

The city at the heart of epigram's social-poetic identity is a stinking, oppressive place, despite its monumental glories. The epigrammatist manages to squeeze out a living, so the story goes, with the stingiest, scrappiest poetry, in a vast metropolis where there is no more space to move. 'There's no place in Rome for a poor man to think or rest' (*nec cogitandi . . . nec quiescendi /*
*in urbe locus est pauperi*), he complains at 12.57.3–4. Senators rub shoulders with moneychangers, hookers and hangers-on in claustrophobic markets, squares and alleyways; thighs touch in steamy public baths and the packed rows of amphitheatres, and disease is rife. Many epigrams feature the victims of gout, coughs and colds, eye ailments, hernias, cancers and curious swellings, as well as the more mundane halitosis, piles, herpes and rotting teeth.[1] Martial is fond of the Dr Death gag, joking that medics, gladiators, undertakers and hit men are all in the same business.[2] He spends much of his time doing the client's social rounds and avoiding a 'plague' of kissers; even if he were cursed himself with 'bright blisters', 'dirty scabs' and a 'dripping nose' (by implication, all the ghastly blemishes he has to nuzzle up to daily), he couldn't put these people off (11.98, cf. 12.59, 10.22 and 7.95).

Yet Martial's fixation on physical defects, infection and the confounding of poison and cure is not simply summed up as capturing the 'real' Rome in the 'grittiest' of verse forms. This urban-poetic landscape, underpinned by the metaphorics of contagion and of the flawed, morbid body, also

---

[1] See 1.78, 1.98, 3.18, 4.65, 4.80, 5.9, 6.47, 6.58, 6.70, 6.78, 6.86, 8.9, 8.25, 10.77, 11.36, 11.61, 11.74, 11.85, 11.91, 11.104, 12.17, 12.83, 12.90; cf. 1.10, 2.26, 4.36, 9.90, 11.28, 11.71, 11.85. On 'figs' (piles), see 1.65, 4.52, 7.71, 12.33. On false invalids see 2.16, 2.40, 7.39, 9.85, 11.86; cf.11.7.11, 11.28, 12.17, 12.56.
[2] On the idea that doctors were murderers or could swap places with undertakers, see e.g. 1.30, 5.9, 8.74, 10.77. For a review of doctors and diseases in Martial see Sullivan (1991) 166–7.

magnifies clichés of post-classical decline, imagining the 'health-bringing', 'fertile' age of Augustus overrun and parodied by an era obsessed with (avoiding) infection and decay. Moreover, Martial's vision of epigram and of the epigram book is integrated into and becomes inseparable from the task of surviving in and making sense of the city. As I'll be exploring in this chapter, the way in which this corpus (often frayed, patched up, soggy at the edges[3]) dips into the vibrant image repertoire of death and disease sets the stage for epigrammatic miscellany. Or, to put it another way, the strategy of *variatio,* Martial's *mixtura iocorum,*[4] performs the (threatening) social mix and mingling at the core of this poet's experience of Flavian Rome. As I outlined in the introduction, the way Martial approaches Rome, (re)makes a world (out) of words, now looks very reminiscent of a post-modern view of the city as text, as a complex surface of activities and interactions, a mass of diverse and opposing voices.[5] The enormous interest in the humanities since the 1970s in the social construction of space, in the way the social is spatially constructed, as well as in the 'grammar' or 'poetics' of urban centres, necessarily frames our study of Martial. So too, the modern awareness of the fact that it is impossible, for instance, to excise *Sex in the City*'s or *Spiderman 2*'s New York from the actual city is an ever-present reminder that there can be no transparent, unmediated access to the 'real' late first-century Rome.[6] In large part, Martial's snappy, dirty little poems *are* Flavian Rome, for us. This *is* it.

THE BODY OF ROME

The *Epigrams* participate in a literary discourse of sickness and health that pervades Augustan and post-Augustan Latin poetry, from Ovid's confla-tion of the saviour emperor with healer god Asclepius at the end of the *Metamorphoses,* to the afflicted, bloated carnival bodies of Persius' *Satires* and Petronius' *Satyricon*, and Lucan's play on snake venom and pestilence as figures for (the effects of) civil war in the *Pharsalia*. Like Petronius and Catullus, Martial exploits the image of nugatory poetry as already decay-ing organic matter (fit for wrapping cheap take-away fish)[7] to allegorise

---

[3] E.g. books are still wet at 4.10, not yet polished at 8.72, read in 'final draft' form with the author's corrections clearly visible at 7.11.

[4] As he puts it in the preface to Book 8.

[5] See e.g. Lehan (1998) ch. 1, and more generally, in relation to modern studies of ancient Rome, Edwards (1996).

[6] A useful summary of post-modern readings of the city can be found in Barker (2000) 290–317.

[7] See e.g. 4.86 and 13.1.

his 'belatedness' and 'stale' regurgitation of the literary canon – in particular the heady 'Golden Age' of Augustan poetry.[8] The idea of poetry, or poetastry, as a disease or *morbus* inflicted on unsuspecting audiences by thick-skinned amateurs is not a new one: it pervades Petronius' novel (the perverse encyclopedism of which is more than matched by Martial's epic output), and can be found in Horace and Plautine comedy. Petronius' poet figure Eumolpus, for example, suffers from gout, and in Horace's *Ars Poetica* (453–6) the frenzied writer is plagued by a rash (*scabies*). But while Petronius' Trimalchio compares the writer to the doctor (both are privy to cancers as yet invisible to the lay eye, *Sat.* 56), in Martial it becomes almost inevitable that poets are, or need to be, chronically *ill*. The figure of the pale, wasted, light-shy poet, most familiar to us from Persius and the Roman love elegists, is made over in the epigrams as a pitiful stereotype drained of its previous smugness and romance. So at 7.4, for example, sick Oppianus starts to compose verses to hide the *real* cause of his deathly pallor. Or at 4.80, orator Maron declaims in a fever which is 'burning up his guts' (*viscera . . . exurit*), as he can't muster up enough red-faced passion any other way. Martial himself goes 'on duty' as a client wearing a plaster on his chin and his lips painted white (suggesting some horrible unsightly malaise), just so Philaenis doesn't try to kiss him (10.22). And the population of Rome is characterised as an unhealthy *pallida turba* ('pallid throng', 10.12.10).[9] It's no accident that this same word, *turba* ('crowd') is also used to describe books of epigrams, in which (we imagine) individual and groups of poems bustle, cluster and compete.[10] As we will be seeing throughout this book, the collapsing of categories (here, social and poetic) into or as a single word or phrase is one of Martial's core strategies for blurring 'inside' and 'outside' and immersing his miniature epigrams in the big, bad, complex world of Rome.

As well as being 'defective', Martial's verses are themselves full of parasites (see 11.1.14: there are 'bookworms breeding' in these *ineptiae*),[11] advertising the poet's own mortality and fleshiness – in contrast, always, to the transcendent immortality of the Augustan *vates*. No wonder he shrinks back

---

[8] On Petronius, see discussions of the Oenothea episode (*Sat.* 136) in Connors (1998) 46 and Rimell (2002) 161–3.

[9] Cf. 1.55.14 (*vivat et urbanis albus in officiis*, 'may he live white-faced amid urban duties').

[10] *Turba* is used fifty-nine times in Martial's corpus, of which two refer to Martial's epigrams: 4.29.1 (the fact that his books make up a *turba* goes against them, as only rarities are prized), and 13.3.1 (the guest gifts make up a *turba* in the crowded dinners and parties of the Saturnalia). As Lehan remarks (1998, 8), 'the city often represents itself metonymically, embodied in the crowd.'

[11] Cf. 13.1.2 (*sordida blatta*).

from sending out his own verse, lest (like a germ-filled handkerchief) it bring back deliveries of more bad poetry in return (5.73, 7.3). Martial's book roll is itself 'dirty' (*sordida*, 10.93.6)[12] as soon as it is read, soiled by being touched by readers' chins (the papyrus was often held under the chin while the book was rolled up); it embodies the poet's fear of the 'pollution' of social kissing. One can never be too cautious in a world in which gossip and invective stain and linger like bad smells. Look for example at 3.28, where Nestor is accused of soiling Marius' ear just by talking into it:

> Auriculam Mario graviter miraris olere.
> tu facis hoc: garris, Nestor, in auriculam.

> You're shocked that Marius' ear smells off.
> Your fault, Nestor: you gabbled into it.

Similarly, at 7.94, Papylus can turn a precious perfume into stinky *garum* just by smelling it, suggesting that he 'contaminates' the scent with his own repulsive body odour. Despite Martial's paranoia, and what Sullivan defines as a deeply conservative, hierarchical depiction of Roman society in which everything and everyone has an allotted place, it is near impossible to 'keep clean' in this city: one of the key things I want to show in this chapter is the extent to which the *Epigrams* are a stunning post-Hellenistic, post-Augustan experiment in poetic interaction within the confines of a book, one which opens up scope for ever more complex relationships that encompass but also go far beyond the usual 'ordering principles' recognised by critics: symmetry, groupings, pairings, oppositions, 'cycles', and so on.[13] We can never forget that whilst they represent and get us to imagine the thrilling, dirty, claustrophobic *turbae* of Rome's streets, these poems themselves make up a 'crowd' jostling within their literary frame.

The ancients didn't conceptualise contagion in the way we do now, of course, but it is clear from Martial and from many other authors that there was a popular understanding of 'pollution' through proximity or

---

[12] The adjective *sordidus* is used multiple times in the *Epigrams*, in many different contexts, referring to dirty and humble clothing (e.g. 1.103.5, 8.3.10, 14.68.1), to streets (e.g. 5.22.6), coins (e.g. 8.33.12) and books (as well as 10.93.6 see 11.15.6).

[13] On poetic 'contexture' generally, see Fraistat (1986) 3–14. On poetic arrangement in the Augustan poetry book see e.g. Anderson (1986). The bibliography on ordering principles in the *Epigrams* is now vast, but almost invariably makes the same routine points about groupings or cycles of epigrams which are then analysed as separate units, and about programmatic and closural epigrams, etc. See e.g. Barwick (1958), Kay (1985, 5–6), Sullivan (1991, 218–19), Merli (1993), Greenwood (1998b), Garthwaite (1990, 1993, 2001), Spisak (2002). Lorenz (2004), although he generally follows the same principles, recognises that there is more to say. Also see Fitzgerald (2007), who focuses especially on the idea of juxtaposition.

touching. At 5.8, for example, a gentleman called Phasis praises Domitian's new law allocating special, separate seating at the theatre to knights.[14] At last the upper classes have regained their *puros ordines* ('undefiled rows', 3), and are no longer 'pressed and soiled by the crowd' (*turba non premimur, nec inquinamur*, 9). Yet Phasis speaks too soon – he isn't really a knight, and is ousted from his seat by an attendant. Neither can Martial escape the defiling masses in the next poem, in which he has much in common with his 'neighbour' in this book, Phasis: when he was ill at home, Symmachus came to visit him accompanied by a hundred pupils, who insisted on 'touching' him with their icy-cold hands (*centum me tetigere manus Aquilone gelatae*, 5.9.3). But as I've already stressed, *turba* (5.8.9) is used twice of Martial's own packed books, which can 'hassle' their audience in just the same way as the poet, and Rome's average citizens, are forced to negotiate (as well as become part of) the mob. Turn, for instance, to 4.29.1–2, addressed to a friend named 'Mr Bashful' (Pudens). Here, Martial apologises for the sheer number of his books, in a culture in which rarities and one-offs are most prized, and reasons that his copious publications 'tire' and 'cloy' the reader:

> Opstat, care Pudens, nostris sua *turba* libellis
>     lectoremque frequens lassat et implet opus.

> Their number, dear Pudens, goes against my little books,
>     and their frequency tires and overfills the reader.

In a crowded market, this mass of epigrams hounds and *invades* its audience (*implere* means literally 'to fill up', even 'to impregnate'[15]), just like the unwashed mob Phasis is desperate to avoid in 5.8.

Public toilets and baths, prime sites for social hobnobbing, recitation, sex and poetic inspiration, are associated in Martial not with evacuation and cleansing but with the unsavoury mingling of classes, influences and bodily fluids. Cotilus prefers to be the first to bathe so that he isn't washing himself in 'irrumated water' at 2.70, and at 6.81 we gawp at Charidemus washing his groin 'all over the bathtub' (Martial jokes that he would rather he washed his head, the implication being that his fellating mouth is the dirtier part). A great many epigrams focus on oral sex (much on offer at the baths), or rather, on a gross union of mouth and genitals which comes

---

[14] Martial refers here to the Roscian Law of 67 BC, which assigned fourteen rows in the theatre to knights only. Domitian reinstituted the law.

[15] OLD s.v. *implere* 4: e.g. Pliny *NH.* 8.172, Ovid *Met.* 6.111. Martial 1.84.4 also plays on this connotation of *implere* (*futuit ancillas / domumque et agros implet equitibus vernis*).

to typify Martial's revulsion at the adulteration of 'clean' by 'unclean'. As Dupont discusses, the theme of 'stinking kisses' recurs again and again in both Greek and Roman satiric epigram, reflecting the ancient idea that the part of the body involved in kissing, the head, is civilised and characterised by its lack of unpleasant odours, while the lower part of the body is ugly and smelly. Hence 'the worst infamy imaginable was to confuse and bring together mouths and sexual parts.'[16] Much of Martial's neurosis about kissing comes from an ever-present suspicion about exactly where those lips have been.[17]

And like their hypochondriac author, the epigrams are nervous about touching and being touched. Epigrams are traditionally 'self-contained', 'independent' entities with sewn-up endings, easily movable in or between books, even between authors. Economically, they cannot afford extravagance of any kind, and epigram's aesthetic depends on clipped syntax, policed borders, each composition repeating a measured acceleration to its final, fast quip. At 7.61, the observation of tidy boundaries is a political as well as poetic imperative. Here, Martial praises Domitian (Germanicus) for his AD 92 edict forbidding stalls from jutting out into the streets and turning the entire city into one sprawling market (7.61):

> Abstulerat totam temerarius institor urbem
>   inque suo nullum **limine limen** erat.
> iussisti tenuis, Germanice, crescere vicos,
>   et modo quae fuerat semita, facta via est.
> nulla catenatis pila est praecincta lagonis
>   nec praetor medio cogitur ire luto,
> stringitur in densa nec caeca novacula turba,
>   occupat aut totas nigra popina vias.
> tonsor, copo, cocus, lanius sua **limina** servant.
>   nunc Roma est, nuper magna taberna fuit.

> Those cocky vendors had stolen the entire town,
> and no threshold kept within its bounds.
> You gave orders for the narrow streets to grow, Germanicus,
> and yesterday's dirt track became today's proper road.
> No column is chained with flagons now, and
> for the praetor, no more wading through the mud;
> Razors aren't drawn blind in the thick of a crowd, and

---

[16] See Dupont (1999) 141ff.

[17] Cunnilingus, in particular, seems to be associated with disease (or vice versa). See Martial 1.77, 11.61.10f. and 11.85. Howell (1980, on 1.77) cites Pliny's thoughts on the poisonous nature of menstrual blood (see *NH.* 7.64f., 28.79f.).

blackened cafs can't monopolise entire streets.
The barber, landlord, cook and butcher all respect their boundaries.
Now this is Rome: it used to be just one enormous shop.

Paradoxically, Domitian reinforces spatial limits in order to open up and create space. His urban planning, we might say, is both congruent and at odds with the project of epigram. The poem itself is hemmed (in?) by *limina* ('thresholds') in the second and penultimate lines (*limine limen / sua limina*), and we might notice that Martial begins his next book (8) with a preface he describes as the *limen* of this obedient, respectful collection, which is dedicated to the emperor (*in ipso libelli huius limine* . . . 8, Pref. 18) – although the same book is conscious of exceeding reasonable limits even as it advocates self-censorship (see 8.3: 'Five had been enough; six or seven books is already too much. Why, Muse, do you want to keep playing?'). The clever polyptoton in line 2 of 7.61 captures the incongruous image of thresholds bumping up against each other, struggling to demarcate space but at the same time cancelling out any such definition. While the epigram performs Domitian's power to liberate and delimit, in many ways, Martial's poetic world is also that of the 'old' Rome – identified with the (Callimachean) narrow path,[18] the bumpy track, the messy complexity of *tota urbs* (this is a phrase that, along with *totus orbis*, occurs multiple times in Martial, usually in connection with the all-encompassing popularity of his verse).[19] Crucially, these poems deal frequently with the *failure* to preserve *limina*, and Martial shows repeatedly how the epigrams themselves interact, rub off, 'infect' each other. Remember that the books are often pictured as slaves, a class of people who conceptually didn't have any physical boundaries, and could legally be used, beaten, penetrated or killed by their masters. Similarly, while the corpus develops an image of epigram as frigid, modest, shrinking back from dirty fingers, many of the poems are imagined as Priapic, drunken revellers, flabby, unfinished compositions that offer their audience the ultimate in carnival entertainment and readerly freedom.

This important paradox is encapsulated in several epigrams. At 1.34, for example, the prostitute Lesbia 'sins on open and unguarded thresholds' (*incustoditis et apertis, Lesbia, semper / liminibus peccas*), displaying her trade

---

[18] Note especially the adjective *tenuis* in line 3 of 7.61, a buzzword for small-scale, elaborate poetry.
[19] *Tota urbs*: see e.g. 1.1.2, 1.86.9, 12.38.2. The phrase is also much used (and inspired) by Ovid (see e.g. *Am.* 1.3.25, 1.15.13, *Her.* 15.28).

(and showing off 'entrances'[20]) to all and sundry. Martial imposes 'harsh strictures' on her activity, advising her to learn some modesty from more 'traditional' whores, who at least take cover in graveyards. Yet the following epigram, 1.35, hits back at a moralist who has attacked his own risqué epigrams: now Cornelius is asked to 'put prudery aside', as if he is a figure for Martial's own severe persona in the previous poem. The first poem in the duo enforces boundaries, while the second walks all over them. Or take 12.57.26–7, a poem I mentioned in the introduction, in which a sleep-deprived Martial moans about noise pollution in central Rome. As we learnt at 1.117, he lives in a pokey attic up three flights of stairs (note that the enclosed private spaces and 'narrow pipe' of neo-Callimachean literary discourse become the crammed public arenas which the lowly poet is *forced* to inhabit).[21] But like the epigrams themselves, recoiling from each other and their environment while at the same time absorbing and regurgitating urban life *en masse,* Martial is boxed into his tiny apartment yet still cannot escape the city: in 12.57.26–7, he is woken up at dawn each morning by the 'laughter of the passing throng'[22] and Rome 'at his bedside' – both trapped in a confined environment *and* fully immersed in the vastness of the city:

> nos transeuntis risus excitat turbae,
> et ad cubile est Roma.

> But the laughter of the passing crowd awakes me,
> and Rome is at my bedside.[23]

Martial *both* suffocates in confined locations *and* struggles to preserve professional and physical boundaries (contrast, again, his Augustan predecessors, in particular the love elegists, who idealised their extra-cultural autonomy). In a life defined by duties, debts, pretence, sycophancy and ever-elusive power, time, as well as space, is restricted. At 10.70, for example, he comments that it is a miracle he finds time to write anything at all (and by definition, what he does manage is banged out, often shabbily, for the bargain bookstore), as most of his day is taken up doing the rounds

---

[20] I.e. Lesbia's legs as well as doors are always open for business. For this use of *limen* see Adams (1982) 89, with (especially) Auson. *Cent. Nupt.* 112, p. 216 P.

[21] Martial also has a 'tiny' country pad (9.18) and at 8.14 is given a 'cubbyhole' (*cella*) to stay in when he visits an old friend in the countryside. Also see 11.18, where he buys a tiny plot of land in the country, a garden so small that a cucumber can't lie straight in it, and its harvest is barely enough to fill a snail's shell.

[22] Or, if we accept Heinsius' conjecture, which makes a lot of sense and really adds to the effect of these lines, the 'thrusting' (*nisus*) of the passing crowd (12.57.26).

[23] It was notoriously difficult to sleep in flats like these in the centre of Rome, particularly as traffic was only allowed through the city during the night.

of patrons' houses, cadging for dinner invites (like many of the subjects he writes about) in the bathhouses, theatres and other public arenas – all places of leisure which, seen through Martial's eyes, are anything but relaxing and pleasurable. Yet whilst the poet must observe and work according to a series of limits, he can exert little of his own control over his environment, which in some ways is rigidly hierarchical and inflexible, in others seemingly chaotic and unmanageable – even violently so. For example, we see the trope of the personified book, used especially in Horace's *Epistles* and Ovid's exile poetry, developed and honed in the epigrams – yet the 'slave-like' *libellus*, manumitted by its master-author and sent out to find its own way (and spread the poet's name) promotes the poet's limited ability to discipline and regulate his work once it reaches the unforgiving and disordered public domain.

Plagiarism is a frequent talking point and threat in the *Epigrams,* emphasising the poems' looseness and penetrability (both literary and sexual). In a world that has inherited the mythic biographies of great authors (immortal Vergil, Horace and Ovid) along with their works, ownership and copyright are now slippery concepts: plagiarists are expert in cutting and pasting stolen epigrams (a varied epigram book, in which strings of poems rework the same theme, lends itself perfectly to this), and these days authorship is up for sale (at 2.20, 'Paulus buys poems and recites them. What you buy, you may rightly call your own'). Poems can seem to 'belong' to whoever recites them (this can go both ways: at 1.52, Martial writes, 'I commend you my little books, Quintinianus, if I can call them mine when someone else recites them', but has just joked at 1.38, 'When you recite my book badly, it begins to belong to you'). This makes Martial passive to false accusation (while at the same time absolving him, potentially, of all such charges): in Book 7, for instance, he twice excuses himself of spite, charging someone else for 'vomiting snake venom' under *his* name (7.12, 7.72). Who the 'author' of these poems is can apparently shift, multiple times, depending on motive and circumstance. This becomes a general point not just related to the threat and reality of plagiarism. For example, poem 51 of Book 7 offers up a warped epigrammatic take on the Ennian image of 'living on in the mouths of men' when it describes a hard-core Martial fan named Pompeius Auctus[24] who 'remembers and recites my little books in their absence so that not a letter is lost to my pages'. He is not a reader, Martial

---

[24] The name plays on *auctor*, 'author', and links *auctor* (which literally means 'one who promotes increase') with *auctus* ('an increasing'): author-stand-in Pompeius (7.51.13–14) doesn't know when to stop reciting.

boasts, he *is* the book itself, and could pass for the author if he wished (thus in some way rendering the real author redundant). In fact all readers are encouraged to make these books their own, deciding on their own cropped version or edited highlights ('you can finish this at any place you choose,' we're told at the beginning of the *Apophoreta*): they are even responsible for these poems' very 'existence', for 'nobody writes, whose poems nobody reads' (3.9.2).

Martial also hints that it is not even clear whether what we come to read is actually what he originally penned, as the moment a manuscript leaves his hands, it must be processed by a (sloppy, hurried, paid by the hour) copyist: we get an 'apology' for this at 2.8, in the style of Ovid's apology for his 'shoddy' Latin at *Tristia* 3.1.17 (the line *non meus est error* in line 3 alludes to the mysterious *error* that earned Ovid a one-way ticket to the Black Sea). And in 4.10, a book sent out in a rush to a friend by slave courier is still damp, and is almost bound to arrive partly smudged (again, Martial's *liturae* caricature the tear stains that blot the tragic letters of Ovid's *Heroides*, as well as the epistolary *Tristia*). A collection of epigrams, in Martial's world, is insecure, vital, ever-changing: its shape and identity, like that of its author, can quickly melt, reform and evanesce.

TOUCH UPS: BOOK I

We have already begun to see how Martial is concerned with both the social realities and poetics of touching. The verb 'to touch', *tangere,* appears several times, in a way that connects epigram's key locations (the baths, dining rooms, theatres, public toilets – themselves sites for public speaking and poetic recitation) with the processes of writing, publishing and funding poetry. We see it used, for example, in the sordid supper enjoyed by Sabidius and friends at 3.17 (nobody wants to touch dessert, *nemo potuit tangere,* once it has been cooled and turned to shit by the host's polluting breath). I've also just mentioned poem 4.10, where this provocative 'still-wet' book is 'afraid to be touched' (*timet tangi*), and 5.9, where Martial shudders at having been pawed by 'a hundred chilled hands' (*centum me tetigere manus gelatae*).

I want to turn now to the 'masterpiece'[25] that is *Epigrams* 1, a collection that presents itself as a stage performance (that is, to be watched, not touched), which can at the same time be 'grasped with one hand' (*me manus una capit* 1.2.4). It also conceives of the process of book production

[25] As Fitzgerald (2007) 68 puts it.

in terms of transfer from one hand (the author's) to another (the reader's): at 1.52, the slavish epigrams are 'discharged' from Martial's hand (*manuque missos*, 1.52.7), *manu*mitted. The *libellus* then cultivates intimacy with its companion-reader, hugging his flesh as it travels in a palm or pocket.[26] That grasping *manus* at the beginning of Book 1 becomes Martial's amanuensis at the closural 1.101 (*illa manus quondam studiorum fida meorum*, 1.101.1). Demetrius is freed on his death bed and so goes to the underworld '*liber*' in line 10 (a free man, but also, implicitly, a figure for Martial's book, *liber*). The verb *contingere* is also used in reference to reading at 1.4: if the emperor happens to 'come into contact' with the epigrams (*contigeris nostros, Caesar, si forte libellos*, 1.4.1), he should react with good humour and 'put aside the frown that rules the world'. The book was itself composed in the close quarters of Martial's pied-à-terre on the Quirinal: we hear in 1.86 that these blocks of flats are built so close together that it is possible for Martial to touch his neighbour Novius 'with his hand' (*manu tangi . . . potest*, 1.86.1–2). Yet Novius might as well be in Egypt, for all Martial sees of him: 'in all of Rome nobody is so near to me yet so far away' (*nec urbe tota / quisquam est tam prope tam proculque nobis*, 9–10). This image is very reminiscent of the classic scene of parted lovers (epitomised by couples Hero and Leander, and Pyramus and Thisbe) who reach out, and can almost touch each other, over a space that is simultaneously tiny and (because unbridgeable) huge.[27] In Martial's deadpan take on this, he and Novius aren't sweethearts, they're 'chums' who happen to live next to each other, or rather are *forced* to inhabit the same sliver of cityspace. Martial recopies Ovid's Callimachean metaphor of the small-big space for his 'epic' epigram.

Moreover, this poem reworks an idea which characterises Book 1 in particular: the paradox of contiguity *without* touching. In many ways, this becomes an epigrammatic ideal, as well as 'trick': tiny poems can inhabit the same 'compressed pages' (*artat brevibus membrana tabellis*, 1.2.3), yet

---

[26] As well as 1.2.4, compare *meque sinus omnes, me manus omnis habet* at 6.60.2, *sufficit in vestras saepe redire manus* in the preface to Book 9 (line 8), and *ecquid te satis aestimas beatum / contingunt tibi si manus minores?* at 11.1.7–8.

[27] Ironically, in Martial's version he *can* actually touch his friend. Compare Pyramus and Thisbe at Ovid *Met.* 4.55ff., neighbours whose houses are separated by a chink of space, and Leander at Ovid *Heroides* 18.179 (*paene manu quod amo, tanta est vicinia, tango*), noting the phrase *tangere manu*, reused by Martial (who also, in line 10, condenses the contrast between *prope* and *procul*, 'near' and 'far', from *Heroides* 18.175–7). In this light, innuendo might well lurk in 1.86.5, *iuncto cui liceat frui sodale* ('when I can enjoy my mate so close by'). See Adams (1982) 179 and 198 on the verbs *iungere* and *fruor*, often used in Latin in reference to sexual intercourse and pleasure in sex; *iungere toto corpore* is the lovers' fantasy at Ovid *Met.* 4.74.

not rub up against each other or invade each other's space. The *lusus* and
*ioci* of this book's spectacle (Pref. 19, 6) are re-performed, for example,
in the 'games and pranks' of the lions in Caesar's arena at poems 6, 14,
22, 48, 51, 60 and 104, where the audience can marvel at the sight of a
hare leaping untouched between a lion's open jaws. As well as being an
original spectacle, this is a civilised move, given that touching is often
associated in Martial with pollution and the abuse of bodily boundaries.
After the image in 1.2, of desiring readers grasping these pages and making
them companions on long journeys, in 1.3 (echoing Horace *Epistles* 1.20)[28]
Martial pictures his *libellus* as a naive slave-boy itching for love (from an
audience) on the streets of Rome: he is bound to get hurt, rewarded for
'throwing kisses' by being speared on the phallic, rhinoceros noses of harsh
critics. This playful book, in contrast to the cunning hare in 1.6 and 1.14,
is not so *tutus* ('safe') cavorting with amphitheatre beasts.[29] In 1.92, we get
another version of sexually violent touching, much inspired by Catullus'
aggressive 'Furius and Aurelius' poems:[30]

> Saepe mihi queritur non siccis Cestos ocellis
> **tangi se digito**, Mamuriane, tuo.
> non opus est digito: totum tibi Ceston habeto,
> si dest nil aliud, Mamuriane, tibi.
> sed si nec focus est nudi nec sponda grabati
> nec curtus Chiones Antiopesve calix,
> cerea si pendet lumbis et scripta lacerna
> dimidiasque nates Gallica paeda tegit,
> pasceris et nigrae solo nidore culinae
> et bibis immundam cum cane pronus aquam:
> non culum, neque enim est culus, qui non cacat olim,
> sed **fodiam digito** qui superest oculum:
> nec me zelotypum nec dixeris esse malignum.
> denique pedica, Mamuriane, satur.

[28] Although Martial in 1.3 focuses on spearing noses rather than grasping hands, Horace warns his book that in the big wide world it will be 'thumbed by vulgar hands and begin to grow soiled' (*contrectatus ubi manibus sordescere volgi / coeperis*, *Epist.* 1.20.11–12). In epigram 1.66, also, work that remains safely locked in its master's book-box (*scrinio* 1.66.6), as Martial recommends in 1.3.2 (*scrinia nostra*), is not yet 'rubbed rough by hard chins' (1.66.8), a similar image of 'pollution'.

[29] Compare 1.3.12 (*sed poteras tutior esse domi*) with 1.6.4 (*tutus et ingenti ludit in ore lepus*). Though ironically, Martial's book is not safe from violence at home, either, where it has to suffer its master's sado-masochistic 'erasures'. Also compare the long epigram that follows the fourth poem in the hare–lion series, 1.49, where Martial fills in his friend Licinianus on the pleasures of life in Bilbilis: here, the 'cunning hare' (*lepus callidus* 25, cf. *lepus improbus* 1.48.7, *lepus ambitiosus* 1.51.2) finally runs out of luck and is killed during a hunt.

[30] Note that Catullus is mentioned as a model in the prefatory epistle to book 1: *sic scribit Catullus . . .* (Pref. 11).

Cestus often complains to me, not dry eyed,
of being poked by your finger, Mamurianus.
No need for the finger: have Cestos whole, if
that is all you lack, Mamurianus.
But if you've got no fire, no bare mattress,
no cracked cup of Chione or Antiope,
if your saggy pants are yellowed and patched up
and a Gallic jacket covers half your butt, if
you dine on the stench of a blackened kitchen
and drink filthy water on your belly like a·dog –
well, it's not your arse I'll dig my finger into (for an arse
that never shits ain't one), but your one remaining eye.
And don't go calling me a jealous bitch.
Just go fuck on a full stomach, Mamurianus.

Here we move from touching poems and neighbours to fingering enemies, from cosy and jovial intimacy to aggressive and satiric poking: Martial takes on Catullus' phallic persona, threatening not just to poke but to 'dig out' (*fodere*) Mamurianus' one remaining eye, presumably in revenge not just for seducing Cestos, but for turning out to be too poor to be blackmailed.[31] Although the books of epigrams invite being handled, Martial makes it difficult to separate physical contact with his poetry, and the sense in which his jabbing verse can physically attack its victims (see also 1.35), from social anxieties about touching endemic in the epigrams. In a very broad sense, we might say, epigram identifies with both Cestos and Mamurianus, shrinking back from dirty fingers and sharp horns (as in 4.10, and 1.3), and at the same time seeking ultimate sensual closeness with its readers. Similarly, Book 1 maintains a double identity as both performance to be watched and enjoyed at a distance, and as codex to be kept in readers' pockets (even while they 'watch' the 'show').

Poem 1.73 unites and plays off these two aspects and senses, touching and spectating:

Nullus in urbe fuit tota qui tangere vellet
    uxorem gratis, Maeciliane, tuam,
dum licuit: sed nunc positis custodibus ingens
    turba fututorum est: ingeniosus homo es.

Not one man in town would have wanted to touch
your wife for free, Maecilianus, as long as she was
public game: but now you've posted guards, the fuckers
are queuing up: you genius.

---

[31] As Citroni (1975) and Howell (1980) note *ad loc.*, the epigram reworks elements from Catullus 15, 21, 23 and 24.

*Tangere,* as commentators note, is often used in Latin in a sexual sense:[32] Martial's city overlaps the vocabulary and imagery of reading, writing, publication, sex and slavery, all of which involve grasping, violent, caressing hands, or pointing, soiled, careful or delving fingers. 1.73 draws on a scenario familiar to us from Greek epigram, satire and Roman elegy – the woman who plays hard to get (making clever use of a guardian, slave-girl or other obstacle) will attract the most men, and keep her lovers entertained the longest.[33] The poem also mirrors 1.34: whereas Lesbia is an exhibitionist who likes to serve clients in full view with the doors open (*incustoditis et apertis . . . liminibus* 1.34.1–2), Maecilianus employs doormen to guard his wife's bedroom (*positis custodibus* 1.73.3). In other words, Maecilianus is precisely the kind of guy we were warned about at the start of the book, and we find here precisely the kind of deceptive stage-production the author *denied* when he announced his Floralia in the preface (*ingeniosus homo es* 1.73.4; cf. *improbe facit qui in alieno libro ingeniosus est,* 'it's a dirty trick to be ingenious with another man's book', *Pref.* 8–9). Yet Maecilianus is an ingenious pimp, not a malicious critic, hinting once more at the paralleling or cross-contamination of categories, literary and sexual. The inhabitants of this city are still afraid of touching, especially when there is obvious risk of 'pollution' (the implication in 1.73 is that Maecilianus' wife is quite repulsive looking: if men could see what they were queuing for, they wouldn't touch her with a bargepole). Yet in this case, reinforcing boundaries doesn't reassure the population by preventing bodily contact. It does precisely the opposite, ensuring that men can't wait to get their hands on this unattractive woman. It's the hidden spectacle, the non-spectacle, that turns out to be a sell-out performance, and setting up limits licenses a limitless imagination. Herein, if we take Martial's bait and play the 'malicious interpreter', lies the irresistible formula for epigram itself.

## THE GOOD, THE BAD AND THE IN-BETWEEN

Yet this discussion begs the question: do poems within Book 1 manage to preserve their 'frigid' borders once readers get their hands on them? Peppered throughout the book, we find a series of poems which advertise or allegorise epigrammatic mixing, and get us thinking about the creative implications and risks of juxtaposition. Look first at 1.16, a neat little couplet warning readers what to expect from this anthology.

[32] See e.g. Catullus 21.8, 89.5, Horace *Sat.* 1.2.28, Ovid *Ars* 2.633, *Met.* 10.343.
[33] See e.g. *AP* 12.102 (Callimachus), Horace *Sat.* 1.2.104–6, Ovid *Am.* 2.19, *Ars* 3.601–2.

*sunt* **bona**, *sunt* quaedam **mediocria**, *sunt* **mala** plura
    quae legis hic: aliter non fit, Avite, liber.

There are good, bad and indifferent poems to read here.
A book ain't made no other way, dear Avitus.

We find very similar two-line poems at 7.81 ('if there are as many good as bad epigrams in this book, Lausus, it's a good book') and 7.90 ('an even book, Creticus, is a bad book'). Yet if a book of epigrams is always a blend of good, bad and middling verses, do the good poems stain the bad ones, or make mediocre poems look good? Such judgements must be *relative,* after all. Is each poem always self-contained and distinct, insertable in any epigram book in any position, or are we often encouraged to imagine sequences, patterns, interactions and mergings? Related to this is the question of how far the writer can control his poems once they leave his hands and are published. When a book leaves the 'safety' of its master's study and is sent out into the big wide world, as Martial imagines it at 1.3, how can he police its borders? In Book 1 in particular, plagiarists hover like vultures over these 'cheap', repetitive, varied *libelli*: anyone can pick up a copy at the local bookshop, do a bit of canny cut-and-pasting, shuffle the order of poems, and pass it off as his own. As I've already suggested, the continual threat of plagiarism in Martial fosters an image of the epigram book as an unstable, fluid and fragmented whole, in contrast to rival imagery promoting epigram as solid tomb-marker, as long-lasting inscription.

But let's look, first of all, at the poems that (almost) touch the edges of the programmatic soundbite of 1.16. After 1.17, a facetious three-liner replying to Titus' advice to start practising advocacy in the courts, we have an epigram addressed to a philistine host named Tucca (an aristocratic name), who serves a grim cocktail of unfermented plonk and fine vintage wine at a dinner party (1.18):

> Quid te, Tucca, iuvat vetulo miscere Falerno
>     in Vaticanis condita musta cadis?
> quid tantum fecere **boni** tibi **pessima** vina?
>     aut quid fecerunt **optima** vina **mali?**
> de nobis *facile est, scelus est* iugulare Falernum
>     et dare Campano toxica saeva <u>mero.</u>
> convivae *meruere* tui fortasse perire:
>     amphora *non meruit* tam pretiosa <u>mori.</u>

> Tucca, what pleasure do you get from mixing must
> stored in Vatican jars with old Falernian?
> What great good have bad wines ever done you?

> Or what great harm have good wines done?
> Never mind about us, it's a crime to murder Falernian
> and put harsh toxins into a Campanian vintage.
> Maybe your guests deserved to perish:
> But so precious a jar did not deserve to die.

This is a pared-down, post-Horatian satire on rich, unsophisticated hosts, reminiscent of Petronius' caricature of super-rich Trimalchio in the *Satyricon*. The topic of 'murdering' anthropomorphized wine has been 'done' already by Catullus, in poem 27, and Martial alludes to this in his first line.[34] The top-quality, 'innocent' Falernian (from Campania, one of the very best Italian wines) is tortured and 'slaughtered', he says, by being mixed in with inferior Vatican. The verb used here, *iugulare* (line 5), means literally 'to cut someone's throat', encouraging us to imagine the rare wine being poured out as gushing blood.[35]

Yet the pertinent point is that, in *this* poem, the mixing of good and bad elements does not produce a mediocre or average result: instead, the Falernian wine is *poisoned* by its Vatican cousin (the 'Campanian vintage' is *saeva toxica* at line 6). Compare the balance of *bona* and *mala,* sandwiching the pivotal *mediocria* in 1.16.1, with the twinning of *pessima* and *optima vina,* doing 'good' and 'harm' (*quid boni . . . mali*) in 1.18.3–4. This opposition and doubling, styled perfectly in elegiac rhythms in both poems, is elaborated in a series of clever patterns in 1.18: the repetitive *facile est: scelus est* at line 5, the cruel quip of the final couplet (*meruere . . . perire / non meruit . . . mori*), and the near-rhymes of *mali, mero* and *mori* at the end of the last three pentameters.

You'll notice that there are several poems about wine, and mixing different kinds of wine, or blending wine with water in Book 1. Bear in mind, in thinking about how 'close' 1.18 gets to 1.16, that wine and water are highly symbolic substances in ancient literature.[36] By Martial's time they have long been used to refer to different literary styles and genres: Hellenistic poetry, for example, talks of 'water-drinking' and 'wine-drinking' poets, and this is picked up in Roman rhetorical theory (where inebriation stands for irrationally inspired, passionate composition). So Cicero, *De Or.* 99, writes that the passionate orator looks like a drunk, while Quintilian chooses a

---

[34] Cat. 27.1: *minister vetuli puer Falerni* (also see Nicarchus, *AP* 11.1, 3f., about wine poured onto the floor).

[35] *Iugulare* is used metaphorically by Martial several times, e.g. at 1.106.9 and 8.50.26. It is also used literally at 3.99.4 and 4.18.8.

[36] On water and wine as metaphors see e.g. Crowther (1979), Knox (1985), Murray and Tecusan (1995), Gutzwiller (1998) 162, 168–9.

description of a boozy dinner party to capture the rhetorical technique of *enargeia*, vivid description (*Inst.* 8.3.66). Similarly Cratinus, later adopted as hero by the adherents of intoxicated inspiration, famously dismissed the sober water-drinkers as inferior poets (fr. 199.2), and later, on the other side of the fence, the sober Callimachus refers to his 'wine-stricken' rival Archilochus (fr. 544). In Propertius and Ovid, the god of wine Bacchus inspires wit in composition (Ov. *Met.* 7.432–3; Prop. 4.6.76), while Horace jokes that the muses always stink of alcohol the morning after a writing session, and that Homer and Ennius were both 'rather fond of the grape' (*Epist.* 1.19.1–11). The metaphor, as befits the Saturnalian or sympotic setting of many of his poems/books, is well developed in Martial too. Book 11 is drunk, 'soaked' in wine (*vino madeat*, 11.15.5), at 10.20.13, a 'tipsy' (*ebria*) volume is delivered to Pliny, and at 10.45.6, a *lagona* (flagon of wine) is a figure for the epigrams. Invective poetry is also described as a *virus,* a poison, much like Tucca's *toxicum,* at 7.12.7, or Fescennia's stinky wine-breath (also a *virus*) at 1.87.5.[37]

This live network of metaphors, then, makes it more tempting to size up the allegorical impact of Tucca's *faux pas* in the context of Book 1. Taken together, 1.16 and 1.18 make a fascinating pseudo-Ovidian diptych (parted only by the brief riddle of 1.17, so that they don't quite 'touch'). They encourage reflection on the problems and *risks* involved in blending good poems with bad or not so good ones (as well as nudging us to contemplate the relative quality of each epigram: is poem 18 the 'better', more imaginative version of the quick couplet knocked out earlier?). In act one of his 'spectacular' collection, it seems, Martial dramatises epigrammatic *variatio* as a mock tragedy – it's an act of aggression, a vicious *scelus*. Mixing bad wine with good doesn't mean Tucca's guests can taste both, and enjoy the contrast, it means that the good wine is destroyed.[38]

We encounter a similar poem to 1.18, with perhaps a similar moral for writing books of epigrams, at 1.56:

> Continuis vexata madet vindemia nimbis:
>    non potes, ut cupias, vendere, copo, merum.

> The grape harvest is soaked, thrashed by constant showers.
> You couldn't sell neat wine if you wanted, innkeeper.

Here a potentially good vintage gets ruined by being mixed up, by accident this time, not with a lesser-quality wine, but with water. Again the wine,

---

[37] *quid quod olet gravius mixtum diapasmate virus* ('the evil stench smells worse when mixed with scented powder').

[38] Compare Fitzgerald (2007) 90.

or grapes, are personified: they are *vexata*, shaken violently, given a good beating, by the rain; and *madet* in line 1 often means in Latin, 'is drunk', as we saw in the example referring to Martial's book at 11.15. The joke is that the grapes themselves are 'soaked', 'drunk' (but with water), meaning, paradoxically, that the customers at the inn where the watery wine will eventually be sold *won't* get drunk so easily. Innkeepers were notorious for trying to fob off customers with watered-down booze – there are several examples of this to be found in Roman satire. The epigram is also paralleled by Martial 9.98 (rains mean Coranus the vintner has made a hundred jars of water not wine) and 3.57, about the city of Ravenna, famed for its wonderful drinking water ('more precious than wine'), where a host cheats his guests by offering neat wine instead of mixing it with water.

In 1.56, the adulteration of fine wine with other liquid (this time water) is a 'torture' that is disappointing for all concerned. And once more, adjacent epigrams both complement and contradict this take on the implications of miscellany and elegiac 'doubling'. Both 1.57 and 1.59 want to retain instead the contrast between 'good' and 'bad' (with 'medium' in between) outlined in poem 1.16. So at 1.59, Martial moans at how ironic it is that the dole he gets at the luxurious seaside resort of Baiae is only 100 farthings. The 'good' and the 'bad' coexist without influencing each other – unfortunately being surrounded by money doesn't increase Martial's pitiful income (*inter delicias quid facit ista fames?* 'What is such hunger doing amid such luxury? . . . *tam **male** cum cenem, cur **bene**, Flacce, laver?* 'When my dinner's this bad, why should my bath be this good?' 1.59.2, 4). Meanwhile the nearer poem, 1.57, also takes us back to 1.16, reshaping poems as *puellae* (this is a move very reminiscent of Ovid's *Ars Amatoria*):

> Qualem, Flacce, velim quaeris nolimve puellam?
>    nolo nimis facilem difficilemque nimis.
> illud quod medium est atque inter utrumque probamus:
>    nec volo quod cruciat nec volo quod satiat.     (1.57)

> You ask me, Flaccus, what sort of girl I want and don't want?
> I don't want one too easy or too difficult.
> I fancy a medium, something between the two:
> I don't want torture, nor satisfaction.

Martial's love life, and his books, are made according to matching formulae: the lover chooses between easy, hard-to-get, and averagely challenging women, just as the reader of epigrams takes his pick of *bona*, *mala* and *mediocria* poems. The addressee Flaccus alludes to Horace (Quintus Horatius Flaccus) and his famous sense of proportion (see especially *Odes* 2.10).

Notice that in this poem, Martial rejects the pain and torture that are the result of collapsed distinctions in epigrams 1.18 and 1.56 (*nec volo quod cruciat*, 'I don't want to be tormented' 1.57.4), and dismisses the winning formula of the well-guarded wife trumpeted in 1.73. This line, *nec volo quod cruciat*, together with the opening question, plays on Catullus 85 – an intertext which also twins 1.57 with 1.32, a more obvious parody of the famous *Odi et amo* poem:

> Odi et amo. quare id faciam, fortasse requiris?
> nescio, sed fieri sentio et excrucior.

> I hate and I love. Why do I do this, you're tempted to ask?
> Don't know, but I feel it and it's torture.

For the pragmatic epigrammatist, love doesn't have to be a torture, nor does it have to be a complicated, confusing 'mixture' of feelings: Catullan love is 'hating and loving' at the same time, but armed with Ovid's textbook, the *Ars Amatoria*, Martial can sidestep neurosis and pick up the ideal girl (a girl who, by the way, is also putting into force Ovid's advice to women in *Ars* 3, especially lines 475–6).[39]

The theme is continued at poem 106, which now explicitly blends the *topoi* of seduction, drinking and mixing spun out in previous epigrams. Here Rufus alternates/mixes wine with water at a dinner party, or drinks diluted wine if forced,[40] because he doesn't want to get so inebriated that he is unable to perform in bed with Naevia. Unfortunately Naevia turns him down, and Martial advises him to get drunk so that he'll at least be able to get some sleep:

> Interponis aquam subinde, Rufe,
> et si cogeris a sodale, raram
> diluti bibis unciam Falerni.
> numquid pollicita est tibi beatam
> noctem Naevia sobriasque mavis
> certae nequitias fututionis?
> suspiras, retices, gemis: negavit.

---

[39] *sed neque te facilem iuveni promitte roganti / nec tamen e duro quod petit ille nega* ('but neither promise yourself too easily to the guy who's trying to pick you up / nor be too stubborn in denying what he asks for').

[40] See Citroni's discussion (1975, *ad loc.*) together with Howell (1980, *ad loc.*) on the meaning of *interponis* in line 1 of this epigram. I have chosen (without absolute conviction) to translate Citroni's way ('you alternate wine with water'), in part because it is so difficult to convey the ambiguity in English. Is it intentional that we are left asking whether Rufus mixes wine with water or drinks them separately, alternating them? As I am stressing, this is certainly a question that *Epigrams* 1 poses, in more general and metaphorical terms.

> crebros ergo bibas licet trientes
> et durum iugules mero dolorem.
> quid parcis tibi, Rufe? dormiendum est.

> You often take water between your wine, Rufus,
> and if forced by a friend, you'll drink a rare
> ounce of watered-down Falernian.
> Is it that Naevia's promised you a night of bliss,
> and so you prefer the sober naughtiness
> of a sure-thing fuck?
> You sigh. You're silent. You groan: she's turned you down.
> Well, now you can down glass after glass
> and slaughter the pain with some hard liquor.
> Why spare yourself, Rufus? You'll need to sleep.

This epigram comes straight after 105, a poem about a fine wine from Nomentum which is so old that its bottle has lost its label. Just as Martial alternates poems about neat wine with poems about (intentionally or unintentionally) watered-down wine, so Rufus in 1.106 'inserts' water between glasses of wine (the verb, *interponere*, in line 1, can be used in Latin of words or arguments, and is used of epigrams at 1.53.4). Crucially, Rufus' clever approach to drinking, which parallels epigrammatic variation and seems to promise a perfect night of hot, semi-sober passion, leads only to disappointment. He should resort to uninterrupted boozing after all, as Martial's *sobriae nequitiae* (106.5–6), his sexy, inhibited poems, are always a contradiction in terms.[41] The sensible choice, the 'medium' *puella*, is perhaps the wildest fantasy of all. Notice that the unusual verb *iugulare* in line 9 connects 106 with poem 18, implying this time a different, contrasting attitude towards neat Falernian: whereas in 18, a poorer wine 'slaughtered' the fine vintage, in 106 downing glass after glass of pure Falernian itself 'slaughters' (now in a positive sense) the pain of rejection.

'Inserted' throughout Book 1, there are also five further epigrams on characters who get drunk on *neat, unmixed* wine. 1.11 and 1.26 concentrate the topic, paired by the tag '*Sextiliane bibis*' ('you drink, Sextilianus').[42] 1.27 and 1.28 focus on the morning after the drunken night/epigram before (*hesterna nocte*, 1.27.1; *hesterno mero*, 1.28.1). In the first of this sequence of poems, 1.11, Martial disapproves of drunkenness, and of drinking wine without adding water. Sextilianus is given tokens at a show entitling him

---

[41] This epigram finds another twin in 1.71: here Martial drinks a measure of wine for each letter of several girls' names. But when he succeeds in meeting, or seducing, none of them, he calls instead on the god of sleep, Somnus, to come to him.

[42] Repeated at 1.11.2, 1.26.1, 1.26.10.

to an allowance of wine, but he drinks much more than he is due. If he had had the good sense to alternate wine with water, as Rufus does at 1.106, the waiters would have run out of the water by now. The same Sextilianus is the subject of poem 26. Martial again marvels at how much he is able to drink, and advises him to choose a cheaper wine instead of 'wasting' all the expensive bottles. He comments, 'You could get drunk on water in such quantities' (*aqua totiens ebrius esse potes*, 1.26.2). Sextilianus' approach to drinking is such that wine and water become interchangeable, another variation on Rufus' unsuccessful strategy (or the paradox of *sobriae nequitiae*) at 1.106, and on neighbouring 1.105, where one fine old wine is indistinguishable from another.

Finally, poem 87, placed at a sensible distance from the 11, 26–8 sequence, is a more developed attack, this time on a drunken woman. Fescennia[43] tries to cover up the stale smell of yesterday's wine (*hesterno vino*, 1, cf. *hesterno mero*, 1.28.1) by adding a further element to the noxious 'mix', scented powder. Instead, she only makes it worse:

> Ne gravis hesterno fragres, Fescennia, vino,
>   pastillos Cosmi luxuriosa voras.
> ista linunt dentes iantacula, sed nihil obstant,
>   extremo ructus cum redit a barathro.
> quid quod olet gravius **mixtum** diapasmate virus
>   atque duplex animae longius exit odor?
> notas ergo nimis fraudes deprensaque furta
>   iam tollas et sis ebria simpliciter.

> In order not to reek of last night's wine, Fescennia,
> you stuff your face with Cosmus' pastilles.
> Such breakfasts coat the teeth, but they're no barrier
> to a belch rising back from the depth of the abyss.
> What's more, the poison smells worse mixed in with the powder
> and the doubled stench of your breath carries further.
> So, enough of this familiar fraud – we're onto your tricks.
> We'd rather you were a simple drunk.

In this poem, Martial experiments with writing a more vivid, more satiric (better?) version of the scenario already described in 28 (Fescennia is like Acerra,[44] but a more interesting case in that she tries to cover up her drunken state the morning after). Here, mixing sweet with rank odours

---

[43] Her name itself alludes to a certain kind of 'drunken' poetry: *versus fescenninus* was a ribald verse apparently sung at weddings (see Sen. *Con.* 7.6.12, Sen. *Med.* 113, Plin. *NH* 15.86).
[44] Acerra means 'incense box' (see e.g. Mart. 4.45.1): instead she reeks of stale wine.

has the effect of highlighting and exacerbating the bad smell, just as cheap dregs overpower and poison the fine wine at 1.18 (*mixtum* 1.87.5, cf. *miscere* 1.18.1).[45] Once again, we are prompted to reconsider the formula of 1.16, and the subtle difference between amalgamation and juxtaposition. In the final line of 1.87, Martial advises Fescennia to 'be a simple drunk' (*sis ebria simpliciter*), recalling the quality of *simplicitas* valued so highly in the preface to the book (Pref. 6–8):

Absit a iocorum nostrorum simplicitate malignus interpres nec epigrammata mea scribat.

I don't want any spiteful critics meddling with the simplicity of my jokes or rewriting my epigrams.

This book is to be 'straightforward', and 'call a spade a spade': it won't use tricks, or cover up its lasciviousness. Martial is the quintessential 'simple drunk', or so he claims. But as we've seen, the 'irregular', 'assorted' character of the epigram book always goes against and unhinges this 'simplicity': even the shortest, bluntest poems, like 1.16, are altered, degraded, enriched, by being read with or over other epigrams. In a sense, we've seen, Martial *invites* readers to play the *malignus interpres*, while reprimanding us in advance for 'over-interpreting', for mixing up the literal and the metaphorical, confusing Callimachean Evian with satiric Beaujolais, and making 'clever' connections. If we read Book 1 'through', as Martial hints we should in his preface (*sic quicumque perlegitur*, Pref. 13), we can see that it offers a number of possible allegories for contrasting, even contradictory, perspectives on the technique of epigrammatic *variatio*. The poems on wine, water and drunkenness, read after 1.16's advertisement of how a book is made, complicate (both in their individual content and interaction) the ideal of distinguishable, integral elements united under one title. The contamination of clean by dirty, sober by drunken, expensive by cheap, classy by common, is the principle, and anxiety, at the heart of both Martial's epigram and epigram's Rome.

STOLEN PLEASURES

I want to take a closer look now at the topic of plagiarism in Book 1. As I said at the beginning of this chapter, the theft and forgery of his work is another way for Martial to explore worries about the instability and potential

---

[45] The verb *miscere* is also used at 1.116.4, where Antulla's parents' ashes are mixed together in a single tomb (*hoc erit Antullae mixtus uterque parens*).

fluidity of the epigrams, including the extent to which each poem is affected by its neighbours, or position within a collection. Plagiarism posed a serious risk to the ancient author, especially in the case of unpublished poems, which could be easily 'stolen'. If a poem was not yet 'out there' in the public domain, it did not officially 'belong' to the writer. That is, he had no legal rights over it. The plagiarist was therefore best off exploiting poems 'known only to the parent of the virgin sheet', as Martial puts it in 1.66:

> Erras, meorum fur avare librorum,
> fieri poetam posse qui putas tanti,
> scriptura quanti constet et tomus vilis:
> non sex paratur aut decem sophos nummis.
> secreta quaere carmina et rudes curas
> quas novit unus scrinioque signatas
> custodit ipse virginis pater chartae,
> quae trita duro non inhorruit mento.
> mutare dominum non potest **liber notus**.
> sed pumicata fronte si quis est nondum
> nec umbilicis cultus atque membrana,
> mercare: **tales habeo**; nec sciet quisquam.
> aliena quisquis recitat et petit famam,
> non emere librum, sed silentium debet.

> You are wrong, greedy thief of my books,
> in thinking it costs no more to become a poet
> than the price of copying and some cheap papyrus.
> You don't get applause for six or ten sesterces.
> Look for private, unpublished poems, work
> known only to the father of the virgin page,
> stuff he keeps sealed up in his desk, not
> yet rubbed rough by bristly chins.
> A well-known book cannot change author.
> But if you find one whose face is not yet pumiced,
> not decorated with bosses and without a cover,
> snap it up: I have such books; nobody will know a thing.
> Whoever seeks fame by reciting other men's work
> should buy not the book, but silence.

This is one of six poems in Book 1 on the theme. In 1.66, in sharp contrast to 1.2, where he is *toto notus in orbe* (cf. *liber notus* 1.66.9), Martial is keen to advertise the fact that he can supply unknown, plagiarism-friendly epigrams: selling on surplus, unpublished work is one way, at least, for him to make some cash. He takes on a sarcastic, pseudo-didactic role here, advising an enemy on how to raise his game. Epigrams are eminently recyclable, of course, not only because of the genre's 'low', 'throwaway' status, but also because a book of epigrams is so patently fragmented and repetitive: who would notice if a poem was missing from a collection, if another author paraphrased one of them, or pinched some lines from different poems and put them together to make a new one? Isn't this precisely what Martial himself is doing? Two poems at the centre of Book 1, 1.44 and 1.45, make jokes of the fact that much material is repeated, both within and between anthologies.[46] And as recent studies of 'intertextual' Martial show, he raids any number of classical texts, quoting and rehashing with more gall even than Ovid (who of all Roman imperial authors makes a special virtue of repetition).[47]

Underlying the plagiarism poems is the idea that readers might not be able to distinguish a fake Martial epigram from a real one – especially if the authentic epigram is one of his 'bad' ones, of which, he admits in 1.16, there are many in a book. Indeed, the literary arena Martial inhabits (or imagines) is so competitive, and so saturated, that it is always difficult for a writer to set himself apart, and for readers to distinguish between one poet and another. In 3.38.9–10, for example, Martial addresses budding poet Sextus, who foresees coming to Rome and winning instant fame with his poetry, which, he says, is as good as Vergil's. Martial bursts his bubble – the city is full of wannabe Ovids and Vergils, all dying of hunger, and he'll just have to get in the queue:

> insanis: omnes gelidis quicumque lacernis
> sunt ibi, Nasones Vergiliosque vides
>
> You're insane: all these guys you see in frosty cloaks,
> they're all Nasos and Vergils.

This is a world in which names and other defining titles (like the illegible labels on old wine bottles at 1.105) are often insecure or imprecise. The plagiarism series in Book 1 explores this uncertainty surrounding ownership and identity in literal terms, yet we're encouraged to envisage these poems less as a separate sequence than as immersed performances of the imagery of touching, mingling and boundary-watching which we've been investigating throughout the book.[48]

---

[46] On 1.45, which has been much disputed, see Howell (1980) *ad loc.*

[47] On intertextuality in Martial, see e.g. Sullivan (1991) 100–14, Hinds (2007).

[48] As Fitzgerald puts it (2007, 105), 'the problematic boundary between book and world is echoed by the problematic boundary between epigrams.'

Of the five other poems in this 'group', four (29, 28, 53 and 72) are addressed to an epigram thief called Fidentinus. In 29, Martial complains that the plagiarist is reciting his epigram books around town as if they were his own. The point seems to be, as Citroni suggests, that the poem is a sort of 'presentation' of the book to this renowned plagiarist. The first couplet refers to his activity before the publication of this book, the second infers that, post-publication, the rules have changed, and that he can no longer get away with his thefts unless he pays up:[49]

> Fama refert nostros te, Fidentine, libellos
>     non aliter populo quam recitare tuos.
> *si mea vis dici*, gratis tibi carmina mittam:
>     *si dici tua vis*, hoc eme, ne mea sint.

> Rumour has it, Fidentinus, that you recite my
> little books in public as if they were your own.
> If you want the poems called mine, I'll send you them for free:
> If you want them called yours, buy this, so they won't be mine.

The implication of the curious last line seems to be that Fidentinus need only buy this book, or pay Martial off, and he can pretend he wrote these *carmina* with impunity. 'Martial's epigrams' can become 'Fidentinus' epigrams' in exchange for the right fee. The two options are barely distinct, as lines 3–4 show: *si dici tua vis* is just a lightly edited, rejigged copy of *si mea vis dici*. This idea, varied a little, is more obvious still in 1.63:

> Ut recitem tibi nostra rogas epigrammata. nolo.
>     non audire, Celer, sed recitare cupis.

> You ask me to recite my epigrams for you. No way.
> You don't want to listen, Celer, you want to recite.

The final line can be taken to mean 'you want to recite my poems as your own' or 'you want to recite your (bad) poems back to me'. The equivocation has the effect of intertwining Martial's epigrams with Celer's. The couplet at 1.38 makes a slightly different point:

> Quem recitas meus est, o Fidentine, libellus:
> sed male cum recitas, incipit esse tuus.

> The little book you're reciting, Fidentinus, is mine:
> But when you recite it badly, it begins to be yours.

---

[49] This reading would also solve the 'problem', as Howell sees it, of the admittedly difficult last line. *Hoc* refers to the present book, or poem, and *carmina* to the epigrams before publication. See also Fitzgerald (2007) 94.

The twist now is that when he hears Fidentinus destroying the epigrams in his clumsy recitation, Martial is tempted to deny (rather than claim) ownership. The point is extended in 1.52, which begins, 'I'm trusting you with my little books, Quintianus, if I can call them mine when your poet friend recites them.' Martial asks Quintianus to declare the poems' freedom and expose his friend's guilt: the plagiarist cannot enslave them when they have already been 'manumitted' by their master-author. If Quintianus keeps on denouncing the crime, eventually the plagiarist will be ashamed of himself (1.52.8–9):

> hoc si terque quaterque clamitaris,
> impones plagiario pudorem.

> If you shout this three or four times,
> You'll shame the kidnapper.

We have heard Martial recommending or imposing *pudor* already in Book 1, naturally in a very different context. At 1.34, Lesbia is told to 'learn some *pudor*' (*disce pudorem* 1.34.7), and the word *furta,* used of her 'tricks' on view in line 2 of this poem, more commonly means 'thefts'.[50] In 1.53, Fidentinus is called a *fur* ('thief'), and Martial's portrait on the cover of a book he tries to pass off as his own 'lays bare the obvious theft' (*traducit manifesto carmina furto*, 3). We may or may not want to make something of this tenuous connection linking (typically) the literary and the sexual in Book 1, a link which is also an opposition (in 1.34 Lesbia is shamed into covering herself up, whilst in 1.52 the plagiarist is shamed into revealing himself, or at least into giving up his deception out of shame). In addition, of course, 1.34 comes paired with its contradiction, 1.35, where Martial fights back against the forces of censorship applied in the previous poem, arguing that epigrams are meant to be phallic and immodest. The point is: Martial promotes a book that seems inconsistent and vacillating, fostering *precisely* the kind of uneven, patchwork effect that is so character-istic of a plagiarist's creation. Indeed, in the very next poem, 1.53, he gives an elaborate description of just such a work. The aptly named Fidentinus[51] has produced a book made up of stolen epigrams by Martial together with one page of his own poetry. 1.53 is the longest and perhaps most interesting of the epigrams in this series:

> Una est in nostris tua, Fidentine, libellis
> pagina, sed certa domini signata figura,
> quae tua traducit manifesto carmina furto.

---

[50] *Furta* is also the word used of Fescennia's mixing tricks at 1.87.7.
[51] *Fides* can mean honour, loyalty, honesty or trustworthiness.

sic **interpositus** villo contaminat uncto
urbica Lingonicus Tyrianthina bardocucullus,
sic Arrentinae violant crystallina testae,
sic niger in ripis errat cum forte Caystri,
inter Ledaeos ridetur corvus olores,
sic ubi multisona fervet sacer Atthide lucus,
inproba Cecropias offendit pica querelas.
indice non opus est nostris nec iudice libris,
stat contra dicitque tibi tua pagina 'fur es.'

There's just one page of yours in my little book, Fidentinus,
but stamped with the sure image of its master,
and it exposes your poems as an obvious theft.
Just as a Lingonian coat put among city tyrianthines
contaminates them with its greasy wool;
just as Arretine pots outrage crystal glasses;
just as a black raven wandering by chance on Cayster's banks
is a laughing stock among Leda's swans;
just as a common magpie insults Cecropian laments
in a sacred grove alive with tuneful nightingales.
My books need no informer, no judge:
Your page stands against you and says, 'You're a thief'.

Fidentinus has inserted one page of his own into the book of plagiarised verse, but its shoddiness immediately gives him away, proving he could not possibly have written the rest. Notice again that the verb *interponere* in line 4 (*interpositus*) is also used at 1.106 of Rufus' plan to alternate wine with water. Yet what reveals Fidentinus' crime is also what we have come to expect from a book of epigrams by Martial. Whilst the first two lines of the poem enforce a clear distinction between Fidentinus' and Martial's work (**tua** *pagina . . . in* **nostris** *libellis*), to what do *tua carmina* refer in line 3? Fidentinus' *own* poems, or what he likes to *call* his poems, which are actually stolen from Martial (in which case *tua carmina* might be read sarcastically)? Much rests on how we translate *manifesto furto* – whether more loosely as 'as an obvious theft', or as 'because of your obvious theft (of *my* poems)'. Pushing the point, we might even say that there is more than one way to read the first line of 1.53: 'There is one page of yours in my little book.' Understood more straightforwardly, this is again sarcastic: 'it's *my* book, actually, not *yours*.' But *nostris libellis* could equally refer to *this* published book, Martial *Epigrams* 1, which includes one 'bad' poem stolen from, or parodying, Fidentinus. In which case we might read line 3 as '(that one page, i.e. this one) holds your poems up to scorn *with* its obvious theft'. 1.53 certainly sticks out like a sore thumb, the only hexameter poem in this book, and practically in the whole of Martial.[52] Is this really authentic Martial, or is our author playing Fidentinus at his own game, plagiarising one of his awful poems, or (at least in part) miming and ridiculing the 'Fidentinian style' in an unmistakable fashion? That would be one way to account for 'low-quality' work, the *mala carmina* Martial admits to in 1.16, and again at the end of the book (1.118), as well as for the bumbling gracelessness of line 5 of 1.53 (*urbica Lingonicus Tyrianthina bardocucullus*). Can all this be dismissed as another poet's rubbish? Of course, there's a great deal of fuel for self-satire here, too. As we saw in 1.29, there isn't, potentially, a great deal of difference between a plagiarist's *libellus* and Martial's 'original'.

Especially when we read on. The string of analogies in lines 5–10 of poem 53 returns us to the questions provoked by Tucca's unfortunate cocktail at 1.18. Fidentinus' page is like a Gallic cloak made of coarse, oily wool, rubbing up against and staining a *Tyrianthina*, a particularly exotic and expensive gown whose rich colour was obtained by dyeing it first violet, and then Tyrian purple. Once more, Martial imagines humanised epigrams jostling for position among city crowds, *turbae*. But stop there: the idea spelt out in the first three lines is that Fidentinus' poem is unmistakably *not* Martial's work. This first analogy, however, describes not just interposition, but contamination. The greasy wool ruins the fine fabric just as surely as Vatican dregs kill off an aged Falernian in 1.18. Suitably, as I've suggested, the line in which the two garments combine, **urbica** Lingonicus **Tyrianthina** *bardocucullus*, is a lumbering tongue-twister of a hexameter – a caricature, perhaps, of 'bad' epic poetry. It may or may not be significant that *bardocucullus* sounds as if it could come from *bardus*, which means both 'bard' and 'stupid'.[53]

In the second simile in 1.53, Fidentinus' poems are shards of red pottery from Arezzo next to Martial's crystal glasses. This line has confused some scholars, as much Arretine clayware is of very good quality. As Howell notes, it was widely exported, and is praised by Pliny (*NH* 35.16). One early historian reasons that Martial must be comparing his own poetry to the pottery, placing *Arrentinae testae* above *crystallina*.[54] This is clearly a mistake, as the use of any sort of pottery tableware was regarded as inferior under the early empire. Nevertheless, the point is that it is not of low quality in itself,

---

[52] There is only one more example of a hexameter poem in Martial's entire corpus (6.64), although 2.73 and 7.98 each consist of just one hexameter. At 6.65, Tucca complains that Martial writes an epigram in hexameters, implicitly an unacceptable metre for the genre.

[53] The suggestion that *bardocucullus* comes from *bardus* is made by Howell (1980) *ad loc.*

[54] See Blümner (1869) 109.

merely rough-looking in relation to fine crystal. So far, then, a fairly logical and effective allegory for the comparison of classy and not so classy poetry. Yet look at the verb used, *violant*, generally euphemised or toned down as 'dishonour', or 'disfigure' in modern translations.[55] *Violare*, more accurately, suggests violent attack involving physical damage, or penetration (it can mean 'to rape'). *Testae* are broken bits of pottery, sharp-edged tiles which implicitly stab (and by definition, shatter) the crystal cups. It's not just that value is relative, then, or that Martial's talent shines out when set alongside Fidentinus' amateur verse. It's that Fidentinus' epigram attacks and destroys, or (in a typical epigrammatic move, as in 1.92) *fucks over* the 'better' poems. It's not necessarily the case that bad poems highlight and *improve* good ones (rather, as the saying goes, 'one bad apple . . .'). Perhaps it would be easier if Martial's pages were identified with the pottery, after all – though his slavish, virginal, depilated epigrams (at least, as imagined in 1.52, 1.66 and 1.117) did perhaps ask for it.[56] In this image, then, the entire book is split into fragments: there are no crystal glasses left, not least because the only way to distinguish crystal from cheaper glass is to examine its clarity and resonance, which can't be done if the glass is cracked, let alone smashed to smithereens.[57]

In the final two examples in lines 7–10, Martial uses birds to signify poetic rivalry, a conventional move for which we can find many parallels in Greek and Latin poetry:[58] a black raven is a laughing stock among Leda's elegant white swans, and a magpie (proverbial for its annoying, squawking chatter) grates on the ears next to the song of a nightingale. Yet an epigram placed later on in Book 1 undoes the certainty that white is better than black. In 1.115, birds are girls instead of poets, and Martial surprises everyone

---

[55] These are, respectively, Shackleton Bailey's (1993) and Howell's (1980) translations. Pott and Wright (1925) simply translate 'is vulgar clay with clearest crystal matched? ', and Scàndola's (1996) translation for the Italian BUR edition uses the verb 'svilire' for '*violare*', meaning 'to shame' or 'put down'.

[56] The 'slave' epigrams are free to be sexually abused by anyone: despite the fact that they have been 'freed' in 1.52, there are still those who try to take advantage of, and 'recapture' them. As Martial warned at the beginning of the book (1.3), his books aren't safe as soon as they leave the confines of their master's care – although it may be the case that they simply swap one kind of abuse for another (at home they suffered their master's 'continual erasures' and 'stern pen', 1.3.9–10). At 1.66, Martial suggests that he too has 'virgin' books to pimp, and at 1.117, he advertises an equally attractive option, a hot-off-the-press edition, 'shaved with pumice and smart with purple' (*rasum pumice purpuraque cultum*, 16): this phrase alludes to Catullus' opening poem which presents his *libellus* as, implicitly, a seductive, depilated boy. Such images of the book of course contrast with e.g. 1.35, where the epigrams are presented as aggressively phallic.

[57] As Howell notes (1980, *ad loc.*), the most valuable *crystallina* were those without blemishes, known as *vasa acenteta*.

[58] See Howell (1980) and Citroni (1975) *ad loc.*, together with Horace *Odes* 2.20, 4.2.25, Persius *Prol.*13–14 and Ovid *Am.* 2.6.

with his penchant for the *nigra puella*. Thus he reverses the conventional comparison in Greek and Roman love poetry between a fair and dark girl (or boy):[59]

> Quaedam me cupit, – invide, Procille! –
> loto candidior puella cycno,
> argento, nive, lilio, ligustro:
> sed quandam volo nocte nigriorem,
> formica, pice, graculo, cicada.
> iam suspendia saeva cogitabas:
> si novi bene te, Procille, vives.

> A certain girl is after me (read this and weep, Procillus!),
> and she's whiter than a washed swan,
> than silver, snow, lilies, privet:
> But I've got the hots for a girl who's darker than night,
> than an ant, pitch, a crow or cricket.
> You're already thinking of the cruel rope:
> If I know you, Procillus, you'll live.

Martial has employed very similar images to those in 1.53.7–8, but elaborates the simile. He also shows off by using two synonyms for each of the birds (*corvus* and *olor* for crow and swan in 1.53, *graculus* and *cycnus* in 1.115). Notice now the word Martial uses for nightingale, *Atthide* at 1.53.9: this is a poetic reference to Philomela, daughter of Pandion, who was metamorphosed into a nightingale after being raped by her brother-in-law Tereus, who also cuts out her tongue. We're reminded, both here and in the previous image of red and white shards in line 6, of Tucca's bloody *scelus* in 1.18. Martial's epigrams might be sweeter in tone, then, but they are still haunted by the images of censorship and rape, and more generally, by the double meaning of *furta* (thefts and sexual tricks) signalled by the nudging up of 1.53 and 1.34. The wood in line 9 '*fervet*', 'is alive', or more specifically 'is seething, or angry' with nightingale song: these birds, and these poems, are furious at having been violated – not least by Fidentinus' Arretine shards in line 6. The noun *querelae* (10), similarly, is associated with elegiac laments (the majority of the epigrams are written in elegiac couplets) and calls to mind the trope of effeminacy and sexual failure in Roman love elegy. As Martial warned his fresh young books at 1.3.3, Rome is a *domina*, an elegiac mistress, ready to whip them into shape.[60] Come

---

[59] See Verg. *Ecl.* 2.15–18, *AP* 12.165 (Meleager), 12.5 and 244 (Strato), Ovid, *Ars* 2.657–8, Juvenal 8.33.
[60] 1.3.3: *Nescis, heu, nescis dominae fastidia Romae* ('how little you know of mistress Rome's scorn – alas, how little you know!').

to think of it, Leda, the proverbial swan in line 8, was also raped by Zeus before her metamorphosis.

We might add that the theme of transformation courses through this poem, and this book. In this expansive *libellus*, forms and perspectives seem to shift and change shape before our very eyes: poets can swap places (and manuscripts), Penelope can become Helen (see 1.62), Minerva plays Venus (1.102), fine wine turns to poison (1.18), and doctors are undertakers (1.30, 1.47); clay pots can rank over crystal, grey clothes hide a taste for red dresses, and black girls are the new blondes. Back in the epistolary preface, Martial also hinted that the proximity of different kinds of readers, or spectators, can alter this book's performance (*Pref.* 14–15):

Epigrammata illis scribuntur qui solent spectare Florales. Non intret Cato theatrum meum, aut si intraverit, spectet.

Epigrams are written for those who are used to watching Flora's games. Let Cato not enter my theatre, or if he comes in, let him watch.

This last line refers to a story told in Valerius Maximus (2.10.8): in 55 BC, apparently, Cato left the theatre on discovering that his presence actually inhibited the actors.[61] Martial, however, encourages him to stay, inviting us to imagine how the epigrams change shape, becoming more or less rude, more or less straightforward, according to who acts as *interpres*, or whose presence is felt on the sidelines. Ultimately, the joke of 1.53 is that we're not at all sure whether this poem is itself an example of a cheap or fine coat, a red pot or a crystal vase, a raven or a swan, a magpie or a nightingale. It's a cop out, but also epigram's greatest coup, to say that it depends on the reader, whom Martial credits for his worldwide fame in 1.1. Martial ends 1.53 by saying that Fidentinus' page confronts him with the accusation that he is a thief, that it 'stands against him'. Yet this poem too seems to 'stand against' Martial, spelling out his hypocrisy, but also advertising the multiple ways of reading the heterogeneity of this book.

In other words, whilst recent critics have tended to understand Martial's *variatio* in terms of 'thematic structures', 'intricate designs', 'cycles' and 'interacting motifs', which unify or set the 'tone' for a book,[62] my reading

---

[61] Val. Max. 2.10.8: *eodem ludos Florales, quos Messius aedilis faciebat, spectante populos ut mimae nudarentur postulare erubuit, quod cum ex Flavonio amicissimo sibi una sedente cognosset, discessit e theatro, ne praesentia sua spectaculi consuetudinem impediret. quem abeuntem ingenti plausu populus prosecutus priscum morem iocorum in scaenam revocavit, confessus se plus maiestatis uni illi tribuere quam sibi universo vindicare.*

[62] I quote from Garthwaite (2001), who wants to extend the critiques of Scherf (1998, 2001) and Merli (1998) in particular. These critics are all, in different ways, offering challenges to White's theory

of *Epigrams* 1 has suggested that the interplay of ideas, poems, imagery and vocabulary in Martial often fails to add up to a comforting sense of wholeness and artistic rationale. And that, the *malignus interpres* might say, is the most contrived stratagem of all. Martial's project takes the difference-in-sameness of *variatio* and pushes it to its most jagged and muddling extremes. He emerges from this collection not just, as critics have recently stressed, as a quasi- or post-Augustan poet, able to craft his books as sophisticated and unified architectural pieces, but also as an aggressive innovator experimenting in a radical way with the chemistry of interconnection, and with the contradiction of jumbled order. We have seen that intermingling and touching in Book 1 involve defilement and corruption, as much as offsetting, (re-)definition or supplementation. Readerly freedom is part of the fun and games of this epigrammatic Floralia (Cato is warned of the *licentia vulgi*, the 'licence of the crowd', at *Pref.* 23), and the transparent claims of 'simplicity' in the preface seem to bait suspicious reading of every *pagina lasciva* (1.4.8). This is an important aspect of Martial's relationship with his reader in the corpus more generally, especially in the 'Saturnalian' books, part and parcel of the all-encompassing scope of his project, his bid to match the intricate cosmic patterning of Ovid's *Metamorphoses,* or Lucretius' *De Rerum Natura.* At the same time, the epigrams repeatedly expose and allegorise the risks of connectivity, in terms of intelligibility, literary reputation, social status and bodily integrity. I have also hinted that the poems on plagiarism threaded through the book do not simply describe or reflect a real or imagined scenario in which Martial's unpublished or recently published poems were vulnerable to manipulation and theft: rather, the book as a whole is invested in performing, mimicking and hyperbolising the plagiarist's guile and the unnerving impact of his (part-)stolen creations. In the first of his twelve numbered books, Martial shows us that design can go along with (and generate) inconsistency, or vice versa, that paradox and metamorphosis will (paradoxically) define this most ambitious of poetic projects.

(see White 1974 and 1996) that rather than being cohesive collections, Martial's books are an often awkward amalgamation of *libelli*, which were initially offered independently to various addressees. For the most powerful general critique of White's position, see Fowler (1995). On 'patterning' in Martial's books see bibliography in n. 13 above.

# CHAPTER 2

# *Vigor mortis: living and dying*

*At non erunt aeterna quae scripsit: non erunt fortasse, ille tamen scripsit*
*tamquam essent futura.*

Pliny *Epist.* 3.21.6

*Epigrams* I has taught us much about how Martial exploits the imagery
and vocabulary of decay and contagion to frame his salty experiments in
visualising (and getting his readers to visualise) the interaction of poems
within a book. We have seen how Martial imagines his books as live acts
and bodies, often greasy and soiled, full of worms that leave trails and eat
holes. Yet this instability and closeness to rot is precisely how epigram swells
over its limits and exceeds all expectations. In this post-Ovidian universe,
the potential for creative, as well as painful, transformation is ever present:
poems can change owners, and (in a curious intuition of late twentieth-
century philosophies of reading) the presence of Martial's audience can
fundamentally alter the text – whether by imposing restrictions (like Cato,
hovering over Book 1), or by flaunting their freedom to slice up books
and poems any way they choose. But more than this, Martial hints that his
audience may even step *into* his books, or inhabit the same conceptual space
as his bitchy, anthropomorphised poems: his *turba* (epigram's metonym
for *urbs*) is made up of theatre-goers, animals, bands of slaves, crowds of
worshippers, actors, scribes, schoolboys, but also of readers, epigrams and
books. Similarly, a book of epigrams can seem to be embodied in a reader,
in a scribe, as well as (a more familiar idea) in its author: we are beginning
to see how all the inherited fleshiness of Latin literature, from Catullus'
penetrative lyrics to Ovid's *viscera* and satire's mixed platters, is summoned
in concentrate to plump up Martial's epigram-as-world.

Yet we are also aware that another crucial aspect of Martial's poetic
programme is epigram's identification with hard, unshiftable inscriptions
that triumph over corporeal mutability. Martial plays extensively on the

connection between epigram and epitaph (epigrams were originally inscriptions on gravestones or other objects) and on the familiar idea of poems as tomb-markers, or as (outlasting) monuments.[1] In particular, his razor-edged reworkings of Augustan poetry often engage with the marriage of text and monument in Augustan Rome, and with the classic poetic ambition to escape mortality (both of the writer himself and of his all too material *opera*) by 'living on in the mouths of men'. The body might decompose, stones may crumble, but reputation, fame, and the orally perpetuated memory of a poet's work, can survive. The basic paradox between fluid spontaneity, tiny lifespan and pitiful prospects on one hand, and grandiose visions and monumental permanence on the other, complicated further by the contradictions that already structure the poetic rhetoric of monumentality in Latin literature, is a fundamental one in Martial. I'm going to be exploring this paradox from various directions in this chapter. In particular, I want to stress how Martial's preoccupation with death intermeshes and overlays apparently diverse domains and perspectives – literal and metaliterary, cultural and poetic, miniaturist and global – seeming to penetrate every aspect of his poetics. Martial is just as interested in what it is for a poem, book or line to end, and when his readers want, or ought, to stop reading, as he is in the demise and survival of friends, rivals, enemies, monuments, eras or dynasties. The literary space of epigram, with its precise rules and markers, and the landscape of Rome, its history, architecture, people and *mores*, are seen to feed off and shape each other, alternately competing and blurring in the epigrammatic imagination.

PLAYING DEAD

It would be strange if Martial's corpus weren't so death-obsessed. As critics have discussed, this appears to be a 'standard topic' in ancient epigram: the collections of Meleager and Philippus contain many poems based on unusual deaths of people and animals, or on quasi-philosophical views about facing up to death and taking the measure of life. Peppered through each of Martial's books, as in the Greek Anthology, we find many varieties of epitaph, poems on unexpected fatalities, escapes from death, death wishes, deadly curses, and multiple takes on the familiar themes of *carpe diem* and *memento mori*.[2] Like his Greek predecessors, Martial preserves many of the

---

[1] On poetic monumentality see especially Fowler (2000) 193–217, Lowrie (1997) on Horace, and Farrell (1999) on Ovid.

[2] Henriksén (2006) attempts to categorise Martial's sepulchral epigrams and use of epigraphic formulae.

generic conventions of epitaphs (the earliest extant epigrams in Latin are also epitaphs), and hones the core paradox of a poetic form that embodies both the still silence of stone, the evolving, everlasting memory of the dead, and the living, chattering body of a reader in motion. We find all kinds of conventional, odd and funny permutations of this idea of life-in-death, or death-in-life, in the *Epigrams*. The poet's stellar career, for example, is already an 'afterlife': he boasts the kind of career success that comes to few poets in their graves (see for instance 1.1 and 5.10), and performs post-mortems on poetic predecessors that bring the past alive (see for example Catullus' 'Venuses and Cupids', buried along with Paris in the epitaph at 11.13). Whereas for Martial at 8.69, Vacerra's opinion that only dead poets deserve praise is not worth dying for, in 2.80, suicide Fannius dies 'to avoid death'.[3] At 10.67, Plutia dies after outliving 'all the crows' (which were said to survive up to nine generations of men), yet still 'bristles with lust' in her tomb alongside bald Melanthio. Similarly, these epigrams are sober written documents that appreciate silence amid the din of gossip and spectacle, yet they also talk, loud and dirty (in the preface to Book 8, for example, the verbs *scribo* and *loquor* are both used of Martial's latest collection, in the same sentence).[4] Drunken books can babble on, unstoppable (Martial has to rein in Book 4: '*ohe, iam satis est, ohe, libelle!*' ('Whoa, little book, that's enough already, whoa!' 4.89.1)), yet a monumental aesthetic often works (and fails) to suppress creeping flesh and wagging tongues; the sheer overwhelming, sleepless *noise* of Rome. 11.102, for instance, features a woman named Lydia who 'spoils her beautiful flesh' by refusing to shut up ('it's a prodigy when a statue starts to speak'), while 9.29, varying the recipe again, celebrates the long-overdue passing of procuress Philaenis, whose name means 'lover of tales': 'Ah, what a tongue is silent,' it exclaims; 'a thousand slave auctions could not drown it out, nor the curly-headed gang of the morning schoolmaster, nor the river bank that rings with Strymon's flock' (5–8). Nevertheless, in a wicked twist on the usual platitude, the final couplet disturbs the peace once more: 'Let the earth lie light upon you and

---

[3] As Watson and Watson (2003) note *ad loc.*, this is based on a well-known paradox, 'Men seek after death while fleeing from it', going back to Democritus (fr. 68 B 203 D-K), where the philosopher comments on the folly of actively seeking death through fear of it. This is an idea especially associated with the Epicureans: cf. Sen. *Ep.* 24.23 (Epicurus), *Ep.* 70.8 and Lucretius 3.79–82.

[4] *Quamvis autem epigrammata a severissimis quoque et summae fortunae viris ita scripta sint ut mimicam verborum licentiam adfectasse videantur, ego tamen illis non permisi tam lascive loqui quam solent* ('furthermore, although epigrams designed to imitate the verbal licence of mime have been written even by the most moral and high-standing of men, I have not allowed these here to talk as naughtily as they are used to,' 8, *Pref.* 11–14). See further discussion of this general point that the epigrams present themselves as 'simultaneously conversation and text' in Fowler (1995).

may soft sand cover you, lest the dogs be unable to dig up your bones'
(11–12).

   Yet there is much more to Martial's development of the paradoxes of
epitaphic rhetoric than ingenious twiddling on a traditional 'theme'. Martial presents epigram as a comment on and culmination of a labyrinthine
history of links between writing and death, text and epitaph in the ancient
world, and in Roman imperial poetry especially. For Martial, the project
of epigram is itself an extended investigation of just how close (successful)
poetry and the (ambitious) author can come to the annihilation and rot
of death. *quid minus esse potest?*, 'what could be more humble?' he says of
epigram at 12.94.9, addressing a rival who keeps on stealing his inspiration,
nudging him down the literary hierarchy, from epic and tragedy to lyric,
satire and 'light' elegy, till he hits rock bottom (*epigrammata fingere coepi*,
'I began to craft epigrams'). Yet in a flash, Tucca is after that trophy, too.
Exasperated, the poet tells his 'friend' to take what he wants – he'll scav-
enge for the scraps, if there are any left. In confining his talents to a poetic
form that represents the last step before career suicide, a genre so small it
is *almost* nothing at all, Martial probes the Derridean idea that any act of
representation evokes absence, loss and death.[5] This kind of poetry is less
a redeemer from decay than an ever-present token of the ephemerality of
paper and poet. In what is constructed as a saturated, backstabbing literary
culture haunted by the inimitable 'golden age' of Augustan poetry, each
*libellus*, as Martial reminds his epigrams at 3.2, is perhaps only moments
away from the grease and soot of a canteen kitchen, a satiric inferno where
papyrus will be recycled as wrapping for cheap take-way fish – itself a
familiar literary image that first enters Latin literature with Catullus.[6] In
this dirty, stingy and expansive genre, Martial dares to confront the limits
and meaning of poetry, showing and asking what poetry can or is forced
to be in a new Rome, and in a new, Flavian age.

---

[5] See Derrida (1978), where he deconstructs the age-old, Platonic concept of poetic language as
presentation rather than representation, showing that even speech cannot contain the truth as
presence, even though that is what it tries to do, and that writing exposes everything that speech
conceals. Also Mills-Courts (1990) e.g. 13: 'the act of representation bears the doubleness of the
epitaphic gesture. Like an inscription on a cenotaph, it proclaims death and an empty core, but that
emptiness is of a peculiar sort: the emptiness of a nothing that seems somehow to signify something.
It is the nothingness of a haunting'; and Foucault (1987), where he illustrates how death is the limit
and centre towards which and against which all strategies of self-representation are directed.

[6] See Martial 3.2.4, and compare Cat. 95.7–8, Pers. 1.43, 4.86.9. As Watson and Watson (2003) note on
3.2, *ad loc.*, the phrase *cito raptus* in line 3 suggests the book's premature death. It must hurry to find
itself a protector, or die a horrible, torturous death, as well as becoming the shrouds or temporary
tombs for dead fish. The kitchen black with smoke (also see 10.66.3 and 1.92.9, with Citroni 1980)
suggests the darkness of Hades.

Martial constantly plays off the lowly status of his epigram against his bid for world renown and monumental glory. This discourse, modernised and complicated by the Augustans against the backdrop of the emperor's spectacular building program and bid to immortalise himself in architecture, has a long and layered literary past. The function of epic poetry since Homer has been to glorify dead leaders and heroes, to commemorate. We might even, as Vernant discusses, trace a 'parallelism or continuity between Greek funerary rituals and epic verse'.[7] At the same time, as Scodel suggests in her reading of the *Iliad,* epitaphs both fall short of and (therefore) symbolise epic monumentality.[8] The Hellenistic poets manipulate the epitaphic form in new and clever ways (especially in epigram), weaving witty dialogues between the living and the dead through the medium of the inscribed gravestone, and composing self-epitaphs, and epitaphs to poetic predecessors, which call on the reader or 'passer-by' to remember them.[9] Virtual epitaphs become sites for literary debate, self-reflection and classification. In Rome, Ennius famously contrasts the vain attempt by kings to win fame and glory by building 'statues and tombs', with the immortality offered by the verses of his *Annals*[10] – an image which is already at least as old as Pindar.[11] His self-epitaph (which ends with the famous line *volito vivus per ora virum* / 'Alive on the mouths of men I fly') is quoted, commented on or alluded to by a string of authors, among them Cicero (*Tusc.* 1.15.34, 1.49.117, *Cato* 73), Vergil (*Georg.* 3.9, *Aen.* 12.234ff.) and Ovid (*Met.* 15.878–9), where the 'monument' of his epic equals even the great bronze tablets on which Rome's fate is carved at *Met.* 15.807–15.[12] Ovid's name will live on in a less fixed but even more everlasting way, as the *Metamorphoses* are recopied, reread and reinterpreted for all time.

'The epitaphic', then, is by no means confined to epigrams, which most closely resemble actual epitaphs. Sepulchral epigram is parodied, recast and embedded in much Roman poetry of the late Republican and Augustan periods, and continues to function as a key instrument and medium for literary self-commentary.[13] We find epitaphs throughout Vergil's *Aeneid*

---

[7] Vernant (1981) 285.    [8] R. Scodel (1992).

[9] For discussion see e.g. Walsh (1991, on Callimachus), Gutzwiller (1998) 93–102, 196–213, 252–73, 307–15, Goldhill (1994) and Bing (1988a).

[10] Book 16 frs. 411–13 Vahlen = 405–7 Skutsch.

[11] See e.g. *Olympian* 6. Lowrie (1997) 70–6 discusses the influence of Pindar's metaphor of monumentality on Horace in the *Odes.*

[12] As Wickkiser discusses (1999, 123–5), the similarities between Ovid's description of the bronze tablets of the fates in this passage and the monument of Ovid's poetry in the final *sphragis* are unmissable.

[13] See further discussion in Thomas (1998), who discusses how 'the poetry of Rome in the late Republican and Augustan periods shows inventive manipulation of the genre of sepulchral epigram'

(marking, for example, the deaths of Creusa, Anchises and Palinurus at the ends of books 2, 3 and 5, and Iris' release of Dido's soul in book 4),[14] and in *Eclogues* 5 and 9, while much has been written about how Horace's *Odes* reconfigure epitaphic rhetoric.[15] We also think of the many virtual epitaphs which eroticise death and poetry in Catullus and the Roman love elegists[16] – from the seductive mourning of Lesbia's sparrow in Catullus 3,[17] or Propertius' nightmare vision of dying unloved at 1.19, to Hypermestra's self-epitaph at the end of *Heroides* 14, or the dedication to dead Tibullus, which ends with a pseudo-inscription, at *Amores* 3.9, following Ovid's lament for his ghost-like, impotent body in *Amores* 3.7.[18] The lover-poet's existence is a kind of living death, yet at the same time never-ending love (or the ever-recurring torture of love, inscribed in the ebb and flow of elegiac couplets) grants him a kind of eternal life, an ideal enshrined in immortalising verse.

The idea that death can be performed, plotted and composed by the poet or poet-figure is hyped up further on the stage of Neronian literature.[19] Stoic Seneca, for example, figures suicide as the final, climactic act in the play of life (*Epist. Mor.* 77.20),[20] and the paradigm of Plato's *Phaedo* (in which Socrates discusses the nature of the soul before swallowing hemlock) is revived at several points in Tacitus and Plutarch in their descriptions of the suicides of Seneca and Thrasea Paetus.[21] The deaths of Lucan and Petronius, as told in Tacitus, are similarly 'scripted', and the two central 'author figures' of the *Satyricon*, Trimalchio and Eumolpus, both associate creative writing with death and rehearse scenes of their own deaths and

---

(222). It's also interesting to note, with Clairmont (1970, xviii), that 'the number of epigrams on grave monuments increases markedly during the Roman as compared with the archaic, classical and Hellenistic periods.'

[14] Also see the sepulchral epigrams to Misenus at 6.164–7, and Caieta at 7.1–4 (marking the transition between the 'Odyssean' and 'Iliadic' *Aeneid*), with R. Scodel (1992). On the dedication of epitaphs to minor heroes in Latin epic, especially the *Aeneid,* see Dinter (2005).

[15] On the *Odes*, see Lowrie (1997).

[16] On embedded epitaphs in Roman love poetry, see Thomas (1998), Foulou (1996) and R. Scodel (1992)

[17] Also see Catullus' epitaph to his brother, 101, which is then embedded in poem 68.19–24 and 91–6.

[18] See also, e.g., Prop. 2.13.35–6, 4.7.85–6, 1.7.24, 2.1.78, Tibullus 1.3.55–6, 3.2.29–30, Ovid *Amores* 2.6.

[19] On this see Connors (1994).

[20] *quomodo fabula, sic vita: non quam diu, sed quam bene acta sit, refert. nihil ad rem pertinet quo loco desinas. quocumque voles desine: tantum bonam clausulam impone* ('as in a play, so in life. What's important is not how long it lasts, but how well it is acted. It doesn't matter when you stop. Stop wherever you like: just put a good clausula at the end'). (*Clausula* can mean both the end of a letter or a play, and the final syllables of a well-crafted sentence: the phrase *clausulam impone,* a cretic and trochee pattern, is precisely the kind of clausula favoured by Cicero.)

[21] Tac. *Ann.* 15.60–4 (Seneca's death by poison), *Ann.* 16.34–5 (the suicide of Thrasea Paetus); Plut. *Cat. min.* 58.2, 70.2 (cf. Sen. *Ep.* 24.6–8), the scene in which Cato reads the *Phaedo* twice in the hours before his suicide.

funerals:[22] in the *Cena*, Trimalchio composes epitaphs, stages his own funeral procession and gives instructions for a huge, ornate mausoleum to be built (even though he has 'thirty years, four months and two days' left to live), while writing the end of his *Bellum Civile* coincides with Eumolpus' near-death experience in the shipwreck at *Sat.* 115. Our manuscripts end with Eumolpus' pseudo death-throes in Croton, where the poet warps the philosophical claim that the soul lives on after death by promising an audience of cannibals that his dead body will 'survive' by being eaten. Nero's own death, according to the famous passage in Suetonius, is preceded by the emperor's elaborate instructions for his burial and tomb, along with his repeated cries of '*qualis artifex pereo*!', 'What an artist dies with me!'[23] And Tacitus' Petronius slips away as he reclines with slit wrists at a dinner party, to a soundtrack of bawdy verse.[24]

By the time Martial is writing, in the shadow of Augustus' Mausoleum, there is no escaping the textualisation and theatricalisation of death, or the web of associations between writing poetry and (transcending) death in Roman culture. Whilst Rome (after the great fire of AD 64) was being 'remonumentalised' in quite dazzling ways,[25] Martial's contemporaries, Pliny the Younger, Silius Italicus, Statius and Tacitus, all add to an evolving dialogue about the role of literature in constructing and perpetuating fame, both of authors and historical figures (not least emperors). Epigram, however, which even more than epic can lay claim to a monumental status, yet at the same time can be scribbled between appointments and thrown away with tonight's dinner, offers *really* fertile turf to test out and elaborate paradoxes that have come to shape Roman, poetic self-definition, especially in relation to imperial power. As the most physical, gritty and 'real' of poetic forms, epigram presents Martial with the ultimate and perhaps most entertaining of literary challenges (crowds always love the underdog, he knows): while Vespasian and his successors strive to trump the grand architectural statements of Augustan Rome, how can the author of the *De Spectaculis*, the poet elected to preserve Rome's new, defining edifices, manage and overcome (or even celebrate) the instability and deadliness ingrained, he imagines, both in imperial literary culture and in epigram itself?

---

[22] See further discussion in Rimell (2007).    [23] Suet. *Nero* 49.1.    [24] Tac. *Ann.* 16.19.
[25] As Boyle writes (2003, 30), 'The Flavians . . . did not simply rebuild; they rebuilt innovatively, grandiosely, and semiotically . . . A new architecture and iconography meant not only a new Rome but a new *romanitas,* one in which "Romanness" was a subject relationship to the Flavian emperor, who was everywhere immanent in the city through buildings and repetitious iconography.' See Boyle (2003) 29–35, Newlands (2002) 8–13, Darwall-Smith (1996) 102–252.

Such contradiction and insecurity are of course *already* part of the discourse of monumentality in Latin literature, and perhaps even define it. When Horace boasts in *Odes* 3.30 that the monument of his lyric verse is 'more lasting than bronze' and 'higher than the regal mass of the pyramids', much has been made of the possible ambiguity of *situs* in line 2, which means 'site' or 'mass', but also 'decay'.[26] This less obvious and more disruptive meaning finds its way into Martial's declaration of his eternal fame at 8.3.5–8:

> et cum rupta **situ** Messalae saxa iacebunt
> altaque cum Licini marmora pulvis erunt,
> me tamen ora legent et secum plurimus hospes
> ad patrias sedes carmina nostra feret.

> And when Messala's stones lie ruined
> and the high marbles of Licinus turn to dust,
> I shall still be read and many a tourist
> will cart my poems home as souvenirs.

For Martial, as for Horace, Ovid and later authors, to say that poetry is a metaphorical *monumentum*, that is, both like and unlike a (real, destructible) monument, is to weaken and unbalance the claim for poetry's transcendence. Epigram 8.3 highlights this point wickedly: in the line just before the passage quoted above, Martial claims that he can rest easy and stop composing, as *teritur noster ubique liber* ('my books are thumbed everywhere now', 8.3.4). Yet *teritur* literally means 'is crushed', 'worn down' or 'used up':[27] while tombs are eroded over time, so are these *libelli*, especially as they are perfect for carrying in your pocket around the city or whilst travelling.[28] As Fowler puts it, referring both to the literary trope and to ancient and modern anxieties about the impermanence and vulnerability of tombs,[29] 'the essence of the monument is paradoxically its lack of monumental stability.'[30] Ovid's *Metamorphoses*, for example, whose spirit lives

---

[26] See discussion in Fowler (2000) 197–8, with Nisbet and Rudd (2004) 369.

[27] Compare e.g. Ovid *Tr.* 4.6.14 (*hoc rigidas silices, hoc adamanta terit*).

[28] *Tero* also has a sexual use ('to rub'), which is hinted at here in 8.3 (see Adams (1982) 183, 219). His books are rough or depilated slaves, perfect for groping.

[29] As Hope explores (2000), the fact that people often feared what would happen to both their tomb and their remains is often attested in surviving inscriptions from the ancient world, which commonly curse and call for fines against those who interfere with graves. Hope argues here that in all likelihood, the tombs and graves of earlier generations were quickly forgotten, and notes that the demands on and changes made to tombs and burial places are well illustrated by the Isola Sacra necropolis, where the epitaphic wishes of the founders of tomb-houses about who would have access to the tomb were often ignored, with burial spaces either given or sold to others over time, and tombs subdivided or disrupted by the introduction of inhumation burials.

[30] Fowler (2000) 211.

on and bubbles through Martial's *Epigrams*, bounces the ideal of poetic permanence and immortality off the creative forces and anxieties of transformation. Martial, as we'll see further in this chapter, takes up Ovid's own strategy in the exile poetry of editing and reframing his epic (as well as his elegiac poetry), ensuring that it 'survives' while implying that its shape might morph beyond recognition. After Ovid, and Petronius (and even Catullus, with his endless stream of kisses), living on 'in the mouths of men' counts as both liberation from the material world and as sardonic full immersion into fluid corporeality.

### SEEING STARS: THE *DE SPECTACULIS*

In order to construct his peculiar behemoth, the monument of epigram, Martial plucks at a nexus of passages in Augustan poetry which are themselves intricate commentaries on the twisted trope of poem as (outlasting) *monumentum*. It comes as little surprise that epigram gets its satiric teeth into the ideal of posthumous *fama* from the outset. This kind of poetry is (in part) far too throwaway and material to set its sights on eternal fame. As I mentioned at the beginning of this chapter, Martial is already busy constructing and basking in his present popularity, and wastes (almost) no time obsessing about future success. He's ahead of the game, enjoying the kind of celebrity few poets can lay claim to *post cineres*, 'after death' (this line, in poem 1.1, is both a jokey reversal of Ovid *Ex Ponto* 4.16.3, *famaque post cineres maior venit* ('fame is greater after death'), and a playful continuation of Ovid's humble arrogance: given that in exile he is effectively 'dead', he can be around to enjoy the boost to his celebrity that death brings to every well-known writer). Near the end of Book 1 (perhaps the 'true' or alternative end, as this anthology far exceeds the 100 items limit intimated in 1.118), Martial rejects the corny gesture of the epic poet who stages the funeral of his own career by burning his books. If he had a patron like Maecenas, and (therefore) the leisure time to spend his days writing, *then* he'd 'try to write works that would live through the centuries' and 'snatch' his name 'from the flames' (1.107.3–6):[31]

> otia da nobis, sed qualia fecerat olim
> Maecenas Flacco Vergilioque suo:

---

[31] This plays on the story that Vergil attempted to burn the *Aeneid* on his deathbed as he would not have time to perfect it. Ovid also jokes around this image and inspires Martial, e.g. in *Tr.* 1.7, where he burns the *Metamorphoses*, only to reveal he has multiple copies.

condere victuras temptem per saecula curas
et nomen flammis eripuisse meum.

Give me leisure time – that is, what Maecenas
guaranteed his Flaccus and Vergil,
and I'd write works that'd last through the centuries,
and snatch my name from the funeral fires.

At points throughout Book 1 and the *De Spectaculis*, his first published collections, Martial often echoes the formulae for poetic and imperial immortality which litter Augustan poetry. In particular, he returns to the familiar cliché of 'soaring to the stars' or 'flying through the air to the stars', mythologised above all in the escape of creative genius Daedalus from his Cretan prison on man-made wings, and in the parallel/counter-model of his son Icarus, the over-ambitious young artist who sails too close to the sun and plunges to his death in a sea that will carry his *nomen* for evermore. The final promise of Ennius' self-epitaph, *volito vivus per ora virum* ('alive on the mouths of men I fly,' quoted by Cicero, *Tusc.* 1.34), resounds through (for example) Horace's predictions for his own immortality at *Odes* 2.20 (*non usitata nec tenui ferar / pinna biformis per liquidum aethera . . .* , 'on no common or feeble wing shall I soar in double form through liquid air . . .', 1–3). Vergil also uses the image of flying or being born to the stars at several points, first at *Eclogues* 5.50–2, where Mopsus and Menalcas compete in immortalising Daphnis (cf. *Ecl.* 9.27–9), and then at *Georgics* 3.8–9, where he looks ahead to the higher pursuits of immortalising epic: . . . *temptanda via est, qua me quoque possim / tollere humo victorque virum volitare per ora* ('I must attempt a path whereby I, too, may rise from the earth and fly victorious on the lips of men'). At *Aeneid* 9.640–1, Apollo addresses young Ascanius after his first day as a soldier, and assures him future stardom: *macte nova virtute, puer, sic itur ad astra* ('blessings on your valour, boy: this is the path to the stars'). And at *Aeneid* 7.98–101, Jupiter predicts the glorious future of the Latin race, saying, *externi venient generi, qui sanguine nostrum / nomen in astra ferant* ('strangers shall come to be your sons, whose blood shall exalt our name to the stars').

Martial's *De Spectaculis*, probably commissioned by Titus to celebrate the inauguration of the Colosseum in AD 80,[32] takes these aspirations to heavenly disembodiment (of which I've mentioned just a few) and transforms them, for a new, bloodthirsty audience, into a sequence of

[32] On the (ultimately unconvincing) possibility that the *De Spectaculis* might, after all, have been written for Domitian, see Coleman (2006) xlv–lxiv.

spectacular, agonising deaths and mutilations. The phrases *ad aethera*, and *in astra*, now become tags for a mischievous and tyrannical perversion of poetic claims to eternal life and fame.[33] We begin at poem 16, where a bull is tossed heavenwards by (we gather from *De Spect.* 17) an elephant:[34]

> Raptus abit media quod ad aethera taurus harena,
>     non fuit hoc artis, sed pietatis opus.

> Snatched from mid-arena, the bull left for the sky.
> This was the work not of art, but of devotion.

This is followed by another bull's not-quite-parallel revenge, as it throws a prisoner kitted out to resemble mythic beast-fighter Hercules high into the air on its horns (16b):

> Vexerat Europen fraterna per aequora taurus:
>     at nunc Alciden taurus in astra tulit.
> Caesaris atque Iovis confer nunc, Fama, iuvencos:
>     par onus ut tulerint, altius iste tulit.

> A bull had carried Europa through his brother's sea:
> but now a bull has raised Alcides to the stars.
> Compare now, Fame, the cattle of Caesar and Jove.
> Even though they bore an equal load, this one threw his higher.

In poem 19, the same bull, which 'had just lifted up dummies and tossed them to the stars' (*sustulerat raptas taurus in astra pilas*, 2)[35] after being tortured by fire 'through the whole arena', is itself killed by the emperor's devoted elephant which appeared in poems 16 and 17. And in *De Spect.* 22, a goaded rhinoceros spears a bull with his double horns, 'just as a bull tosses dummies to the stars' (*iactat ut impositas taurus in astra pilas*, 22.6). Typically, Martial has summoned all the demonic magic of Ovidian metamorphosis to turn artists into beasts (Ovid's *natus homo est*, 'so man was born' at *Met.* 1.78, becomes *nata fera est*, 'so a beast was born', in the triptych on the birthing-dying sow at *De Spect.* 12.8 and 13.6).[36] Heroes become victims; the prisoner playing Daedalus is ripped apart by a bear

---

[33] Also note the precedent of Seneca, *Thyestes* 885–7, where the tyrannical Atreus, his hands bloody from slaughtering Thyestes' sons, describes himself as reaching up to the stars and knocking the gods off their thrones.

[34] The poem also contains the joke of (re-)creating the cosmos: we 'see' how the constellation *taurus* came to be in the sky.

[35] The participle *raptus* traces a pattern of violence and revenge: in poem 16, the idea that the bull is *raptus* (seized, or 'raped') jokes on the myth of the bull raping Pasiphae, which is restaged in the arena at *De Spect.* 5. In 19, the bull again does the 'raping', but is then attacked once more by a larger beast, speared (if Housman's conjecture *cornuto ore* is correct) by a 'horned mouth'.

[36] See further discussion of Martial's use of Ovid *Met.* 1 in the *De Spectaculis* in Rimell (forthcoming).

in poem 8 (*quam cuperes pinnas nunc habuisse tuas!* 'how you wish you had your wings now!' Martial sneers), as is another poetic icon, Orpheus, at poem 21. In this scene, an acid cutting-down and revision of Ovid's extended account at the beginning of *Metamorphoses* 11,[37] birds soar above the bard not because they are enchanted by his song, but because they are waiting to peck at his sorry corpse. Is the bear that savages these two has-been artists the same one that in poem 11 seems to 'fly' and is caught like a bird in sticky lime? Here, what was once a Daedalean miracle of flight is aped by a dumb, heavy, nameless animal which doesn't so much soar as get hurled across the arena. The goddess Fama now judges beasts, not poets, in the competition for glory (16b.3). Yet this 'fame' is cheap entertainment and lasts but a second. So many gored bodies are 'tossed to the stars' that even that spectacular thrill gets downgraded to the trivial. In short, there could be no better stage than the bloodied arena for showing off Martial's tactic of reducing everything he touches to epigram's bargain-basement level, and for enacting epigram's need to grapple with the grim reality of (literary) death. The Colosseum serves as a microcosm for both Titus' empire and Martial's epigrammatic world. It is also itself a kind of giant tomb, putting Augustus' Mausoleum to shame (see *De Spect.* 1.5), while at the same time mirroring its circular shape, and replacing its one honoured corpse with many dead actor-heroes.

The contrast between Titus' architectural feat, which will surpass all other monuments, and the disposable, easily forgotten lives and snapshot deaths of the victims on display within it, is cleverly mirrored in Martial's branding of epigram as both memorialising and ephemeral, as obsessed both with repeated closure and with living to the full, as well as living on. Poems such as 12–14, the triptych on a sow which dies just as one of her litter is born by 'Caesarian section', is a perfect showpiece for epigram's knotting of death and life, killing off and preservation, modernism and nostalgia. Throughout the *De Spectaculis*, Martial both debunks and hyperbolises traditional claims to eternal fame. In part, the message is loud and clear that the emperor alone has the prerogative on celebrity and magic making, and poets (at least, the poet figures of old) must settle for humbler goals. The poet's world of myth, especially, is more than trumped by the *real* grotesque artifices of the arena.[38] At the same time, these epigrammatic games gain monumental gravitas by association, and even compete with Titus' spectacles, offering up action-packed highlights with extra features

[37] See also discussion in Hinds (2007).    [38] See especially poems 5, 6b, 7, 27.

(poetic tricks galore) for an impatient crowd. There are no intervals in this fast-paced show: *i nunc et lentas corripe, turba, moras!* ('go crowd, complain now of boring delays!' 22.12). Martial reinvents as well as parodies monumentality in this book: with epigram as his camera, he can take epitaphic snapshots which preserve his subjects (as if) in stone just as surely as a real statue or tomb, while at the same time making us see great mausolea wobble. This is precisely the effect of the reuse of *aëre vacuo pendentia Mausolea,* 'the Mausoleum poised in empty air' (*De Spect.* 1.5) in the scene of a hunter appearing to snare a clumsy bear mid-air, in the same line of poem 11: *deprendat vacuo venator in aëre praedam* ('let the hunter catch his prey in the empty air'). Augustus' tomb is 'hanging' in 'empty' space, seeming to totter in the metaphorical glare of Titus' opus, whilst epigram's eye can move quickly enough to let us see the most unlikely of beasts pinned down as it 'flies'.

Not that we leave these deadly amphitheatrics behind when we launch into *Epigrams* 1. The first poem, after 1.1's drum roll, and the commercial break of 1.2, sees Martial's beat-up slave of a book determined to pimp a living in the arena that is Rome (1.3):

> Argiletanas mavis habitare tabernas,
>     cum tibi, parve liber, scrinia nostra vacent?
> nescis, heu, nescis dominae fastidia Romae:
>     crede mihi, nimium Martia turba sapit.
> maiores nusquam rhonci: iuvenesque senesque
>     et pueri nasum rhinocerotis habent.
> audieris cum grande sophos, dum basia iactas,
>     ibis ab excusso missus in astra sago.
> sed tu ne totiens domini patiare lituras
>     neve notet lusus tristis harundo tuos,
> aetherias, lascive, cupis volitare per auras:
>     i, fuge; sed poteras tutior esse domi.

> Would you rather live in the shops of Argiletum, little book,
> when my desk has all this empty space for you?
> You've absolutely no idea how scornful a mistress Rome can be:
> Trust me, Mars' rabble is far *too* smart these days.
> You won't hear louder snorts anywhere:
> young men, old men, kids, all with rhinoceros noses.
> They'll be clapping you off, but just as you're throwing your kisses,
> you'll be tossed to the stars from a shaken cloak.
> But you, you little raver, fancy soaring through the airs of heaven –
> anything but suffer your master's endless edits,
> and his cruel pen slicing through your jokes.

> Go on then, get out of here – just bear in mind
> you might have been much safer stuck at home.

It's a dangerous, foreign world out there, a world that evolves out of a past defined here in terms of Augustan poetry. Yet it is also scarily new. 1.3 is most obviously inspired by two (interactive) classics from the Augustan period: first Horace *Epistles* 1.20, where the personified book yearns for public life, though its master did his best to discourage such plebeian tendencies, and is sent out into the city, risking ruin, enslavement and degradation, with instructions to talk up its author's rags-to-riches story. And secondly, Ovid's first poem in the *Tristia*, where the exiled poet sends his little book to Rome as his representative, to plead the case for his return. Unlike Horace, Ovid encourages the book to appear rough and dog-eared (this is the fate Horace's *libellus* is threatened with), as it is in mourning for its 'dead' author-father, and warns it not to shy away from the common crowd. Martial picks up Ovid's *parve liber* (*Tr.* 1.1.1, cf. Martial 1.3.2), and *ibis* (*Tr.* 1.1.1, cf. 1.3.8), and marks his debt to the exilic *Tristia* with his 'sad pen' (*tristis harundo*) in line 10. Though now, of course, Martial plays emperor doling out over-harsh punishments, and his *liturae* ('blots', line 9, cf. *Tr.* 1.1.13, *neve liturarum pudeat*) are not caused by the tears of an anguished poet, but refer to the 'continual erasures' of a sadistic master. Furthermore, here and elsewhere, Martial collapses what in Ovid are the remotest reaches of the empire with the Romanized provinces and the city of Rome itself. The Colosseum's gigantic structure, which can contain and order (representatives from) the whole empire (as *De Spect.* 3 describes) has become a metaphor both for how the empire has expanded under the Flavians (so that what once were the furthest margins are now fully Romanised – colourful, quaint suburbs of a cosmopolitan centre), and for the way in which Martial's 'tiny' epigram wants to swallow and package up the Roman world. In a city thronging with Sarmatians, Arabs, Ethiopians and even the occasional Brit (*De Spect.* 3), making one's debut on the streets of Rome is akin to travelling the globe. Yet in Martial's vision, characterised as always by flipsiding and paradox, it also works the other way around: the rules and cruelty of Rome's favourite spectator sport penetrate everyday life far beyond the Colosseum, as if the arena exports its own violent norms as well as importing and unifying what lies outside it.

*Epigrams* 1.3 sees Martial, or his book, caught between inside and out-side, private and public, past and present. Ovid's dream of return set out in *Tristia* 1.1 gestures towards Martial's own literary backtracking and reminiscence in this poem. The idea of poetry belonging to a small private world, of the poet shunning public life and writing in enclosed, inside spaces, immediately evokes the kind of imagery used in Horace and other Augustan poetry. In urging his book to stay indoors, Martial presents himself as still reluctant, in this programmatic piece, to enter Flavian Rome and the Rome of epigram, and impresses upon readers just how attached this project will be to the shapes, vocabulary and ideals of his predecessors. The book itself is still eager to flit through the heavens, *volitare per auras* (contrast the down-to-earth living fame vaunted in 1.1), yet with Horace's warnings still reverberating in the background, it is more likely to suffer the literal star-tossing of beasts and prisoners in the arena. Its dream of immortal fame is now an anachronistic concept: the audiences in today's recitals (which might as well be *munera*) have critical noses as sharp as rhinoceros' horns. Not that, in Martial's universe, there is much difference between the sado-masochistic den of the poet's study and the cruel bookshops of today's dominatrix Rome (*domina Roma* 1.3.3). This little book might well *not* have been better off 'at home' (1.3.12).

### LIVING ON, AND ON: BOOK 10

At this point in the discussion of Martial's tomb-like books, I want to fastforward to Book 10, or rather to Book 10 (second edition), sent back to the drawing board, edited, patched up and polished after Domitian's murder and *damnatio memoriae* in AD 96. In terms of my discussions in this chapter, *Epigrams* 10 is in at the deep end, a fault line in Martial's twelve-book epic tome which teaches us to keep looking backwards and forwards, to (re)read *everything* differently. Book 10 is also where we'll find a cluster of epigrammatic soundbites on poetry's epitaphic function. As 10.2.11–12 put it,

> at chartis nec furta nocent et saecula prosunt,
>   solaque non norunt haec monumenta mori.
>
> But thefts don't harm paper and time is a boon.
> These are the only monuments that cannot die.

We soon see this formula reapplied. 10.26 is an epitaph to Varus, a military commander who has died in action somewhere on the banks of the Nile, where his body still lies unburied. Even though he cannot be entombed or mourned in a funeral, this 'eternal poem' will grant him a 'name that will live on' (*sed datur aeterno victurum carmine nomen*, 10.26.7). In 10.63.1–2,[39] similarly, the marble poem that we (like passing travellers) are reading is small, yet, in a throwback to the majestic Colosseum in *De Spect.* 1, as well as to Horace *Odes* 3.30, it 'will not yield to the stones of Mausolus and the pyramids':

> Marmora parva quidem sed non cessura, viator,
> Mausoli saxis pyramidumque legis.

> The marble you read is small indeed, dear traveller,
> but will outlast Mausolus' stones, and the pyramids.

Amidst such stiffened soundbites, the collection chews over the passage of time, celebrating birthdays (e.g. 10.24, 10.27, 10.87), and debating what it is to think about and approach mortality at crucial life junctures. We'll find here an epigrammatic gamut of deaths: a selection of epitaphs (as well as 10.26 and 63, Martial builds gravestones out of words for charioteer Scorpus at 10.50, for Erotion at 61, Plutia at 67, and Rabirius' parents at 71); premature deaths (Scorpus and Erotion), and deaths long overdue (Plutia); deaths foiled (Numa at 10.97), plotted and imagined (Martial's paradise at 10.24, the drawn-out agony of 'someone' at 10.5), and one man's imagined return from the Elysian fields in 10.101. Epigram's deadpan humour spills over at 10.16 (death is a neoteric *lusus* when boarish Mr Aper plays Cupid, piercing his wife's heart with an arrow, or *pen, harundo*), at 10.43 (serial monogamist Phil-eros buries his seventh wife on his own land – no farmer gets a better return than he does) and at 10.77 (Carus dies of a nasty fever, but Martial wishes it had been less fatal, so his enemy might have survived to see his doctor – the implication being that this way he would have died a slow, excruciating death).

All this and more is framed and complicated by the presentation of Book 10 as a second edition: the first was 'published too hastily', and Martial recalled it, killing off some poems, reviving others and adding lots more (10.2.1–4). Domitian has been assassinated, hailing a new era and prompting a complete rethink of what Book 10 should look like, what epigram should do and memorialise *now*. While the ex-tyrant's existence is being erased from public monuments, Martial implicitly edits out his

---

[39] This 'inscription', which we read in perusing this book just as a roadside tomb catches the eye of a passing traveller, is spoken by the ideal *univira*, a Roman matron of unblemished reputation who has only ever had one husband and who also has the unlikely good fortune to have outlived all ten of her children, five boys and five girls. Martial lines up the epitaphic markers (the address to a passer-by, the small tomb, contrasted with the greatness of its occupant), only to crack all solemnity with the sharp last line: out of this chaste mouth come the words, '*una pudicitiae mentula nota meae*', 'my chastity knew only one cock'.

Domitian poems, backtracking and excising all that filthy flattery. As he puts it in 10.72, 'I am not about to speak of "Lord and God". There is no place for all that in this city.' Domitian is succeeded by senator Nerva in 96 (*iustissimus omnium senator*, 'the most just of all senators', 10.72.9), who dies in 98 after an epigrammatic reign, leaving his newly adopted son, the Spanish-born Trajan, to take his place. The book apparently spans this period of rollercoaster uncertainty. It's clear from the start that while this second edition hails, in some sense, a new poetic freedom, and marks the canny survival of Martial's fluid edifice when other stones and inscriptions are crumbling, or being smashed, it also performs its scarred and split character, and pressures the metaphor of poetic monumentality until it cracks open. The book is an engrossing palimpsest that invites us to expose strata of allusions to literary epitaphs, epilogues and endings of all kinds. The epigrams in it pick constantly at tensions between stony writtenness and winged orality, between past and present, deaths and rebeginnings, nostalgia and forgetting. What's more, as we'll be seeing in a moment, the book is especially marked by its mixing up of beginnings and endings, so that they inhabit the same space and are inseparable. Each and every one of these poems, we suspect, is invested in some way in enacting a book in limbo, strung between eras and languages, death and life, full of tight and ragged seams, or like the plagiarist's latest at 10.100, 'arguing with itself'. This is, as Boyle puts it, 'a hard book to read' – though perhaps not in all senses of the word.[40]

Let's look first at the poems chosen to front this intriguing 'double' collection. Suitably, we notice, 10.1 and 10.2 are written in elegiacs, the metre that (especially after Ovid) looks most 'bitty' – couplets jigsawed together, each one a lopsided partnership of 'the one' and 'the other', hexameter and pentameter, or two hexameters, the second cropped to fit. Before the eulogy to monumentalising reading in 10.2, Martial inserts a note to readers, inviting us to re-edit the new draft, to turn big into small as we see fit. We're reminded of Ovid's reaffirmed devotion to elegy at the beginning of his third book of *Amores* (*ergo ades et longis versibus adde brevis* 3.1.66): notice how the first hexameter of 10.1 is tagged with the word *longus*, the last pentameter with *brevis*:

> Si nimius videor seraque coronide longus
> esse liber, legito pauca: libellus ero.
> terque quaterque mihi finitur carmine parva
> pagina: fac tibi me quam cupis esse brevem.

---

[40] Boyle (1995a) 266. As Henderson (2001) also goes a very long way to showing.

> If I seem too big and long a book whose end page
> comes too late, just read a bit: then I'll be little.
> Quite often, my tiny pages end with a poem's
> end: so make me as short for yourself as you like.

Was 10.1 an add-on, slipped in at the end? The ingenious pull of Book
10 is that we're always wondering what's new and what's old, and whether
it's supposed to show. This opening gambit helps get us into the spirit: we
can join in with Martial (ed.) and erase what we like. But that's skipping
ahead. Only in 10.2 do we stop, rewind, and hear the longer story (unless
we've already decided to ignore this one, and take a shortcut to the next,
or last, page):[41]

> Festinata prior, decimi mihi cura libelli
>     elapsum manibus nunc revocavit opus.
> nota leges quaedam sed lima rasa recenti:
>     pars nova maior erit: lector, utrique fave,
> lector, opes nostrae: quem cum mihi Roma dedisset,
>     'nil tibi quod demus maius habemus' ait.
> 'pigra per hunc fugies ingratae flumina Lethes
>     et meliore tui parte superstes eris.
> marmora Messallae findit caprificus et audax
>     dimidios Crispi mulio ridet equos:
> at chartis nec furta nocent et saecula prosunt,
>     solaque non norunt haec monumenta mori.'

> Booklet number ten, edition one, was far too hurried:
> It slipped from my hands, but now it's been recalled.
> Some pieces you'll read here are known, just polished up of late,
> but most stuff is brand-new: look kindly on both, dear reader –
> you *are* my fame and fortune. When Rome gave you to me,
> she said, 'I could grant you nothing greater. Through him,
> you'll dodge the lazy waves of thankless Lethe,
> and live on in the better part of you.
> The fig tree splits Messalla's marble, the bold
> mule-driver mocks Crispus' half-horses.
> But thefts don't harm paper and time is a boon:
> These are the only monuments that cannot die.'

If we don't fastforward, 10.2 is our second chance at ending this book, quick.
In the excitement of reshuffling, and inspired by an impatient model reader,
this poem is patched together from a number of famous past epilogues,
blended in with Martial old and new. To begin with, Rome's prophecy for

---

[41] Henderson (2001) makes this point.

Martial's afterlife synthesises (at least) three end poems by Ovid. Compare *et meliore tui parte superstes eris* (10.2.8) with *Amores* 1.15.41–2 (the last lines):[42]

> ergo etiam cum me supremus adederit ignis
> vivam, parsque mei multa superstes erit.

> Once the last fire has devoured me, I too
> shall live, and the great part of me shall survive.

and *Amores* 3.15.19–20 (the last lines):

> inbelles elegi, genialis Musa, valete,
> post mea mansurum fata superstes opus!

> Unwarlike elegies, kind muse, farewell –
> my work will survive and live on after me.

and finally (?) *Metamorphoses* 15.871–9, the culmination of all that's gone before:

> Iamque opus exegi, quod nec Iovis ira nec ignis
> nec poterit ferrum nec edax abolere vetustas.
> cum volet, illa dies, quae nil nisi corporis huius
> ius habet, incerti spatium mihi finiat aevi:
> **parte tamen meliore mei** super alta perennis
> astra ferar, **nomenque erit indelebile nostrum,**
> quaque patet domitis Romana potentia terris,
> ore legar populi, perque omnia saecula fama,
> (siquid habent veri vatum praesagia) **vivam.**

> And now my work is done, which neither the wrath of Jove, nor fire,
> nor sword, nor the gnawing tooth of time shall have power to destroy.
> When it wants, let that day come which has no law except over
> this body, and end the span of my uncertain years;
> yet in my better part I shall be borne immortal beyond the
> lofty stars, and my name shall live on for evermore.
> Wherever Rome's might extends over conquered lands,
> I shall be read on the mouths of men, and through all the ages,
> if there is any truth in the prophecies of bards, I shall live in fame.

---

[42] Martial has previously used another line from the end poem *Amores* 1.15 to begin a book, and to begin his entire epic collection of twelve books. See 1.1.2, *toto notus in orbe Martialis*, cf. *Am.* 1.15.8, *in toto semper ut orbe canar*, itself a selfish remake of *Am.* 1.3.25–6 (*nos quoque per totum pariter cantabimur orbem, / iunctaque semper erunt nomina nostra tuis.*) See C. Williams (2002a) on traces of *Amores* 1.15 in the epigrams. As Williams summarises (424), 'Ovidian and Horatian reflections on lasting poetic fame placed at the end of a book, collection, or epic have become a declaration of immortality authoritatively uttered in the voice of a personified Rome and confidently placed at the beginning of the book.'

These last lines of the *Metamorphoses* resonate, like Martial's, with two
other crucial passages in Latin literature which rehearse the image of poem
as (surpassing) monument: Ennius' self-epitaph (see especially the parting
phrase *volito vivus per ora virum*), and Horace *Odes* 3.30, again the last
poem of the book, especially lines 1–8:

> Exegi monumentum aere perennius
> regalique situ pyramidum altius,
> quod non imber edax, non Aquilo impotens
> possit diruere aut innumerabilis
> annorum series et fuga temporum.
> non omnis moriar multaque pars mei
> vitabit Libitinam: usque ego postera
> crescam laude recens.

> I have built a monument more lasting than bronze
> and higher than the pyramids' regal pile,
> one that no biting rain, no mad North wind
> can destroy, nor the countless chain of
> years and the flight of time.
> The whole of me shan't die, but a great part of me
> will escape the grave: on and on I'll grow,
> renewed by future praise.

I've already mentioned that 10.63 also reuses the model of *Odes* 3.30 (the
matron's small grave is greater than 'the stones of Mausolus or the pyramids'), while the line I quoted above from 10.26 (*sed datur aeterno victurum carmine nomen*) almost repeats Ovid addressing Elegy at *Amores*
3.1.65 (*altera das nostro victurum nomen amori*, 'the other, you grant eternal fame to my love'), a poem which marks a new beginning and rein-
vention after talk of ending it all (the goddess Elegia asks her poet at
3.1.15, *ecquis erit tibi finis amandi?* ('Will there ever be an end to your
loving?')).

10.2, meanwhile, is at saturation point: How 'long' can it get? We're
already getting nostalgic for the *festinatus* version (though at the same time
we're learning for the nth time that poems short in length can be long
to read).[43] Edition number one 'slipped away' (*elapsum manibus*, 2), but
Martial has dragged its corpse back from the dead (*revocavit*, 2), or at least
part of it (*pars maior*, 4), the part which will survive (*et meliore tui parte*

---

[43] As always in Martial, the reverse is also just as likely: long can seem short, e.g. in 10.71, where
Rabirius feels that he is laying his parents to rest 'in his earliest years', even though they are ancient
and he far from young. Time, and the length or size of poems, is relative, and their assessment
subjective.

*superstes eris*, 8). But we're bound to ask (this *is* epigram): in buffing up edition number two, did he also cheat and import 'new' poems from old books? 10.2, after all, is very similar to 8.3, part of an introductory series in a book dedicated and devoted to the now dead emperor, Domitian (compare especially 10.2.9–10, which use as an example the magnificent tomb of Messalla, a freedman of Augustus, with 8.3.5–6, which I quoted earlier in this chapter). 10.1 also seems designed to be set alongside 8.3, which is well aware that six or seven books of epigrams were already too much, *nimium* (cf. *nimius* 10.1.1): two book tens are *really* going overboard. This beginning of Book 10 which (for the impatient reader) could be the end, a rebeginning that marks the passing of this book's non-identical twin, is enriched by a classic library of ends that promise never-endingness, or ends which are (re)beginnings, or beginnings which call for an end (8.3.3 requested *sit pudor et finis*, 'let there be some shame, and an end', before the ninth sister fate urged Martial to continue). As 10.1 promises, this book is already ending and ending again (*terque quaterque finitur . . . pagina*, 3), yet within the same epigram as well as after each page of poems. Again, elegiac couplets, which can seem so self-contained, reinforce this effect: books are divided into 'parts' (*pars nova maior erit*, 10.2.4), but so are poems, and poets (*meliore tui parte superstes eris*, 10.2.8). So far, Martial's monument reglorifies snippets of the Augustan greats, 'Ovid and Horace on monuments', whilst proving that poetry really does die. Or rather, it (only? ) survives in chipped-off bits.

What's more, Martial's winged, oral monument, embodied in his 'fans', the epigram readers of Rome in 10.2, is already being menaced in the next poem, 10.3 (in limping scazons this time, changing the tone). Here the poet faces the flipside of fame, and of an orally perpetuated reputation. Gossip is circulating that Martial is the author of some vulgar, nasty poems, and his white wings are threatened by *nigra fama* (9). So much for 'thefts doing no harm', as 10.2.11 claimed: Martial's *nomen* is flying out of his control, and he himself is suffering a kind of *damnatio memoriae*. Except that instead of destroying his *fama* by suppressing and erasing his work, some clandestine poet (*poeta quidam clancularius*, 5) is ruining Martial's reputation by spreading malicious verse under his name. The poem concludes (10.3.11–12):

> cur ego laborem notus esse tam prave,
> constare gratis cum silentium possit?

> why should I make such perverse bids for fame,
> when silence can be had for free?

The *damnatio memoriae* of Domitian is a campaign of silencing which leads Martial to muffle and scrawl over his own writings *on* Domitian. Yet the implication here is that he doesn't have to write abusive poems when silence, what is left out and unsaid, can say much more than a thousand tongues.[44] Paradigmatically, then, within the frame of Domitian's excision from Book 10, Martial takes the idea of deadly silence and makes it come alive as a series of fascinating gaps that elicit much more gossip, much more pernicious *fama*, than a host of provocative tabloid headlines. Except this way, there is no solid evidence to prove what he (perhaps) implies, only (as 10.2 boasts) a curious reader whispering endless rumours. Even in the most tight-lipped and epitaphic of poetic forms, Martial always manages, in some crooked way (*tam prave* 10.3.11) to stay alive on the mouths of men.

We're also reminded that there's no such thing as a straightforward, painless death, or an abrupt separation of life from death in Book 10. As the curse of 10.5 howls, after the end-beginnings advertised in 10.1 (*finitur pagina*), and the slipping away and partial resuscitation of the book in 10.2 (*elapsum manibus nunc revocavit opus*), 'don't let his punishments end in a suppliant's death'[45] (10.5.13) – that is, in a quick, simple death. We can never forget, as devoted readers and Martial's one big hope for longevity, that we are perusing poems revived from a dead edition, reshuffled with new ones. 10.5 forms a natural bond with 10.3, and may even be addressed to the same poet. Now a certain 'someone' has 'harmed with impious verses those he ought to respect' (is this victim Martial? We're held forever in suspense). He gets it in the neck with this curse poem, itself an example of the kind of deadly verse it attacks:

> Quisquis stolaeve purpuraeve contemptor
> quos colere debet laesit impio versu,
> erret per urbem pontis exul et clivi,
> interque raucos ultimus rogatores
> oret caninas panis inprobi buccas
> illi December longus et madens bruma
> clususque fornix triste frigus extendat:
> vocet beatos clamitetque felices
> Orciniana qui feruntur in sponda.

---

[44] There are other poems that touch on the idea of silence or silencing in Book 10: see e.g. 10.18 (Martial's customary jests are silent for this Saturnalia).

[45] Or as Shackleton Bailey conjectures (1993, *ad loc.*), 'in a simple death' (*simplici poenae*), which even if not correct is the sense of lines 13ff.: he shouldn't die quickly, but should suffer many drawn-out tortures first.

at cum supremae fila venerint horae
diesque tardus, sentiat canum litem
abigatque moto noxias aves panno.
nec finiantur morte supplicis poenae,
sed modo severi sectus Aeaci loris,
nunc inquieti monte Sisyphi pressus,
nunc inter undas garruli senis siccus
delasset omnis fabulas poetarum:
et cum fateri Furia iusserit verum,
prodente clamet conscientia, 'scripsi.'

Whoever he is, who holds the stole and purple in contempt,
who has attacked with tasteless verses those he ought to honour –
let him wander through the city, exiled from bridge and slope,
and end up last among the raw-voiced tramps, begging paltry
scraps of bread fit only for the dogs.
Here's hoping he enjoys a long December, a wet winter, and
a closed archway that drags out the miserable cold.
He should learn to envy those born in a pauper's bier,
consider their lot a happy one.
But when the threads of his final hour have come,
that day he's longed for for so long,
let him hear the snarling dogs, let him be forced to flap his rags
to drive the vicious birds away.
Nor should his punishments end in a simple death:
may he rehearse the poets' nightmares one by one,
now cut by cruel Aeacus' thongs,
now crushed by tortured Sisyphus' hill,
now dry amid loud-mouth Tantalus' waves.
And when the Fury orders his confession,
may his guilty conscience make him blab, 'I wrote it.'

10.5

This is a bold and funny take-off of Ovid's exilic *Ibis*. Both poems jab an angry finger at *quisquis* (10.5.1, cf. *Ibis* 9, *quisquis is est*), and like Ovid, Martial wants his enemy's death to be drawn out and *long* (the sadistic drive to torture and prolong plays off 10.2's invitation to crop and cut to the chase, as well as the *morae dulces* and *longus pulvis* trailing behind the new emperor amid joyful crowds in 10.6). But it's all relative, of course, and, that's where Martial gets the first laughs: compared to 644 lines of vitriol in *Ibis*, this epigrammatic curse doesn't even scratch the surface, though it does allude to how Ovid manages to do in his enemy just by torturing him with infinite mythic exempla (which are reduced in Martial to three, Aeacus, Sisyphus and Tantalus, and summarised in line 17: *delasset*

*omnis fabulas poetarum* ('let him exhaust all the stories of poets')).[46] 10.5
also synthesises both of Ovid's collections of exilic letters, the *Tristia* and
*Epistulae ex Ponto*, which are woven in code into the epigram, in lines 3
(*erret per urbam pontis exul et clivi*) and 7 (*triste frigus*). Martial hopes this
poet will wander through the city as an exile (*exul*), in that even beggars
will shun him. Ovid makes a similar wish in the *Ibis* (113), yet the difference
here is that Rome itself is the site of 'exile'. Pain, death, torture and poverty
are always to be found right on Martial's doorstep.

Martial's summoning of Ovid's *Ibis* and exilic letters in Book 10 is apt
and intriguing for several reasons. 10.5's deadly curse feeds into the invisible
background of Domitian's murder and the parallel 'killing off' of the first
edition of the book. It also encapsulates in literal terms the idea of a death
that is not a death, a life brought repeatedly to the agonising brink of
death, that spans this book full of endings and rebeginnings which has
itself been hauled back from the dead (10.2.2). Moreover, this paradox can
now be enhanced by shadows of Ovid's repeated description of exile as
a living death, and by the perverse endlessness of *Ibis*' vivisection.[47] But
more provocatively, 10.5 must surely be, we suspect, a sarcastic and slippery
comment on the relationship between poet and emperor as exemplified
by exiled Ovid. Ovid was of course the first to show how silence (as we
explored in 10.3) can function as a satiric weapon in the assertion of a poet's
power: he refuses to reveal his enemy's identity in the *Ibis* (*nam nomen adhuc
utcumque tacebo*, 9), while basking in the certainty that everyone, not least
the addressee, knows full well who it is, or at least is full of suspicions, yet
can never prove it. Martial relies on the same trick, whilst suggesting that
a Flavian poet might well disapprove of the kind of bard who composes an
*Ibis*. 10.5 sees him both stepping into Ovid's shoes and, possibly, standing
up to curse him back. This 'somebody' has 'attacked with impious verses
those whom he ought to respect', says 10.5.2, piously. Perhaps this is where
we might begin to wonder whether this epigram is a hangover or not
from edition number one. It seems out of synch with 10.72, for instance,
which separates old, compliant lingo from the new 'truth'. Are we still
amid (the relics of) edition number one here, a book that, like *Epigrams*
8, felt duty-bound to honour and cultivate a good relationship with the
emperor Domitian, and tick off anyone found not towing the line? Have

---

[46] Martial also alludes to *Ibis* 113–14 (*exul, inops erres, alienaque limina lustres / exiguumque petas ore
tremente cibum*), at 10.5.3–5 (*erret per urbem pontis exul et clivi, / interque raucos ultimus rogatores /
oret caninas panis inprobi buccas*).

[47] See esp. *Ibis* 123–4 ('May you have reason to die, but no means of dying. May your life be forced to
flee the death it longs for').

the rules changed, and if so, is all this talk of pious poets an old rule or a new one? And if we get busy pushing the parallel, and one of the suspects in this multi-part whodunnit is Ovid himself, is Martial also hinting that the *Ibis'* curse was directed at Ovid's emperor, Augustus? No, he never said any such thing. What's more, it would be difficult to make a strong case for 10.5 wishing on *quisquis* an Ovidian exile, even though there are so many pointers towards this (apart from the encoding of *Ex Ponto* and *Tristia*, witness the talk of extreme winters and Tantalean agonies,[48] all reminiscent of Ovid's suffering in the exile poetry), simply because there is so much overlap with the punishments Ovid himself wishes on *his* mystery enemy. *Quisquis* could even be (shock!) Martial himself (as well as his enemy) unleashing some venom through Ovid's ghost in still uncertain times. There are clues, if you look (readers make Martial, that's the other excuse): doesn't the hiss of someone's confession, *'scripsi'* (19), sound rather like all that snaky, spat-out hate in lines 13–17? Listen to the following:

> Nec finiantur morte *S*upplicis poenae,
> sed modo severi se*C*tus Aeaci loris
> nunc inquieti monte *S*isyphi p*R*essus,
> nunc inter undas garruli sen*I*s siccus
> delasset omnis fabulas *P*oetarum:
> et cum fateri Furia iu*Ss*er*I*t verum,
> prodente clamet conscientia 'Scripsi.'

Of course, the case is weak and unconvincing: time to move on. But before we do, we should note that the plot of 10.5 gets thicker still when we begin to make connections with other uses of (Ovidian) exile and exile poetry in Book 10. If we go back to the multi-layered palimpsest of 10.2, we might note a further important model for lines 7–10. Compare again:

> 'pigra per hunc fugies ingratae flumina Lethes
> et meliore tui parte superstes eris.
> marmora Messallae findit caprificus et audax
> dimidios Crispi mulio ridet equos.'

with Ovid *Tristia* 1.2.41–4:

> o bene, quod non sum mecum conscendere passus,
> ne mihi mors misero bis patienda foret!
> at nunc, ut peream, quoniam caret illa periclo,
> dimidia certe parte superstes ero.

---

[48] On horribly cold winters on the Black Sea, see e.g. *Tr.* 4.7.1, or *Ex P.* 4.9.85–6.

> Thank goodness I didn't have to see her board with me,
> so wasn't forced, poor victim, to suffer death twice over!
> But even though I perish now, the fact that she is safe
> means I can live, or at least half survive.

Ovid consoles himself with the idea that even though he has suffered the 'death' of exile,[49] at least his wife was not punished with him, so he 'half-survives' through her. Martial's second edition takes this idea literally: Book 10 'half-survived' – its original form is lost, but some of its components remain. Martial will live on, in part: as we've seen, that's his sardonic take, adding to Ovid's in exile, on the ecstatic ending to *Metamorphoses* 15, which in turn evokes Horace *Odes* 3.30 in claiming that the poet will live on in the 'greater or better part of himself'. Moreover, while in *Tristia* 1.2, as in Horace *Odes* 1.3 (addressed to Horace's beloved Vergil, 'half of his own soul'), the image of a split self or *fama* is an erotic one (we reminisce in the *Tristia* about the beginnings of Ovid's career, where his name is entwined with that of other-half Corinna),[50] in Martial, it is statues of horses that are split, not people or souls.[51] The only (albeit narcissistic) love affair we'll find in Martial is with his readers.

Other poems in *Epigrams* 10 are also involved in marking their similarity to/difference from *Tristia* 1.2's paradigm for deathly living. For example, while Ovid narrowly escapes dying twice (*bis*) in *Tristia* 1.2.41–2, Antonius Primus in 10.23 can look back with such joy at his tranquil life, he feels he has lived twice over, just like this book (*hoc est / vivere bis, vita posse priore frui*, 10.23.7–8).[52] The celebration of Martial's own birthday in the next poem, 10.24, casts this and its predecessor as a pair, and we realise now, if we haven't already, that Book 10's revision of itself is less a jarring anomaly than old hat, a new, flamboyant take on epigrammatic *variatio*, the skill in rewriting the same. While Antonius Primus, the *numero uno* of this diptych, 'lives twice' on his birthday because this for him is a day for looking back and remembering the past (*praeteritosque dies et tutos respicit annos*, 10.23.3), Martial in 10.24.6–11 marks his fifty-seventh year by looking to the future and asking for a new lease of life:

---

[49] Also see *Tristia* 3.7.50 (*me tamen extincto fama superstes erit*). Exilic 'death', for Ovid, provides the stage for a 'posthumous' retrospective of his entire writing career: the poet plays the part of a devoted reader who reframes, repeats and monumentalises his work for future generations.

[50] A similar idea is explored in Callimachus *Epigram* 42 ('half of my soul still lives, but I don't know whether love or death has stolen it').

[51] This conversion of men into beasts, as we saw in the *De Spectaculis*, is typical of the degrading strategies of Martial's epigram.

[52] He's Antonius Primus and Secundus.

his vos, si tamen expedit roganti,
annos addite **bis**, precor, novenos,
ut nondum nimia piger senecta
sed vitae tribus arcubus peractis
lucos Elysiae petam puellae.
post hunc Nestora nec diem rogabo.

To these years, but only if I ask what's good for me,
add twice nine more, I beg of you,
so that, not yet slowed up by late old age,
but with three arcs of my life complete
I might seek out the groves of the Elysian girl.
Beyond this Nestor[53] I shan't ask a single day.

Both Martial and Antonius multiply by two, but in different, in a sense opposing, ways. The celebration of seventy-fifth and fifty-seventh birthdays side by side perfects the mirror image. Both men enlarge their lifespan, but whilst (Book?) number one works with what he's got, his successor in 10.24 builds by moving on. Nevertheless, we can't help remembering the years (and books) to which Martial wants to add: the closing promise of 10.24 not to exceed a certain age is all too reminiscent of this poet's measured, numbered volumes – 10.1's fear of being 'too much', *nimius*, as seen through the past life of 8.3 (*iam sex septemve libelli / est nimium*, 'six or seven books is already too much', 1–2). This elastic tension between backtracking and creating anew runs throughout Book 10. It's no surprise that two-faced Janus has a presence here (see 10.28), or that new years and months can take us forwards or backwards each time: Martial sees in the new year with a new consul who makes him nostalgic for the old one in 10.10; Proculeia divorces her husband and wipes the slate clean as Janus' month begins at 10.41; the summer rolls in in 10.51 as Taurus looks back at Aries (*respicit*, 10.51.1, cf. *respicit*, 10.23.3), and Diodorus' birthday at 10.27 seems to cancel out rather than reaffirm his existence, as a 'new start' erases past, present and future. Add to this the small gathering of 'before and after' epigrams: 10.28, 10.29, 10.32 and 10.57. Incidentally, the keyword of this book, *bis,* crops up again in 10.63's everlasting tomb: this matron's life was 'twice approved' (*bis mea Romano spectata est vita Tarento*, 3). So too in 10.71, where (again with metapoetic force), Rabirius' two parents are burned on one pyre and buried in one tomb, after coming to the end of 'twice six lusters' of wedded bliss (*bis sex lustra tori nox mitis et ultima clusit*, 5). And Martial can't resist giving the dirty take on doing things twice in

---

[53] I.e. 'length of days'.

10.81 (prostitute Phyllis has two clients for the morning, each hoping to be first in the queue: instead of doing it twice, she accommodates both at the same time).

From the very beginning of Book 10, then, Ovid's 'double life', 'near double-death', or 'deathly life' in exile becomes a privileged shorthand for edition one's half-survival and rebirth. In another flashback, we realise that Martial has used Ovidian exile before to elaborate his post-Ovidian commentary on posthumous fame. For example, another of his grandest statements about the monumentality of his poetry, in 7.84, echoes *Tristia* 1.7, where Ovid sends on six new lines to be placed at the head of *Metamorphoses* 1. In this epigram, Martial sends his book to a friend at 'Getic Peuce and prostrate Hister', a reversal of Ovid's mailing of his *libellus back* from Getic lands to Rome to plead on his behalf. While an artist prepares his portrait on canvas, this book, Martial says, will display the author's face more clearly (*certior in nostro carmine vultus erit*, 6). And in lines 7–8, unlike the actual portrait:

> casibus hic nullis, nullis delebilis annis
> vivet, Apelleum cum morietur opus.
>
> No accidents, no erosion of time will destroy it;
> it shall live, when Apelles' work shall die.

This recalls the first fourteen lines of *Tristia* 1.7, where Ovid reminds friends to treasure the portraits they have of him, and to pity him in exile. However, Ovid adds that his poetry, especially the *Metamorphoses*, whose writing was interrupted by exile, 'are a more striking portrait'. Before he left, he threw his epic on the fire, in an affected imitation of Vergil, yet it was an empty gesture, as he has many more copies. Now he prays that they may live, *ut vivant,* echoing his epilogue to Book 15.

Like Ovid in the exile poetry (and in *Tristia* 1.7 in particular), Martial in Book 10 returns to and rewrites a work which (again just like the *Metamorphoses*) is a half-dying, living, growing organism (*non sunt penitus sublata, sed extant,* 'these verses were not utterly destroyed, they still exist', *Tr.*1.7.23; *adhuc crescens carmen,* 'the poem was still growing', *Tr.* 1.7.22). Yet this second edition (emblematic of going back and rewriting the past more generally) is also symptomatic of how Martial emphasises the enormous distance and contrast between himself and Ovid. While Ovid's *carmen et error* help frame Martial's awkward and evolving relationship with imperial authority, Martial has the luxury of being able to do what Ovid can never literally manage in his obsessively retrospective *Tristia* and

*Ex Ponto*: recall an edition and rework it to suit a new political climate. If only Ovid had been able to half-erase and edit the *Ars Amatoria*, and thus at least mitigate his 'crime', or more to the point, if only Augustus had been murdered just as Ovid's exile had begun (as perhaps the *Ibis* hopes), allowing his dream of return to be fulfilled . . . Martial enjoys all the perks of exiled Ovid's 'afterlife in life', without having to leave the city that sustains his existence (even his enemy is exiled *in* Rome in 10.5).[54]

If we turn to the end poem of the book, we can read some culminating examples of Martial's remapping of Ovid's empire as seen from the horrors of the Black Sea. 10.103 addresses the people of Bilbilis, and asks whether they rejoice in the celebrity of a poet who has lived for thirty years 'among the beautiful walls of mistress Rome' (*moenia dum colimus dominae pulcherrima Romae*, 9). If they want him back, he's happy to oblige (though he'll want a fanfare); if they're not bothered, he can return to Rome (*redire licet*, 12). 10.104 sees Martial sending off the book instead, *Tristia*-style, not back to Rome but back, from Martial's 'exile' as a Spaniard in Rome, to 'the heights of Spanish Tarraco':

> I nostro comes, i, libelle, Flavo
> longum per mare, sed faventis undae.
> et cursu facili tuisque ventis
> Hispanae pete Tarraconis arces:
> illinc te rota tollet et citatus
> altam Bilbilin et tuum Salonem
> quinto forsitan essedo videbis.
> quid mandem tibi quaeris? ut sodales
> paucos, sed veteres et ante brumas
> triginta mihi quattuorque visos
> ipsa protinus a via salutes,
> et nostrum admoneas subinde Flavum
> iucundos mihi nec laboriosos
> secessus pretio paret salubri,
> qui pigrum faciant tuum parentem.
> haec sunt. iam tumidus vocat magister
> castigatque moras, et aura protum
> laxavit melior. vale, libelle:
> navem, scis puto, non moratur unus.
>
> Go little book, go with my Flavus
> over distant seas, but may the waves be kind,

---

[54] For discussion of Martial's reception of the *Ars,* also see Casali (2005), 19–36, and Hinds (2007).

and fair winds make for an easy trip
to the heights of Spanish Tarraco:
wheels will take you on from there – you'll make
quick progress, and perhaps get a view at the
fifth stage of lofty Bilbilis and your Salo.
You ask what your duties are? Just to greet a few old friends
not seen for four and thirty winters; also,
from time to time, remind my good friend Flavus
to find me a nice place – no fixer-upper, decent price –
where your old Pa can put his feet up.
That's it. Now the pompous skipper calls
and curses our delays, and a better breeze
has opened up the port. Goodbye, my little book –
a ship, you know, won't wait for just one passenger.

Yet while Rome, for Martial, is the new 'place of exile', where life is dark and dangerous and poetic talent threatened and worn down by the daily grind, 'August' Bilbilis (10.103.1), it seems, is in part the new (Augustan?) Rome, as defined by Martial's nostalgia for a lost world of *otium*, gentle breezes and writers' retreats. In 1.104, as in *Tristia* 1.1, Martial is the father of his new generation of books that carry his *nomen* (10.104.15), yet this journey is not a depressing funeral cortège, the vision of a tortured soul. Martial uses his book not as a defence lawyer and diplomat, but as a personal assistant sent ahead to organise three-star accommodation. It won't be encountering savage natives, just friends Martial hasn't seen for an age and presumably doesn't have the time to visit himself (for one thing, he's far too famous).

The poem ends with a sequence of *Ars Amatoria*-style innuendoes: the skipper about to sail in line 16 is *tumidus* ('pompous', but also, post-Ovid, 'aroused', 'swollen') as he complains of delays, and a fair breeze has 'opened up the harbour'. There is no mistaking the nod here to Ovid's metaphors of sailing and docking in the *Ars*, which refer both to sexual adventure and climax/conquest, and to the ending of the books that instruct lovers. *Ars* 1 begins with the comparison between sailing or rowing boats, or steering chariots, and directing the project of *amor*, while it ends with Ovid throwing anchor, after his parting comments on fishing women from erotic seas. This *magister* sounds just like an impatient young lover who can't wait to try out his skills on the high seas – though at the same time that word, *magister*, is used in the *Ars* for the master of love himself, Ovid, whose ghost calls out to Martial's *libellus* in this epigram.[55] Again, we also

---

[55] See e.g. *Ars* 3.811–12 (*ut quondam iuvenes, ita nunc, mea turba, puellae / inscribant spoliis "NASO MAGISTER ERAT"*).

sense the backdrop of Horace *Epistles* 1.20, where the poet scolds his book for wanting to flaunt itself on the streets (it'll regret it when its 'sated lover grows tired', 8). The joke of 10.104, of course, is that Martial is apparently free to regurgitate the naughtiness of Ovid's *Ars* in his remake of *Tristia* 1.1, a product of Ovid's punishment for that same provocative *carmen*. For Martial even more than Ovid, the metaphor of literary exile becomes a vantage point from which to re-evaluate and remake the past, as well as to vaunt future fame after death. This end-as-rebeginning makes an entertaining coda for a book which has experimented in a galaxy of ways with flicking between past and future, between before and after, first and second editions, death and living on.

As a coda to this section, we might note the slight surprise that, in the game of one and two, first and second, forward-looking 10.104 mimics the ending not to the *second* book of Ovid's *Ars*, but to the first. Another way of marking out this ending as pointing towards another beginning, we might say, extending the joke of 10.1, after 8.3, that Martial's volumes are simply going on and on. Just noticing this pulls us back into the midst of Book 10, almost bang in the middle in fact, to epigram 50. This is the epitaph to chariot-racer Scorpus, who has died in his prime. Martial can't resist milking Ovid's chariot-racing metaphor and pun from *Ars* 1.39–40,[56] put into action in the climax to *Ars* 2. He writes (10.50.7–8):

> curribus illa tuis semper properata brevisque
>  cur fuit et vitae tam prope meta tuae?

> The goal, ever quickly reached by your hastening chariot –
>  your life's goal too, why was it so close?

Compare the lovers at the end of *Ars* 2, instructed *ad metam properate simul*, 'rush to the goalpost together' (727). Just as Scorpus comes to the end of the race, so he comes to the end of his life, and so Martial's readers are also offered the option of ending Book 10 here. However, after his encouragement to shorten and skip where we want (*fac tibi me quam cupis ipse brevem*, 10.1.4), this ending-as-death is marked as premature: Scorpus dies too soon (his goal was *brevis*, as well as *properata*, 10.50.7, which recalls the *festinata* first edition, 10.2.1 – even though this poem mimics the end to Ovid's *second* book of the *Ars*).[57] Should we really stop

---

[56] *Hic modus, haec nostro signabitur area curru: / haec erit admissa meta terenda rota.*
[57] This testing out of premature endings that underlines both the repeated endings and beginnings that make up an epigram book, and the extent to which epigram more generally must continually confront (its own) death, is by no means an isolated feature of Book 10. For example, poem 1.101 explores the idea of this book rotting and dying through the figure of Martial's scribe, Demetrius,

reading now? Compare 10.59, where Martial warns that readers are missing a 'feast furnished from every market' if they just handpick the epigrams they like rather than reading a book from beginning to end.[58] We all know that such an 'ending' can serve as a rebeginning, and this is spelt out by Martial's implicit reuse of Ovid's pun on *meta*, which can mean either end post or turning post.[59] It makes sense that although Scorpus is (in parallel with edition number one) 'cheated of first youth' (*prima fraudatus, Scorpe, iuventa*, 5), he comes back to talk from the dead in 10.53, is referred to as alive and well (and a big earner) at 10.74, and is gossiped about in the very first poem of the next new book, 11.1 (lines 15–16). The epigrams cut off Scorpus in his prime, yet his celebrity lives on, and on.

## AMBER TOMBS AND THE OCEAN OF ROME: BOOK 4

As my all too brief reading of Book 10 shows, it is often difficult, and beside the point, to isolate single epigrams in Martial's volumes for analysis, or to consider individual poems in the light of distinct 'aspects' of Martial's project – despite the fact that this is what any critic is bound to do. Martial's constant zigzagging between categories, his bewildering accumulation of perspectives on the same set of images or ideas, even on a single word, often seem to mock critical attempts to describe, separate and define. Even (or, the *very*) epigrams which seem to exemplify miniaturisation, solidification, monumentalisation, also seem to drain through fingers and ooze over borders as soon as they are touched by curious readers.

To illustrate this further, I want to turn now to a fascinating couple of epitaphs inset into Book 4, one of the volumes apparently composed for Rome's December carnival, the Saturnalia. These two famous epigrams, at 4.32 and 59, which appear as neat icons for the gem-like brilliance and epitaphic drive of Martial's poetry,[60] describe the glorious deaths of a bee and a viper each caught in a drop of sticky amber, which hardens

who comes to embody the epigrams of his master. He is freed after his death at just nineteen years of age, and Martial puns on *liber* (meaning both 'free' and 'book' depending on the length of the first syllable): when Demetrius dies, he in a sense carries this book with him to the underworld. Book 1 nevertheless 'lives on' for another 17 poems.

[58] Also see e.g. 8.29 ('he who writes couplets wants to please by brevity. But tell me, what good is brevity, when it's a book?').

[59] See discussion in Sharrock (1994) 19–20.

[60] Cf. Fitzgerald (2007) 119 on Martial 6.15. It is also interesting to note (although the poems themselves don't mention it) that bees and vipers sting (just like epigram), yet their sting is both preserved and rendered harmless by the amber casting. Does imperial epigram always have to contain its power to sting? Also see 13.2, where Martial has the perfect antidote to readers' venom.

around their compliant bodies like a perfect, transparent tomb – a process mirrored in the neat encasing of these beautiful deaths in monumental epigram. Although the poems can be seen to pick up the 'theme' of unusual or miraculous deaths in Greek epigram, there is nothing quite like this in the Palatine Anthology. Yet whether this idea is original to Martial or not, the choice of amber as a material to fashion the most stunning of epigrammatic graves is an interesting one. The notion, dramatised in both poems, as in the similar 6.15 (on an ant in amber), that amber metamorphoses from a liquid into a solid, from viscous to smooth before our very eyes, becomes symbolic of Martial's epitaphic poetics. As we have been seeing throughout this chapter, Martial is interested in exploring the paradoxes of monumentality, or the ways in which poetry (not least epigram) struggles to escape a fragile material world and the vicissitudes of corporeality. This struggle is reinvigorated, and made fun of, in Book 4's jesting and chemical experiments around water and other liquids, which seem to seep right into Martial's amber tombs before they have time to set.

First comes 4.32, a two-couplet elegy about a bee who finds herself imprisoned as if in her own nectar:

> Et latet et lucet Phaethontide condita gutta,
>      ut videatur apis nectare clusa suo.
> dignum tantorum pretium tulit illa laborum:
>     credibile est ipsam sic voluisse mori.

> Entombed in Phaethon's drop, the bee both hides and shines,
> imprisoned, it seems, in her own nectar.
> She is well rewarded for her sufferings:
> you might believe she chose to die like this.

4.59, one couplet longer than its predecessor, features a viper trapped by a drop of amber that flows into its path on a branch:

> Flentibus Heliadum ramis dum vipera repit,
>     fluxit in opstantem sucina gemma[61] feram:
> quae dum miratur pingui se rore teneri,

---

[61] Note that *gemma* ('gem', or 'bud'), is the reading of manuscript T, in the $\alpha$ branch, while $\beta\gamma$ has *gutta* ('drop'). With *fluxit, gutta* makes a lot more sense, and is clearly the *lectio facilior* (it perhaps gets picked up from 4.32.1, or from 6.15.2: *inplicuit tenuem sucina gutta feram*): 'How can a gem/bud flow?' we are bound to ask. However, the two competing versions capture and reflect the curious qualities of amber, which is both solid and liquid, and do even more to evoke the spirit of (post-Ovidian) metamorphosis which surrounds amber and which Martial is ingenious in exploiting, especially if *gemma* is what he wrote: *gutta/gemma* flows yet is rock-hard, is both a living part of the tree and a separate, inanimate entity (just as the snake both crawls, *repit,* and stands still, *obstans,* in lines 1–2).

concreto riguit vincta repente gelu.
ne tibi regali placeas, Cleopatra, sepulchro,
vipera si tumulo nobiliore iacet.

While a viper crept among the Heliads' weeping boughs
a bud of amber flowed into its path:
and while it marvelled at the sticky fluid taking hold,
it stiffened, chained all at once by hardened ice.
Don't be too pleased with *your* royal tomb, Cleopatra,
if a snake lies in a nobler grave.

Both tiny *monumenta* act out a cluster of paradoxes. The bee in 4.32 is hidden, or hides away, and at the same time shines through the transparent amber; she is buried alive, yet also seems to have engineered her own death. In 4.59, there are miracles of scale: a snake is trapped by one drop of amber (a comically unbelievable idea if read literally), and Cleopatra's tomb is less impressive than this palm-sized objet d'art. The Callimachean cliché that even small and humble genres can reach epic heights is replayed multiple times in Martial, and Book 4, a relatively petite collection of just eighty-nine poems,[62] has already flagged the influence of Callimachus' epigrams at 4.23 (although Martial claims here that Callimachus himself conceded that Bruttianus was better than him). Martial delights readers with surprising juxtapositions or pairings of opposites: the sinuous, rippling viper stands still while the amber flows: *fluxit in opstantem sucina gemma feram*, 2; Cleopatra, who was killed by an asp, should envy the tomb of a snake who meets an equally memorable fate. And finally, in 4.59, we get to watch the amazing mutation, or mutations: the Heliads' tears become the rich, liquid amber, which becomes in an instant a lump of 'congealed ice' in the staccato tautology of line 4: *concreto riguit vincta repente gelu*.

In 4.32, the insignificant death of an insect becomes a poignant lesson in self-sacrifice, and a glorious culmination of 'so many' epic labours (*tantorum pretium laborum*, 3). The honey-coloured drop of amber is 'Phaethon's', evoking the sun-god, Helios, and the sun itself, another outrageous magnification. In 4.59, the epigram's epic ambition to confer *kleos* on the smallest of beings evokes an entire scene from an epic poem which is itself an epigrammatic remake of a more famous epic. 4.59.4 seems to be inspired by a section from Eumolpus' *Bellum Civile* in Petronius' *Satyricon*, which seems

---

[62] Despite the fact that the book itself wants to keep going at 4.89, and Martial has to stop it in its tracks (*'ohe, iam satis est, ohe, libelle!'* 4.89.1). At 4.82, Martial offers Rufus Books 3 and 4 as a gift, and suggests a way to make them (even) shorter: 'if two are too much to read, you can fold up one of the rolls. Divided in this way, the work will become short' (4.82.7–8).

to be modelled, for want of a better word, on Lucan's epic of the same name. Martial compares the solidifying amber to ice in a phrase that recalls the fate of Caesar's army crossing the ice-bound Alps. Flick back once more to that memorable line: *concreto riguit vincta repente gelu*. We pick up at line 150 of Petronius' poem, where Caesar's troops face ground 'chained with frost' (*sed glacie concreta rigent hiemisque pruinis*). Then, as they begin to march, although 'at first, the ground chained with white frost did not fight them' (*prima quidem glacies et cana vincta pruina / non pugnavit*, 185–6),[63] the horses then fall through the shattering ice, and 'new-born rivers rolled from the mountain heights'. Those rivers, too, 'stood still as if by some command, the waves stopped, the destructive floods enchained (*stabant, et vincta fluctus stupuere ruina*), and the water that ran a moment before now halted, stiff enough to cut' (189–92). In short, Martial injects into this tiny drop of amber all the elemental chaos and unnerving metamorphosis that captures civil war in Petronius' remake of Lucan's *Bellum Civile*. What's especially interesting is that the solidification of amber in 4.59 evokes a scene in which water not only freezes in a flash, but can be unchained just as easily. In the same way, we find that the Heliads' stiffened tears and Phaethon's hard drop of sunshine remelt in adjacent epigrams. Martial weaves together a number of poems in Book 4 in which water 'metamorphoses' or bears multiple, contrasting associations.[64] It was always tricky for a viper to fit neatly inside a teardrop:[65] this amber jewel spills out, is reborn and snakes throughout Book 4.

To begin with, 4.59 is bordered by the couplet on Galla, who does not cry for her husband (in contrast/parallel to the mourning Heliads, whose tears are 'frozen'), and 4.60, where Curiatius (not saved by any congealing waters) dies a watery death in the river Tibur. 4.63 also describes a death by drowning, and at 4.73, a dying Vestinus is about to 'pass through the waters of the Styx'. The next poem, 4.61, which asks Mancinus to shut up about his abundant wealth, lists among his treasures 'a genuine sardonyx decorated with three lines and two gems like sea-waves' (*duasque similes fluctibus maris gemmas*, 7), a neater recasting of the amber jewel that

---

[63] Martial 4.59.4 is a hybrid of Petronius *Bellum Civile* 150 and 185. *Fluxit* at 4.59.2 also picks up *fluctus* at *BC* 191.

[64] Also see Lorenz (2004), who discusses water imagery in Book 4 as a 'leitmotif'.

[65] As Watson and Watson (2003 *ad loc.*) note, the snake would have to be coiled, which seems unlikely given the image of it sliding along a branch and meeting a drop of amber in its path. Perhaps we are encouraged to imagine the snake as complicit in its own death, coiling itself up neatly to fit its Callimachean tomb, just like the bee at 4.32 (*credibile est ipsam sic voluisse mori*, 4). Also see P. Watson (2001).

once flowed like liquid (*fluxit*, 4.59.2). *Gemma*, suitably, is also a literary term for stylistic adornment, used by Martial at 5.11.3 to describe Stella's poetry.[66] Meanwhile, the mention of Cleopatra at 4.59.5 takes us back to 4.22, a remake of the Hermaphroditus myth[67] starring a certain virginal Cleopatra who dives into a gleaming pool to escape the advances of her amorous new husband. In the transparent waters, she is 'covered' yet still 'shines', just like the bee trapped in amber at 4.32. Compare 4.32.1–2:

> Et latet et lucet Phaethontide condita gutta,
>    ut videatur apis nectare clusa suo.

> Entombed in Phaethon's drop, the bee both hides and shines,
> imprisoned, it seems, in her own nectar.

with 4.22.3–6:

> sed prodidit unda latentem;
>    lucebat, totis cum tegeretur aquis:
> condita sic puro numerantur lilia vitro,
>    sic prohibet tenuis gemma latere rosas.

> But the water gave away her hiding place.
> She shone, even as the waters shrouded her:
> So lilies enclosed in transparent glass are counted,
> and thin crystal does not let roses hide.

Whereas the amber in 4.59 goes from liquid to solid (like ice), Cleopatra's pool is turned metaphorically from water to crystal, which is then (re)broken when the poet dives in, Salmacis-like, to 'steal reluctant kisses' (7–8), only to be curtailed by the 'transparent waters' (8). These *perspicuae aquae* are then exchanged for a *perspicuus calix* at 4.85, a transparent glass that is used by Ponticus but not his guests, in case they discover they are drinking a lesser wine.

Elsewhere in Book 4, the *gelu concretum* image and sudden freezing at 4.59.4 is reworked (or vice versa) in 4.2 and 4.3, when snow falls from the sky during a show, so that Horatius' poor black cloak turns pure white (4.2) and the emperor is drenched (4.3). The marvel is 'sudden' in 4.2.5 (*repente*, cf. *repente* 4.59.4), whilst in 4.3 the emperor laughs at the *concretas aquas* icing up his head (4.3.4, cf. *concreto riguit . . . gelu* 4.59.4). Once more, Martial

---

[66] *Multas in digitis, plures in carmine gemmas / invenies.*

[67] See Ovid *Met.* 4.297ff. The pool into which Hermaphroditus dives is also crystal clear (*videt hic stagnum lucentis ad imum*, 4.297), its waters 'transparent' (*perspicuus liquor est*, 300). Martial takes from Ovid the simile comparing the beautiful body immersed in clear water to white lilies in translucent glass (*Met.* 4.354–5). Also, Martial 4.22.7–8 echoes *Met.* 4.358, *luctantiaque oscula carpit.*

exploits the paradox of an element (like amber) that can be so many things at once: snow, frost, water, congealed moisture, even both wet and dry (*quis siccis lascivit aquis et ab aethere ludit?* 'who sports with dry waters and plays games from heaven?' 4.3.7).[68] In an epigrammatic blink, the emperor's head is simultaneously and paradoxically drenched with a (we imagine, a solid white) *vellus*, 'fleece', of flowing water (1–2), paralysed by stiff white ice (3–4), and left dripping with melted ice (*madidis comis*, 6). While Martial gently mocks his Caesar as a carnival clown, his face running with metaphorical custard pie, he also imagines the emperor as a great, snow-capped mountain, a Latinus-like rock towering over the other theatre-goers (his head is the peak, *vertex*, 3), and reminding us again of the allusion to the icy Alps traversed by (Julius) Caesar at 4.59.4 (*concreto riguit vincta repente gelu*). These chains and knots of associations continue in, for example, 4.18, where the dripping of a wet stone (*madet lapis*, 4.18.2) produces a killer icicle that slits a child's throat and 'melts' in the warm wound (the water is 'heavy with winter ice', *hiberno praegravis gelu*, 4.18.4);[69] at 4.10, where this very book is still damp, and accompanied by a wet sponge, or 4.14.12, in which Martial's *libelli* are 'soaked with naughty jokes' (*lascivis madidos iocis*), spelling out together both the multiple associations of a wet-dry (icy-warm) book, and the ingenious reshapings of water imagery within it.[70]

In chapter one, we saw via Book 1 how water and wine lubricate social and poetic interaction in epigram's Rome. And in this short reading of Book 4, we have homed in on two miniature epitaphs which exemplify, in their role in performing the carnival entertainment of this volume as a whole, the fame-making tricks Martial turns around the trope of unstable and self-transforming tombs. 'Wetness', more generally (the key verb is *madeo*), is integral to Martial's landscapes of icy, wet, carnival winters, of public baths, of dinner parties, taverns and brothels where mouths are greasy with food and sex, heads swim with booze, and hair drips with

---

[68] Cf. a marsh is paradoxically 'dry' in 4.4.1.

[69] With Greenwood (1998b), I also note Laurens' observation (1989, 256) that 'Martial ne nomme point le glaçon (en latin: *stiria*), préfère la périphrase qui conserve sa nature liquide à l'eau qui ne s'est congelée que le temps de tuer, puisqu'elle fond aussitôt dans la plaie brûlante. Or sur cette métonymie (eau pour glaçon), c'est à dire sur cette légère tromperie poétique repose la pointe de l'épigramme, le paradoxisme que l'eau égorge.'

[70] Greenwood (1998b) highlights what he identifies as an unnoticed 'cycle' of epigrams relating to water in Book 4 (poems 18, 22 and 63), which 'provide us with a further, comparatively unusual example of the epigrammatist's acknowledged fondness for cyclical arrangement' (371). This is an excellent example of how critics' attempts to fence off 'cycles' in Martial's books have tended to oversimplify the modality of interaction in the *Epigrams*: the element of water, as I show here, is of all things the least likely not to 'leak' into surrounding poems.

perfume, as well as to his descriptions of the pathetic client, forced to wait on doorsteps and kiss patrons in the rain and cold. Soaked, blotchy epigrams also identify themselves with tearful, tearstained elegy, and in particular with the *liturae* which smudge Ovid's papyrus in the *Heroides* and exile poetry. And as we also saw in chapter 1, water is traditionally associated with a certain type of refined, sober, (post-)Callimachean poetry, often opposed to the kind of verse composed by the 'wine-drinkers'.

Martial hints frequently at a (pseudo-)Callimachean poetics of water, but also experiments with bigger, epic rivers and oceans, as well as mixing his drinks. He produces hybrid books that can't be pinned down to one element or the other, even though they are also engaged in doing just that. 'Pure streams' of Callimachean-style inspiration are blended, too, with versions of the old joke about bad poems deserving to be drenched or drowned.[71] The corpus includes numerous poems describing books as actually or potentially wet, or 'soaked' (*madidus,* a much-used word in Martial, also means 'drunk'). Book 4, as I mentioned above, is 'steeped' in jests (*madidi libelli,* 4.14.12), and Book 11 soaked in wine for the Saturnalia (*vino madeat,* 11.15.5); in 7.72, poems 'dripping' with venom are attributed (falsely, he says), to Martial (*atro carmina quae madent veneno,* 13), while Book 3 risks becoming sodden papyrus for sardines at 3.2.4 (*cordylas madida tegas papyro*). The end poem of this book, 3.100, recounts how Martial sent a volume to Rufus via a runner, who got caught in a rainstorm and was wet through (together, presumably, with the poems) when he arrived (*cursorem . . . carmina quem madidum nostra tulisse reor,* 1–2). The last line quips, 'that book deserved to be sent in no other way'. There are four more poems on the same theme: at 4.10, Martial sends out his fresh book still damp, and accompanied by a sponge, so that implicitly it can be smudged or erased. Martial attacks a fellow poet using a similar image in 5.53 (he should write about Deucalion, another pointer towards the floods of *Metamorphoses* 1, as his work is only fit to be sponged out). At 9.58, Martial tries dedicating his book to the Nymphs, only to get in reply the following put-down: 'Whoever gives his poems to the Nymphs' temples is telling us himself what ought to be done with his books' (9.58.7–8), the implication again being that his epigram should just be thrown into the water. And finally, 14.196, labelled 'Calvus on the use of cold water', from the collection of Saturnalian *Apophoreta,* reads: 'these pages that tell you of

---

[71] Howell (1995) 137. See Cicero *Q.FR* 2.13.1, and Tibullus 1.9.50.

fountains and the names of waters would have been better off swimming in their own waters.'

Yet as we have seen in Book 4, Martial uses water and other liquids, in various forms, to achieve a range of different effects, not just to imply low-quality verse. This image system seems to embrace and define the whole of epigram's Rome: as Martial imagines in 10.58, whilst bemoaning the cruel pace of urban living, 'I am tossed on the city's ocean': *iactamur in alto / urbis*, 7–8. In recalling the third line of Vergil's *Aeneid* here (*terris iactatus et alto*),[72] the poet appears both as an epic hero, after Aeneas, the great hope of his people driven in exile *towards* Rome, and at the same time a directionless loser almost drowning in a punishing metropolis. The epigram pays homage to Horace *Epistles* 2.2, where the poet turns to a rustic life of philosophical contemplation, recalling the 'waves and storms' of the city (85), which made it impossible to write; Martial, by contrast, is thrust passively back into the urban jungle. A similar scenario is threatened in 1.5, where (apparently) the emperor, who has just put on a *naumachia,* tells his poet that if he keeps on writing epigrams, he is asking to be thrown into the water along with his books. The ocean-like city also reminds us, perhaps, of the horrors of Titus' arena in the *De Spectaculis*, flooded in seconds for a *naumachia* that drowns wretched animals and people. See especially *De Spect.* 24, where a spectator arrives late to find a naval battle going on in the Colosseum (*'hic modo terra fuit'*, 'just now, all this was land', 3), an allusion to Ovid's description of Jupiter's flood sent to punish wicked men in *Metamorphoses* 1. More generally, Martial evokes the metaphorics of flux that permeate the *Metamorphoses*, as a way of colouring both the unpredictability of tyranny, transformed into popular entertainment in the microcosmic Colosseum, and the oily, deadly wit of his epigrams, on show in this book-sized *lusus*.[73] The greatest monument in history, its core filled with water, quickly forgotten victims and brief sparks of sordid fame, becomes the ultimate visual metaphor for epigram's contrary relationship with death and with poetic visions of the afterlife.

OVERGROWN GRAVES: 1.88

In the final section of this chapter, I want to turn back to Book 1 once more, to read an epitaph in which Martial shows off his skill in building liquid, everlasting graves in a different way. In 1.88, Martial offers his slave

---

[72] This is another example of a 'rebeginning' in Book 10, this time echoing Vergil's epic.
[73] For more on this see Rimell (forthcoming).

Alcimus a tomb which will last forever, since it takes the form of a garden. Instead of 'tottering masses of Parian stone', which will eventually crumble, the slave will have a cheap boxwood coffin set in green meadows, which will be irrigated by his master's tears:

> Alcime, quem raptum domino crescentibus annis
>     Labicana levi caespite velat humus,
> accipe non Pario nutantia pondera saxo,
>     quae cineri vanus dat ruitura labor,
> sed faciles buxos et opacas palmitis umbras
>     quaeque virent lacrimis roscida prata meis
> accipe, care puer, nostri monimenta doloris:
>     hic tibi perpetuo tempore vivet honor.
> cum mihi supremos Lachesis perneverit annos,
>     non aliter cineres mando iacere meos.

> Alcimus, snatched from your master in your prime,
> now that the light soil of Labican earth covers you,
> take no tottering weights of Parian stone,
> gifts of vain labour doomed to fall.
> Instead, accept this pliant wood and the vine's dark shades,
> and green meadows watered by my tears.
> Take these gifts, dear boy, as momuments to my grief:
> this is an honour that will live on, for you, in time eternal.
> When Lachesis spins out my final years,
> I'll want my ashes laid to rest just so, and in no other way.

Martial revisits here the conventional idea that tombs are perishable compared to immortal works of literature. The second couplet steals inspiration from Ovid *Ex Ponto* 4.8.31–2, where Ovid states that he wants to honour Germanicus in verse, not by building monuments, as all his wealth now lies in poetry:

> nec tibi de Pario statuam, Germanice, templum
>     marmore: carpsit opes illa ruina meas.

> I will build you no temple of Parian marble, Germanicus:
> That disastrous event tore away my wealth.

Yet of course, Martial is not promising Alcimus immortal verse,[74] at least not directly. Marble *mausolea* are now rivalled by shabby boxwood, vines and overgrown meadows. *Faciles*, the adjective describing *buxos* in line 5, was used of water in the *De Spectaculis* (26.2), and means 'yielding', 'malleable': this wood is still young and moist, hardly an inanimate material

---

[74] On the topos of immortal poetry as a memorial to the dead, see e.g. Horace *Odes* 3.30, Prop.3.2.17–18, Martial 8.3.

at all. While Ovid in his *Epistulae ex Ponto* calls his poetry '*nostri monimenta laboris*', 'the monuments of my toil' (4.14.25), in literal terms it is Martial's makeshift graveyard that shall serve as his equivalent memorial (*nostri monimenta doloris*, 5). Yet this epigram is also a homage to, and exercise in perpetuating, poetic fame. Martial marks Alcimus' short life and death by embroidering his epitaph with the beginnings and endings of two famous epics, by Vergil and Ovid. We saw him using similar tactics in 10.2. 1.88 is a clever comment on how poetry can live on in readers' imaginations, and a programme for how Martial plans to cheat the odds and find a way to survive with the best of them.

Let's return first to line 7 of 1.88 (*accipe, care puer, nostri monumenta doloris*). Martial evokes Ovid's phrase at *Ex Ponto* 4.14.25, as I've said, but the line is modelled more closely on Virgil *Aeneid* 3.486–7. This is where the Trojans are about to set sail for Italy, where the voyage of this epic begins. Andromache, to assuage her grief at their departure, offers gifts she has made herself to young Ascanius, who is now the spitting image of her son Astyanax at the point at which he died. She says,

> Accipe et haec, manuum tibi quae monumenta mearum
> sint, puer.

> Take these things, dear boy. May they remind you forever of the
> hands that made them.

As Alcimus dies, his youth remembered in one beautiful teenager who lives, and in another who dies but whose memory lives on, so Martial fuels the lifespan of his poem by relaunching Vergil's epic in the shape of his own garden of memory. Yet at the same time, Martial's *nostri monumenta doloris* also closely recalls one of the final lines of the *Aeneid*, 12.945: *saevi monimenta doloris*. This refers to Turnus' swordbelt, which depicts the horrific scene of the Danaids slaughtering their would-be husbands. Turnus had taken the belt as booty after killing Pallas, and for Aeneas, seeing it brings back in a flash all the raw trauma of that loss, linked now to Andromache's grief for her beloved Astyanax. The ending to the *Aeneid* is notoriously difficult and inconclusive – cut off just as our pious hero rams his sword into a suppliant Turnus, whom we never see buried or mourned. Just as Aeneas is overwhelmed by the still-vibrant past, so Vergil's readers are thrust back into the epic. The final lines are full of ghosts, from Pallas and the Danaids, to Hector, Dido, Andromache and Astyanax. This is precisely what Martial conjures up again here: Alcimus will live on in this garden, just as the *Aeneid* and its characters still haunt Martial's pages.

Meanwhile, line 8 of the poem crams in the beginning and ending of the next big Roman epic, Ovid's *Metamorphoses*. Compare Martial's *hic tibi* **perpetuo tempore vivet** *honor* with *Metamorphoses* 1.2–4:

> di, coeptis (nam vos mutastis et illas)
> aspirate meis primaque ab origine mundi
> ad mea **perpetuum** deducite **tempora** carmen

> Gods (for you yourselves have made these changes)
> breathe on the work I have begun, and bring down my song
> unbroken from the world's beginning to the present time.

And the final line of the *Metamorphoses* (15.879):

> (siquid habent veri vatum praesagia) **vivam**.

> If there is any truth in the prophecies of bards, I shall live.

Notice how Martial puts *perpetuum* and *tempus* together, creating 'perpetual time', without a beginning or end goal.[75] In this reshaping, and in the epigram as a whole, the influence of Ovidian metamorphosis is plain to see. Ovid's Callimachean epic tale of mutating bodies is an aspirational model for Martial's epic-scale project made up of tiny pieces, a myriad of endings and rebeginnings. Martial hints that Alcimus' corpse will rot to become part of the garden, feeding and even metamorphosing into its trees and plants. The vocative *Alcime*, the first word of the poem, is already quite close to the *lacrimae* in line 6 that will metaphorically drip onto his grave, joining master and slave in death (again, the element of water facilitates epigrammatic tricks and transformations). Martial blatantly spells out, then, what Ovid implies: that a cosmos or ecosystem that is self-renewing, that embraces death as part of the cycle of life, can in turn bring to life the poet's quest to reconcile the deathliness of representation with the commemorative power of poetry. Paradoxically, in 1.88, what is most ephemeral turns out to be most 'permanent' and long-lived. Notice also that in line 1 (*crescentibus annis*) Martial doesn't miss the chance to nod towards Ovid's own re-editing of the still *crescens Metamorphoses* in *Tristia* 1.7, where he evokes the scenes of primordial chaos in *Metamorphoses* 1, before adding a new six-line heading to that book.

Yet the phrase *crescentibus annis* also decorates Alcimus' death with another beginning, this time of Ovid's epic-in-elegy, the *Ars Amatoria*.

---

[75] In this sense, Martial takes up Ovid's idea in *Met.* 1 of creating his own idiosyncratic poetic time (*mea tempora*), of placing primal chaos at the heart 'even of established natural time' (Feeney 1999, 24). See Feeney (1999) *passim* for further discussion.

This is where Martial really starts experimenting in seeing how his poetry can mutate alongside his living monument. Compare the following hard sell at *Ars* 1.61–2:

> seu caperis primis et adhuc crescentibus annis,
>     ante oculos veniet vera puella tuos.
>
> Are you attracted by youth and still ripening years?
> A real girl will appear before your eyes.

Suddenly the poem takes on a different complexion, and we begin to join the dots. Alcimus was 'taken from his master in his prime', yet echoes of cynical seduction in the *Ars* might make us read *raptum* as 'taken' in a different sense, even 'raped', and the ablative *domino* as 'by' rather than 'from' his master. Especially as the phrase '*rapta sit puella*' is used by Ovid at *Ars* 1.54 (referring to Paris' abduction of Helen). Martial's vocabulary and images now look cornily reminiscent of Roman love elegy: the master–slave dynamic, all that weeping, the poor man's gifts. How does Martial remember the relationship between Aeneas and Pallas? What did he get out of reading the *Ars Amatoria*, which was all about men chasing *women*? How far can 1.88 metamorphose into a poem that reminisces about picking up a boy? As ever, Martial mixes death with lust, and lowers the tone even (or especially) while pirouetting among literary greats.

   This eco-epitaph flaunts this poet's mischievous plot to honour Ovid's legacy by treating all classical verse as if it were putty in his hands. In Martial's corpus, 1.88 offers itself as perhaps the neatest and most entertaining paradigm for the epigrammatic strategies I have been exploring throughout this chapter, strategies which, so characteristically, manipulate strata and concatenations of paradoxes. While burying Augustan poetry in a cheap, facile grave, Martial at the same time recopies and reinvents the Horatian-Ovidian metaphor of monumentality. He bends into these trim ten lines the whole of Roman history and Augustan poetry, from the beginnings of Aeneas' voyage to Italy and the epic *Aeneid* to Ovid's nostalgic, morbid letters from exile, while also echoing and warping the initial seductions and the thrilling new Augustan city of that criminal *carmen*, the *Ars Amatoria*. He makes Alcimus return from the dead, and grow on in the shape of tears, by digging up a living corpus of texts, and ensuring that beginnings and endings, prologues and epilogues, together with literal and figurative bodies, will (in this narrow world) always have to converge in the same space.

CHAPTER 3

# Poetic economies: figuring out Martial's maths

*Tu quoque de nostris releges quemcumque libellis,*
*esse puta solum: sic tibi pluris erit.*

*Ep.* 4.29.9–10

One of the most basic dynamics of Martial's poetics, which we have seen operating in all kinds of contexts so far, is its simultaneous shrinking down of big to small, and magnification or elevation of the small. In this way the most lowly genre can aim for epic status, and objective measurements are utterly subjectivised, when it suits: short can seem long, a thin book can become fat in the reading, and vice versa, and simplicity can be deceptive. One of the ways in which the epigrams advertise their rank as the smallest and lowest common denominator of literary forms is through numbers, which are the focus of this chapter. In Martial poetry, and the poet's job, are reduced to simple counting. Metrics are what make verse, we're reminded, and epigram must do much in a tiny space – in this genre size matters, and budgets are *the* issue.[1] Not least because Callimachean poverty and moderation are now constraining realities, Martial imagines, not hallmarks of cerebral artistry, or accessories for a bohemian lifestyle. The snappiness and tight form of epigram seem perfectly designed to tap out sums, which play a graphic role in shaping Martial's aesthetics. At the same time, the job of totting up metres and measuring verse to fit merges, in epigram's world, with a materialistic Rome inhabited by hungry and desparate consumers – legacy-hunters, fortune-seekers and thiefs, misers, gluttons, bankrupts and crooks – as if epigram were the *only* poetry that could encompass and express its environs. Martial shows us how fundamental little figures are to

---

[1] There is evidence of an ongoing debate among Greek epigrammatists over the proper measure for an epigram. E.g. Plato *Leg.* 958e insists that funerary epigrams should not be longer than four verses, and Philip of Thessalonica, editor of the *Garland of Philip*, writes (like Callimachus) in praise of brevity in epigram (*AP* 4.2.10–11, cf. Parmenion *AP* 9.342). Also see *AP* 9.369 ('the couplet makes a fine epigram. But if you go over three, that's called a rhapsody, not an epigram').

shaping and representing real and poetic worlds and times, spanning the whole of human experience from the quotidian to the life-defining, from the atomic to the galactic.

## CALCULATED MOVES

We're regularly reminded of where we're at, numerically, in Martial's oeuvre, encouraged to get with the rhythm ('I, Martial, known to the people for my verses of eleven feet and eleven syllables', 10.9.1–3),[2] to measure out the time it takes to read with the same exactitude as the poet has timed his writing sessions (time, of course, is money: the scribe at 2.8 is paid for the number of verses he copies in a certain time, so hurries to '*adnumerare versus*').[3] Books 2, 5, 6, 8, 10 and 12 are all numbered as such in prefaces or introductory epigrams.[4] Martial knows (groan) that he has exceeded his 'limit', at 1.118 ('he for whom reading 100 epigrams is not enough will never have enough of a bad thing'); 300 epigrams in a book is far too much (2.1.1), and this *libellus*, he recommends, is accurately calibrated to take the same time to read as it does to wait for a slave to mix five measures of wine at dinner and set down the glass, before its contents begin to cool (2.1.9–10). This is in contrast to the dinner party Martial attends at 3.50, where host Ligurinus serves up indigestible volume after volume with each of the five, painfully counted courses (*protinus . . . alter . . . tertius . . . quartum . . . et quintum denique*). Martial is often aware that the sheer number of his poems, and books, might go against him, joking that he's boring us, tiring us out, and giving us rather more than we bargained for: 8.3, which I discussed briefly in chapter 2, and its echo in 10.2, lay it on thick that we've already had it up to *here* with Martial, which might also mean that we're working up to a twelve-book epic masterpiece. 8.3.1–2: 'Five was already enough: six or seven little books is already going overboard: why do you love playing on, dear Muse?' are followed in what seems a jiffy by 10.1, apologising again for possibly appearing *nimius*, 'too much' (10.1.1). In this unforgiving, high-pressured town, excess is a common complaint: one can

---

[2] This self-promotion alludes to Catullus 42.1 (*adeste, hendecasyllabi . . . /* 'come, eleven-syllable lines . . .'), cf. Cat. 12.10, and to Ovid *Am.* 1.1.30 (*Musa per undenos emodulanda pedes /* 'O Muse, to be set to the tune of eleven feet'), cf. *Fasti.* 2.567–8.

[3] *Adnumerare* is a financial term ('to pay out' *OLD* s.v. 1). See C. Williams (2004) and Watson and Watson (2003) *ad loc.* On time pressures felt by Martial, see e.g. 11.24: with all the social duties he has to attend to, Martial barely has time to write: 'in almost thirty days I have scarcely finished a page. Such is life when a poet doesn't want to dine at home' (13–15).

[4] Also see discussion in Henderson (2002) 79–82.

even be 'too much' of a poet (*nimis poeta*), as Martial warns Ligurinus
(3.44.4), who force-feeds him verse wherever he goes, from the public
toilets to the baths to dinner, even to bed.

This stunted genre at the bottom of the literary pile (12.94), less poetry
than trivial, surface, formulaic, material *thing,* is presented as epitomising
the relative dwarfing of poet alongside the wealth and grandiosity of Flavian
culture (and, especially, alongside the god-like omniscient emperor), the
reduction of *all* literature to ephemeral merchandise circulating in the
system of Rome. Many of Martial's figures involve money, and we are
constantly reminded of what poetry costs and earns, the extent to which
patronage boils down to *economics.*[5] Amidst the magnificent opulence of
the capital's bathhouses, villas, courts and amphitheatres, poets (especially
epigrammatists) go hungry and obsess over riches that always remain just
out of reach. As Martial complains at 1.59, a poem we glanced at in chapter 1:
'the dole at Baiae presents me with 100 farthings. What is such poverty
doing amid luxury?' Several epigrams describe the drag of eking out a
living as a client, dashing from doorstep to doorstep to maximise patrons'
handouts. In 10.74, for example, this existence is made all the more painful
by the thought that rich guys like Scorpus can cart off fifteen bags of gold
hot from the mint in a single hour. Martial expends much energy sniping
at the kind of man who flaunts or seems to have walked into wealth. In
4.61, for instance, he addresses Mancinus, who constantly boasts about the
amount of money he has been loaned, the value of the gift he has just
received, the legacies he has recently been allotted. He's told: 'take pity on
us, cruel man, and at long last shut up. Or if that tongue of yours can't be
still, finally tell us something that we want to hear' (4.61.14–16). Similarly, at
4.37, we only discover in the sixth line that the by now familiar enumeration
of debts ('Coranus owes a 100,000, Mancinus 200,000, Titius 300,000'
and so on) is actually a quote from the nauseatingly dull and loaded Afer.
Martial demands that he should be paid if he is to endure any more of it
('I can't listen to all this gratis, Afer', 10).

Yet naturally, these are precisely the kind of calculations Martial's poetry
obsesses over, and which in many ways stamp out epigram's 'concreteness',
its precision wit. Numbers help give epigram the prosaic drumbeat and
street-consciousness of a rap – they map out the Real. And as Quintilian

---

[5] For an overview of the role of money in Martial, see Gold (2003), who draws on the discussions of
scholars such as Kurke (1991) and Carson (1999) regarding the development of gift-exchange culture
and poetry about money in sixth- and fifth-century Greece, especially in Simonides and Pindar.
Gold concludes (612) that Martial was 'very aware of his place in the historical continuum of the
gift-exchange culture'.

stressed in his *Institutio Oratoria*, an affinity for maths makes the good orator better, ensures that politics persuade (*Inst.* 1.10.6). The powerful certainty conveyed by accounts of accounts is exploited at length by Pliny at the beginning of his *Natural History*, as well as, more famously, by Augustus in his *Res Gestae*, which lays down a whole chunk of history in numbers, quantifying money spent, statistics relating to population, imperial territories, senators, consuls, priests and spectacles, and marking the age and rank at which the emperor realised each duty or ambition. This same power to quantify is satirised by Petronius in the figure of Trimalchio, who boasts of the number of silver cups and decanters he owns (*Sat.* 52.1), his 100-year-old wine (34.6), and the fact that he has 'thirty years, four months and two days left to live' (77.2), a precision he has also instilled in his staff (a slave announces that three white pigs are two, three and six years old respectively at 47.8, while at 53, a clerk reads out statistics on Trimalchio's estate from the daily gazette[6]). In Cicero's *Tusculans*, the grand theories of Greek geometry are contrasted with the Roman shrinking down of this honourable art to 'the practical purposes of measuring and calculation' (*Tusc.* 1.2.5),[7] while Horace's *Ars Poetica*, meanwhile, sees Roman maths as the antithesis of Greek learning, and of all artistic sensibility. With a sardonic smile, Martial more than lives up to Horace's image of the unpoetic Roman soul, stained by all those boring fractions learnt at school (*Ars Poetica* 323–32):

> Grais ingenium, Grais dedit ore rotundo
> musa loqui, praeter laudem nullius avaris.
> Romani pueri longis rationibus assem
> discunt in partis centum diducere. 'dicat
> filius Albani: si de quincunce remota est
> uncia, quid superat? poteras dixisse.' 'triens.' 'eu!
> rem poteris servare tuam. redit uncia, quid fit?'
> 'semis.' an haec animos aerugo et cura peculi
> cum semel imbuerit, speramus carmina fingi
> posse linenda cedro et levi servanda cupresso?

> To the Greeks the Muse gave native wit, to the Greeks
> she gave well-rounded turns of phrase, and they craved only glory.
> Our Romans learn from boyhood lengthy calculations to
> split the *as* into a hundred parts. 'Albinus' son to answer this:

---

[6] The passage, marked '26 July', lists the 30 boys and 40 girls born, the 5,000 pecks of wheat taken up from the threshing floor, the 500 oxen broken in, and 10,000,000 sesterces which could not be spent placed in the safe.

[7] Compare Plutarch *Life of Marcellus* 305.4–6, and see discussion in Cuomo (2001) ch. 6.

if you subtract one ounce from five-twelfths, what's left? Come on boy.'
'A third.' 'Good! You'll take care of yourself, you will. Add an ounce,
what does that make?' 'A half.' And once this rot and lust for petty coins
has stained the soul, what hope is there of writing verse that warrants
cedar oil and a polished cypress cover?

Martial's numbers may stand, on one hand, for Horace's stereotype of
Roman pragmatism and of plodding, bad poetry, yet they also punctu-
ate precisely the kind of slender, witty, entertaining verse Horace then
goes on to commend (*Ars Poetica* 332ff.). Indeed, the topic of 'numbers
in Latin literature' suits epigram's big-smallness because it is unexpect-
edly enormous in scope, encompassing connotations of seductive magic
and mystery alongside dour scientific reason, evoking Pythagorean and
religious symbolism alongside the accounts of imperial triumph[8] and the
petty greed and hard bargains of the far-reaching Roman business world.
Ancient mathematics is bound up, as Cuomo discusses, with knowledge
and power, with political and moral (dis)order.[9] In literary terms, Martial's corpus churns up a universe of numbers and counting games that
span epic poetry (with its play on totalising oneness and violent duels),[10]
Greek epigram, Roman erotic verse, ancient histories, calendars, textbooks
and satire. We're reminded of the dozens of mathematical problems and
puns in the fourth-century epigrams of Metrodorus, collected in Book 14
of the Palatine Anthology, as well as the witty computations of various
Hellenistic epigrams (for instance Posidippus, *AP* 5.183, Asclepiades *AP*
5.185, Leonidas *AP* 6.129 and Simonides *AP* 6.214, or, playing rather more
sophisticated games, Antipater of Sidon at *AP* 7.427).[11] Martial is especially indebted to several Latin poets before him who experimented with
displaying the arithmetic of metre, with enumerating books and works, and
with the erotics of (not) counting. We think in particular of Ovid, who
famously subtracts two books from his five-book *Amores* to make three,
crops a foot from hexameter number one to make pentameter number two
$(6 - 1 = 5)$ in *Amores* 1.1,[12] and tots up girls and sexual positions by the

---

[8]  On the connection between numbers and the occult in antiquity see e.g. Dilke (1987) and Cuomo
(2001).

[9]  See Cuomo (2001), *passim*.

[10]  On oneness and duality in the Roman epic tradition, see Hardie (1993) 2–11, and my discussion
below.

[11]  See the interesting discussion of *AP* 7.427 in Gutzwiller (1998) 270–1. Other Greek epigrams which
play on numbers and counting include *AP* 11.225 (Strato) and *AP* 13.14 (Simonides): compare the
use of the verb ἀριθμῆσαι in line 5 of this poem to Martial's use of *annumerare*. On the trope of
economy in Simonides see Carson (1999).

[12]  These numbers are spelt out in *Am.* 1.1.27 (*sex mihi surgat opus numeris, in quinque residat*).

thousand (*mille*);[13] also, the number-rich rituals of Horace's *Carmen Saec-ulare*[14] and Ovid's *Fasti*, or Catullus, who adds up pointy hendecasyllables but whose kisses for Lesbia in poems 5 and 7 are too many to number.[15] Yet whilst Catullus and the Roman love elegists rate love and art over material wealth and make enemies of penny-pinching moralists and rich suitors who 'buy' their women with expensive gifts, Martial counts cash along-side and in place of metrical feet, lines of verse, and books of poems. It is through plain numbers that he evokes the rampant culture of consumerism we visualise through Statius' *Silvae*, where, in contrast to Martial's cheap books, Statius' collections are expensive items carrying a high price tag.[16]

There is no escaping counting in Martial's Rome, and lifetimes, gov-ernments, time, people and friendships are gauged in just the same way as poetry is plotted out in feet. Again, Ovid's well-worked pun on the human/metrical *pes* is partly to blame. Women are notches on the bedpost, marks out of ten, and often come in ball-park units, ranked in order.[17] Men, too, can be just as conveniently numbered: 5.21 features Decimus ('the tenth'), flattered (or cut down to size?) by rhetor Apollodotus, who persists in calling him Quintus ('fifth'), and Martial swops Quintus for

---

[13] *Mille modi* is a much used phrase in Ovid. See e.g. *Ars* 1.756 (*mille animos excipe mille modis*), cf. 2.679–80 and 3.787, and *Am.* 3.14.23–4 (*illic purpureis condatur lingua labellis / inque modos Venerem mille figuret amor*). As Hinds points out (2007), Martial also uses the phrase at 9.67.3 (*fessus mille modis illud puerile poposci*), but actually spells out, in no uncertain terms, what it means, overriding Ovidian euphemism.

[14] See Barchiesi (2005a) 157–60. Barchiesi highlights Horace's mention of the number seven, *septem*, in line 7 of the poem, and the numbers ten and eleven in line 21, which reminds him of the Alexandrian tradition of *carmina figurata*. The Ludi Saeculares contained a great deal of numerology. Barchiesi also points out that the number seven connects Rome (with its seven hills) and the gods Apollo and Diana, who are associated in various ways with the number.

[15] Catullus: see 5 and 7, plus 12.10–11 (*quare aut hendecasyllabos trecentos / exspecta*), 16, 48 and 11.17 (*quos simul complexa tenet trecentos*). As C. Williams mentions (2004, 281), explicit references to the number of books a poet has written are unusual before Martial. As well as the *Amores*, see *Ars Amatoria* 1.35–40, *Fasti* 1.723–4, Propertius 2.13.25. See also Statius, *Silvae* 3, Pref. 8 (*securus itaque tertius hic silvarum nostrarum liber ad te mittitur*).

[16] See Statius *Silv.* 4.9.7–9 (the book is expensively decorated and cost ten asses), with discussion in Newlands (2002) 257–9.

[17] See e.g. 1.71, where each of Martial's girls is numbered by the exact amount of wine in his cup: 'let Laevia be drunk in six measures, and Justina in seven, Lycis in five, Lyde in four, Ida in three' (1–2). In 1.57, he measures up his ideal woman as a 'medium' (3). At 11.97, Martial can get it up four times in one night but can't cope with Telesilla once in four years. In 9.32 he is looking for a sixpenny prostitute, not one *poscentem nummos*. And in 10.55, Marulla is the model of Martial's statistical precision when she weighs an erect penis with her skilled hands and pronounces the measure in pounds, scruples and sextules (i.e. to one twenty-fourth of an ounce), reminding us of the Priapus from the vestibule of the House of the Vetii in Pompeii, who weighs his giant penis against a money bag. See Beard and Henderson (2001, 35) on the possible verbal pun on *penis* and *pendere* visualised here.

Sextus ('sixth', another common first name) at 3.11.[18] Even the Flavian emperors can all fit into one elegiac couplet when they are simply termed 'first', 'second' and 'third' (see the epigram sometimes attached to the end of the *De Spectaculis,* where it almost certainly does not belong: 'Flavian race, how much the third heir stole from you! It would almost have been worth it not to have the other two!'[19]). We can list dozens upon dozens of poems which (explicitly or implicitly) measure, or concern applications for financial loans, loans that have not been granted, debts owed and due, salaries, fortunes and inheritances. What's left of *otium,* in the wake of Julio-Claudian poetry, must be scientifically tallied: in 12.34, for example, Martial reminisces that he's had thirty-four summers with Julius. Some were sweet, some bitter (experiences are mingled to mime this book's mis-cellanies); yet if the counting pebbles were sorted into two piles, one black and one white, the white heap would outnumber the black (5–7). The poem itself neatly divides and patterns (*mihi,* 1; *tecum,* 2; *huc et illuc,* 5; *vincet candida turba nigriorem,* 7). It ends with advice on the difficult bal-ancing act of friendship: if you don't make yourself too much of a friend (*nulli te facias nimis sodalem,* 10), you'll get less pleasure (*gaudebis minus*), but also less pain (*minus dolebis*). In short, subtract an unspecified amount from *nimis,* and you'll get two minuses, which may well make a plus.[20] In 2.44, the character Sextus seems to exemplify the contagiously nervous, penny-pinching mentality which infects Martial's city, and from which the poet himself is never immune. Just as a starving man cannot stop thinking about the hunger gnawing at his belly, so the *hoi polloi* of Rome, mired in a poverty, real or imagined, relative to surrounding riches, focus compul-sively on the activity of counting: in this epigram, then, whenever Martial makes a purchase, Sextus is maddened with the fear that he will be asked

---

[18] In this poem, Martial plays on the idea that all names have a metrical quantity, and that in poetry names may be chosen because they are of the right 'measure'. Names of the same quantity are thus, in a sense, interchangeable: so here, Martial writes Thais to stand for Lais (*pro Laide Thaida dixi,* 3). How can Quintus think that Martial is really referring to his girlfriend Hermione, a name with a different metrical quantity? To ensure he can't possibly think this, Martial will even change the name Quintus in 3.8 to Sextus, a name which has the same metrical quantity but paradoxically represents a different number. However, the joke is perhaps that as soon as you say that Sextus (sixth) can stand in for Quintus (fifth), then a name of two syllables or four letters (like Lais) can potentially stand in for a name of four syllables, or seven letters (like Hermione). Martial is likely hinting that 3.8 was in fact aimed at Quintus and his girlfriend after all, even as he denies it.

[19] In Lindsay's Oxford text the poem is numbered 33. Friedländer places it at the end of Book 11.

[20] Compare the many birthday epigrams, in which friends and enemies are reminded of the measure of mortal life, the ticking clock: e.g. 10.24 (on Martial's own fifty-seventh birthday, he resolves to add two times nine years to this sum so that life's three courses are properly, exactly run), or 10.38, where model husband Calenus has enjoyed 15 years of marital bliss, each hour marked out by pebbles from India's shore. I discussed both these poems in chapter 2.

to pay off *his* debts, and begins processing figures ('that's seven thousand I owe Secundus, Phoebus four, Philetus eleven, and I don't have a penny in my piggy bank'). If someone somewhere makes a loss, it is all too easy to get swept along in the aggressive domino effect of borrowing and repayment: at 11.76, for instance, Paetus forces Martial to pay him 10,000 sesterces, because Bucco has just lost him 200,000. The inevitability of being in debt to *someone*, and hence part of a complex invisible chain that binds the whole of Roman society, entails that you can always be made to suffer for sins you have not committed, as the poet bewails here. The deal is always: *quisquis magna dedit, voluit sibi magna remitti* ('whoever gives a lot wants a lot in return', 5.59.3). Once you accept a loan, or place a down payment, you are at the mercy of your debtor.

Martial is at pains to stress that reading, too, cannot operate outside these vicious circles of social reciprocity into which the poet is locked: readers enter into a contract when they pick up these *libelli*, are duty-bound to pay up if they want to read on, regardless of the value judgements they may make along the way. In the third introductory poem of the *Xenia*, 13.3, Martial picks up the carnival buzz of the Saturnalia by bargaining with his customers: 'this little book', he says, in the voice of a canny street hawker, 'will cost ya four sesterces.' He imagines our reluctance, we're already going on our way. Quick as a flash, he'll halve it ('it could cost two'), or rather (it's not his stall, after all), the bookstore could sell it for that much, and still make a profit. But this is itself a clever sales pitch: sympathise with Martial, being fleeced by his own bookseller, just as poor as you; and now that you're onside and already reaching for your wallet, know that you can make further savings – you don't have to read it through, just skip anything not to your taste! (*praetereas, si quid non facit ad stomachum*, 13.3.8). In price and size, if you play your cards right, this book comes reduced by half. The reader at 11.108, however, is trying to con the poet, get away with more, not less. He immediately ups the price, and the smart reader fakes deafness, at which point Martial cuts off his services, and this book.[21]

> Quamvis tam longo possis satur esse libello,
>   lector, adhuc a me disticha pauca petis.
> sed Lupus usuram puerique diaria poscunt.
>   lector, solve. taces dissimulasque? vale.

[21] The joke being that the scene of the still hungry reader seems highly improbable (invented by an unpopular poet trying to drum up business *somehow*), after 11.106 (Vibius Maximus passes this poem by, as well as the rest of the book) and 11.107 (Septicianus claims he has read the book Martial sent him from beginning to end. Right, comes the reply – just like I read every line of *your* books).

Though you might be satiated with so long a little book,
dear reader, you ask me for a few couplets more.
But Lupus demands interest and the boys need their rations.
Pay up, dear reader. Silent, eh? Gone deaf? *Ciao.*

Pliny in *Epistles* 3.21 responds in quietly satiric tones to Martial's vision of
the obligations of reading. If Martial sends you something, you have to
send him something back in return: so Pliny replies in kind to *Epigrams*
10.19, which instructed the muse to send Pliny a book of epigrams, or
rather the epigrammatic combination/parallel gift of cash and poetry (he
mentions that he had repaid friendship and verses by giving Martial his
travel expenses when he left Rome for Bilbilis, 3.21.2). Pliny concludes
his assessment of Martial's poem about him by alluding to and reiterating
the tension between wanting more and having to settle for less that runs
through epigram's accounts: *dedit enim mihi quantum maximum potuit,
daturus amplius si potuisset. tametsi quid homini potest dari maius, quam
gloria et laus et aeternitas?* ('he gave the very most he could, and would
have given more had he been able. Though surely, what more can you give a
man than glory, fame and immortality?' 3.21.6). The string of comparatives
and superlatives here, hinting sardonically at inadequacy, mirror (in a neat,
quasi-epigrammatic structure) the initial statements of this obituary, which
condense Martial within a rhetorical frame of 'the most' and 'the less' (*erat
homo ingeniosus acutus acer, et qui plurimum in scribendo et salis haberet et
fellis, nec candoris minus,* 'he was a very talented man, with a sharp and
penetrating mind, the sort whose writing had the most salt and bile, and
no less sincerity to boot,' 3.21.1). As Henderson puts it, 'Pliny sums up the
summer-upper'.[22]

For critics, too, it seems almost impossible to comment on Martial's
books at all without (descending into) numbering – as the introduction
to this book has already helped to show. When we're dealing with such a
huge, variegated, unmanageable mass of poetry, how else can we categorise
and make judgements? Sullivan epitomises our compulsion to count up
Martial in his discussion of *Epigrams* 1:

Martial produces in Book I an interwoven pattern of epigrams on a variety of
topics, which will recur throughout the rest of the books . . . There are about
fifty satiric epigrams criticising physical defects, sexual deviations, improper social

[22] Henderson (2001) 62. On this poem also see Garthwaite (1998a), who takes both Pliny and Martial
rather literally on the subject of immortality, and Roman (2001, 117), who discusses the dialogue
between Pliny and Martial in terms of the contradictory aesthetics of epigram.

behaviour, such as legacy- and dowry-hunting, avarice, ostentation, drunkenness and so on. (Of these about fifteen might be regarded as indecent.)

Epigrams concerning publication, the nature of poetry and the habits of its practitioners, such as plagiarism, add up to twenty-seven. These are often tendentiously self-conscious, and have an affinity with even more personal epigrams relating to the poet's own life or his status as a client, including erotic and convivial themes. Of these there are fourteen in all.[23]

We can find similar statistics in many other books, articles and commentaries on Martial.[24] What I want to stress here, which will come to the fore in my reading of *Epigrams* 2 towards the end of this chapter, is just how infectious Martial's mathematics become, especially for the critic – who has already been sized up by the poet as enemy number one. Numbers span the literary and the real, or 'real'; they also become figures, in another sense, for readers' entry into Martial, our introduction into what makes this poetry tick, as well as into the workings of power and materialistic desire in Flavian Rome.

### SOMETHING FOR NOTHING

If we want to summarise (with the awareness that we're bound to be caught out this way), we might say that epigram more often counts down than up. Martial constructs epigram as continually striving for more, yet as painfully conscious of the poetic constraints which are both contingent on and emblematic of the social, political and financial straitjacketing of its author. These epigrams will always want to be 'epic', yet the sums just don't add up (or do they?). Bigger poetry, surely, needs heavyweight financial backing: without a Maecenas,[25] *vel sim.*, in a literary culture in which every other small-time scribbler reckons he's the next Vergil,[26] epigrams earn pocket change[27] – at least, that's the spin. Self-deprecation in Martial often takes the form of pricing-down. So at 4.72, Quintus is quite right, Martial confesses, in refusing to pay for his books. At 1.117, Lupercus asks for his latest volume of epigrams, and Martial points towards the nearest bookshop, whose doorposts are covered with ads for poets (you can find

[23] Sullivan (1991) 22.

[24] E.g. Watson and Watson (2003) 25, 28, 30–1, C. Williams (2004) 9, Holzberg (2002) 136,

[25] Martial longs for, and explains the repercussions of not having, a Maecenas, in 1.107, 8.55, 11.3.

[26] See especially 3.38 ('all these people you see here in frozen cloaks, they're all Nasos and Virgils. "*atria magna colam*": that line hardly fed three or four, the rest of the crowd is pale with hunger', 9–12).

[27] See e.g. 11.3: here, Martial boasts that his books are read worldwide, even in Britain. Even so, 'what's the use?' he complains, *nescit sacculus ista meus* ('my wallet knows nothing of all that', 6).

him among the long list). A pumice-shaved copy will cost him five *denarii*. But he predicts Lupercus will say he's not worth the price, and agrees: '*sapis, Luperce*' – 'you're a smart chap, Lupercus!' (18). Likewise, there is much advice in Martial on how to be his best editor, how to cut out what bores or grates. We can do as he does, when in the *Apophoreta* he compresses the whole of Livy into 'tiny skins' (*pellibus exiguis*, 14.190), and dispatches Virgil's lifework in a single distich ('how small a quantity of parchment has comprised vast Maro!' 14.186.1). So reader Venuleius at 4.82 can fold one of the rolls that make up Books 3 and 4 in half, if two books are too much (*nimis*) for him: *divisum sic breve fiet opus* ('thus divided, the work becomes short', 4.82.8). Or at the end of Book 2, in a different take on division, Martial's second volume can become the first (if Regulus has missed or wants to skip *Epigrams* I), with the simple act of removing one iota from the title (II – I = I). We should make Book 10 (edition 2) as small as we like (10.1.4), and pick and mix as the mood takes us (e.g. 6.65, 13.3.8, 14.2). The compact book has its own unique virtues, and can be construed as the ideal product for consumption in a marketplace where leisure time is scanty, and life is short.

So (in parallel to the spatial paradoxes we touched upon in chapter 1), despite its ever-present awareness and cheeky delight in exceeding borders, in becoming much more than it seems, Martial's epigram often shrinks back and down, using a sliding scale to nought as a potent tool both for satiric put-downs, and for self-victimisation. Poem 10.75, for example, devalues Galla with subtractions that keep on going: at first this prostitute asks the poet for 20,000, because she's worth it (or rather, as Martial comments, *magno non erat illa nimis*, 'she wasn't too much of a high price,' 2). After passing up the opportunity, a year goes by and she asks again, this time for 10,000, which paradoxically makes him feel as if she is asking for more; the price dips to 2,000, and he barters at 1,000, which she does not accept – yet two Kalends later, the unsolicited Galla requests four gold pieces, then 100 sesterces, then 100 farthings, before going down all the way to zero, and then finally offers to pay *him*, if he'll have her.[28] He declines, as the cheap bargain seems worthless.[29] Martial documents many more losses and broken promises of loans than gains, and emphasises the disproportionate expenditure of (precisely reckoned) units of time, effort and cash to achieve the smallest result: in 2.5, for example, he bemoans how he walks the two miles to and from Decianus' house, only to find he

---

[28] *ultro dat mihi Galla* (14): *dare* means both to give money and to put out sexually.
[29] Similar poems include 11.105 and 10.57.

is not at home when he said he would be, or does not have time to see his client. Or in 9.6, the poet travels 'twice and three times' to visit Afer for five successive days only to be turned away. Likewise, even huge sums of money can be squandered in a moment, as if the epigrammatic imagination itself shrinks down everything it touches: at 4.66, Linus has accomplished the astounding task of gambling away the million he inherited from his mother. In parallel with the imagined reception of his *Apophoreta*, which Martial jokes would be more trashy than trash if only critics could find the vocabulary (14.1), the poverty-stricken poet is on a steep downward slope to bankruptcy, and is constantly subtracting rather than adding up, being paid or given less and less: in 4.76, for example, the poet complains that a patron sent him 6,000 when he asked for 12,000; in 8.17, Sextus has only sent 1,000 sesterces when 2,000 were due. Or 8.71, where we are told that Postumianus used to send Martial four pounds of silver, but then began to send only two pounds, followed by decreasing amounts in the third and fourth years, just one pound in the fifth, until in the sixth he was presented with an eight-ounce dish, in the seventh a half-pound cup, in the eighth a spoon weighing less than two ounces, and in the ninth a snail-pick lighter than a needle. We know what's on the horizon: *quod mittat nobis decimus iam non habet annus* ('for the tenth year he doesn't have a penny to send,' 11).[30]

Ultimately, the epigrammatic drive to reduce and miniaturise pushes for, or risks, invisibility. Martial's poems are advertised as 'nothings' themselves (e.g. in 5.6.17, Martial wants his personified book presented to the emperor *sic tamquam nihil*, 'as if it were nothing'). We get the sense that Martial is trying to liberate himself from the pressures of literary and social exchange, as though coming to nothing is a way of halting the infinite pattern of recycling and debt, a declaration of bankruptcy. When all gifts are hooks, when giving in general is never an altruistic gesture, it is much more generous to donate nothing (5.18.9–10: *quotiens amico diviti nihil donat, / o Quintiane, liberalis est pauper*). Similarly, Martial's promise to recite *nihil* at dinner makes the invitation far more attractive to Julius Cerealis at 11.52.16. At 5.59, Martial snaps the chain of reciprocity by sending the poet Stella *no* gifts of silver and gold, because whoever gives a lot wants a lot in

---

[30] Other similar poems include 9.8 (Fabius, to whom Bithynicus used to give 6,000 a year, has left him nothing in his will: Martial calculates that Bithynicus will in fact be richer as a result). Misers are also the theme of *AP* 11.165–73, while *AP* 11.174–84 concentrate on thieves. Many of these epigrams are by Lucillius, the Neronian epigrammatist whose deadpan humour can often be felt in Martial. On the relationship between Martial and Lucillius, see e.g. Sullivan (1991) 85–90.

return.[31] This poem finds its twin in 5.73, where Martial writes instead about the depressing implications of handing out his *libelli* as gifts:[32]

> Non donem tibi cur meos libellos
> oranti totiens et exigenti
> miraris, Theodore? magna causa est:
> dones tu mihi ne tuos libellos.
>
> Do you wonder, Theodorus, why
> I don't give you my little books,
> though you beg and ask so often?
> For good reason: I don't want *yours* back.

This, and many other of Martial's epigrams, embody the idea that books offered (like lines of poetry, like favours) are liable to boomerang back to the giver, in a different form: *non donem tibi* in the first line becomes *dones tu mihi* in the last, coming full circle to sew up this neat sample of Martial's poetic technique. Wrapped up in the middle of the parcel, the name Theodorus is a sly pun: this poet is 'god-given', or as Kay comments, '(not) God's gift to poetry'.[33] In this mini-tale about not-giving, or non-giving, even gifts from the gods are negated, and come to nothing.

Indeed, *nihil* ('nothing') is a trademark in the epigrams, orbited by multiple narratives and jokes.[34] For a start, of course, we can't escape the irony that to trace how this word is used involves enumerating lots of examples, and asking what lots of noughts add up to. Through his twelve numbered books, Martial accumulates dozens of poems that hinge on the threat or promise of nothingness. In Book 8, which begins by apologising for well exceeding all decent boundaries, 8.9 advises on clawing back ground that's about to be lost. Here, half-blind Hylas is indebted to Quintus: when he was shortsighted, he wanted to pay back just three-quarters of the money; now he's lost sight altogether in one eye and so wants it reduced to half. Martial advises Quintus to take up the offer: if he goes completely blind, he'll pay *nil*. 9.8 addresses a certain Bithynicus, who has been left *nil* by Fabius in his will, despite the fact that Bithynicus used to give his old friend

---

[31] This implicitly literary exchange, from one materialist to another, contains the dig that Stella would not be able to match the great gift Martial could give, so should not be embarrassed by the initial gesture – as well as suggesting that Martial himself does not possess poetic jewels to donate.

[32] The theme recurs at 7.3 ('why don't I send you my little books, Pontilianus? So that you don't send me yours, Pontilianus').

[33] See Kay (1985) on 11.93, where the name Theodorus is used for a bad poet.

[34] Martial may be in part inspired by *AP* 11.167 (Pollianus), which plays on the idea of a lot being perceived as nothing, οὐδέν: 'You have money, but I will tell you how it is you have nothing. You lent it all; so that in order that somebody else may have some, you have none yourself.'

6,000 sesterces a year. Martial consoles him that at least he'll get to keep this money, so will effectively be richer anyway. In Book 12, a sequence of poems toys further with the question of how to define nothing: 12.48 sees Martial snarling at a dinner host who tries to buy favours with a stingy platter of Lucrine oysters (it's a fine supper today, but tomorrow it is worth *nil*, 6); 12.71 addresses Lygdus, who refuses Martial nothing; this innuendo is revisited at 12.79 (lover Atticilla pesters Martial for something, which he refuses to give, for *quisquis nil negat, Atticilla, fellat* ('Whoever refuses nothing, Atticilla, sucks')). And 12.76 jokes that given the low market price of wine and wheat, the farmer with a good harvest has, effectively, nothing. In 2.64, addressed to a man named Laurus who can't make up his mind on a career, *nihil esse,* to be nothing (10) means 'to be dead', and this is what Martial often seems to be moving towards, or falling just short of. In death we're all a number, a great big zero. Poem 1.19, for example, features an old toothless woman with a nasty cough (people with coughs in Martial are usually diseased, often watched intently by legacy hunters waiting for them to keel over[35]). The epigram counts down decrepit Aelia to imminent death:

> Si memini, fuerant tibi quattuor, Aelia, dentes:
>     expulit una duos tussis et una duos.
> iam secura potes totis tussire diebus:
>     nil istic quod agat tertia tussis habet.

> If I remember rightly, Aelia, you had four teeth:
> one cough spat out two, another one two more.
> You can rest easy now, and cough all day:
> A third cough can have no effect.

Martial writes four lines for four teeth (in two couplets, one for each of the two coughs which expel two teeth each). Yet the comedy coughs, and their description, are over by line two: after this neat division (two into one, twice), further coughs and verses look redundant. There is nothing interesting coming out of Aelia's mouth, or out of Martial's – just nothing, *nil.* We don't even count to four, properly ($2 \times 2$ is epigram's neater shortcut), and the poem hangs on *tertia tussis*, cough number 3 (= 0 entertainment). The minus implicit in *se-cura* ('free from care') is the pay-off for further, irrelevant additions, which can produce no more subtractions.[36] This mocking, premature epitaph combines the idea that to make someone

---

[35] E.g. 1.10 ('Gemellus is wooing Maronilla . . . what's so attractive about her? Her cough . . .').
[36] Thanks to John Henderson for this add-on.

just a number is to dehumanise, objectify and diminish them to next to nothing, with the idea that we might remember old Aelia precisely because she is a (just about) living exemplum of division and multiplication.[37]

In listing these examples, however, we've already begun to see that *nihil* can often amount to more than nothing in the epigrams. This diminutive, low-value genre has big ambitions to revalorise the small, even the non-existent, and to reframe 'tedious' enumerations as concentrated, value-for-money language play. While Martial exploits the objectiveness of figures to sharpen our impression of the pragmatic tautness of epigram, he also conjures up a city, and a poetics, in which it is easy to lose count, where numbers *are* art, and can be dubious tools for figuring reality. It's the dice, that symbol of gaming and unpredictability, that defines 'verses written in December',[38] which covers much of Martial's output. Epigram's Rome is inhabited by gamblers and cheats, all bent on grabbing *more* than they are due ('folk these days think nothing is big enough,' 4.64.31), on miscalculating in ingenious ways for the benefit of their own purses. Loans are taken but not repaid (*sex sestertia, Paete, perdidisti,* 'Paetus, you have wasted six thousand sesterces,' 6.30.7, cf. 6.5), presents sold back to the givers (7.16), properties razed to profit from insurance claims (3.52), birthdays celebrated eight times a year to rake in the gifts (8.64), last testaments sealed again and again to lure the legacy hunters (5.39), and house buyers conned by designer furniture which isn't included in the asking price (12.66).

*Nihil*s pile up, and negatives cancel each other out. Hence when Thais refuses nothing in 4.12, this means she has no limits on what she accepts to do:

> Nulli, Thaï, negas; sed si te non pudet istud,
>    hoc saltem pudeat, Thaï, negare nihil.

> You refuse nobody, Thais; but if there's no shame in that,
>    at least be ashamed of this, Thais: there's nothing you refuse.

12.71, which I mentioned above, makes the same joke ('there is nothing you do not refuse me when I ask, Lygdus. But one time, Lygdus, you refused me nothing'). Ultimately, there is no opting out of a social system grounded

---

37 It is quite common for epitaphs, which sum up the dead, enumerate achievements and mark the measure of life, to include figures, and several Hellenistic sepulchral epigrams represent the randomness of life and death in terms of number, often using the image of a dice. See e.g. Leonidas *AP* 7.422, Antipater *AP* 7.427 and Alcaeus *AP* 7.429, with Gutzwiller (1998) 267–8, 270–1, 275. Martial 3.93 gives ancient Vetustilla a push towards the grave by burying her with figures ('you've got 300 consuls, Vetustilla, plus three hairs and four teeth,' 1–2).

[38] Cf. Ovid *Tr.* 2.491.

in the bargaining ethic of reciprocity: at 5.36, for example, the poet is cheated when a certain party to whom he (literally) paid a compliment plays innocent as though he owes him nothing. 'I know these efforts of mine are nothing, *nihil*,' he says in 13.2, 'and yet they are not altogether nothing' – *non tamen hoc nimium nihil est.* The words *nimium/nimis*, 'too much', and *nihil*, 'nothing', are frequently juxtaposed, becoming a structuring paradox in Martial's poetics. To say that something is nothing is sometimes (always?) just a rhetorical ploy, exposed, for example, in 3.61. Here Martial complains that whatever Cinna asks for, he says it is nothing:

> Esse nihil dicis quidquid petis, inprobe Cinna:
>   si nil, Cinna, petis, nil tibi, Cinna, nego.

> Hateful Cinna, whatever you ask for you say it's nothing:
> If you ask for nothing, Cinna, then nothing I'll deny you.

Martial will deny Cinna nothing, which should mean that he'll give any-thing or everything, yet in Cinna's logic, *nihil = quicquid petis.* Presum-ably Martial will play him at his own game, but reverse the trick: while Cinna asked for a lot (which he calls 'nothing'), Martial will offer nothing (which Cinna has now defined as 'a lot'), so that 'I'll deny you noth-ing' really means 'I'll deny you everything'. *Nihil* also manages to look like something at 10.102: Avitus writes nothing but is still a poet (just as Philinus never fucks but is still a father), because he plagiarises other people's verse.

There are several more epigrams in which sex, or even masturbation, becomes a surprise lesson in multiplication, a making of something from nothing. At 9.41, Ponticus, like Philinus in 10.102, never has sex – at least, not with anyone other than himself. Martial reprimands him with some statistics on what he is missing: for what he thinks is *nihil* is actually a tragic crime of huge proportions:

> Pontice, quod numquam futuis, sed paelice laeva
>   uteris et Veneri servit amica manus,
> hoc nihil esse putas? scelus est, mihi crede, sed ingens,
>   quantum vix animo concipis ipse tuo.
> nempe semel futuit, generaret Horatius ut tres;
>   Mars semel, ut geminos Ilia casta daret.
> omnia perdiderat, si masturbatus uterque
>   mandasset manibus gaudia foeda suis.
> ipsam crede tibi naturam dicere rerum:
>   'istud quod digitis, Pontile, perdis, homo est.'

> Ponticus, you think it's *nothing* that you never fuck when
> your left hand is your mistress, a kind slave to your lust?
> This is a crime, believe me, and one of huge proportions,
> such that *your* brain can scarcely comprehend. The facts are these:
> that Horatius had three kids from shagging one time only,
> and Mars scored twins by doing virgin Ilia just once.
> Just think – all these lives eradicated if just those two had wanked away,
> consigning filthy pleasures to their hands.
> Believe it, the very nature of things is telling you,
> 'what you waste with your fingers, Ponticus, is a human life.'

Lines 5–6 of the epigram allude to Ovid *Amores* 2.14, the comic pro-life elegy which reminds Corinna that if Thetis, Ilia and Venus had aborted their babies, then Priam, Romulus, Remus and Aeneas would not have been born to make history (compare especially *Am.* 2.14.15–16: *Ilia si tumido geminos in ventre necasset, / casurus dominae conditor Urbis erat* ('If Ilia had murdered her twins in her swollen belly, the founder of mistress Rome would have been doomed')). Martial takes Ovid's mock-tragic tirade to even more ridiculous extremes, suggesting that Ponticus is effectively murdering his unborn offspring as he masturbates. The poem jokes that there are two ways to use your hand – as a counting tool or as a wanking tool. The final line (*istud quod digitis, Pontice, perdis, homo est*) refers not only to the 'waste' of masturbation, but to the act of miscounting using the fingers (because presumably you can't count accurately if your fingers are busy elsewhere).[39] Ponticus is encouraged to think about counting (how many children he *could* be conceiving), a calculation made more difficult and interesting by the possibility of multiple births: his *nihil* is *ingens*, and it only takes 'one time' (*semel*) to make two or even three babies. Martial expands his point by cranking up the epic references: in this single little poem we'll find not just Ovid's *Amores*, but also Lucretius' *De Rerum Natura* (rearranged as *naturam dicere rerum* in line 9).[40] Martial uses epigram's microscope

---

[39] Quint. *Inst.* 1.10.35 characterises the bad orator as someone 'who contradicts his calculations by shaky and inappropriate movements of the fingers' (*si digitorum saltem incerto aut indecoro gestu a computatione dissentit, iudicatur indoctus*). Russell (2001, *ad loc.*) notes that this refers to the conventional system of indicating numbers and doing calculations by various positions and movements of the fingers (see also Quint. *Inst.* 11.3.117, Juv. 10.249, Apuleius, *Apol.* 89). Fingers were used to count large numbers, not just one to ten: units of ten were expressed by the left hand, hundreds and thousands by the right, while higher numbers involved moving one hand or the other about. E.g. Nestor, in Juv. 10.249, is 'beginning to count his years on the right hand'. Russell notes that the rules for digital counting were complex and easily confused.

[40] Several more epigrams multiply individuals, another take on the theme of one as many, or once = many times. E.g. 1.68 (Rufus is so devoted to his Naevia, he thinks she is *una*, the only woman in

to show you all the little moving seeds the universe is made of, just like Lucretius.[41] Yet the joke is also that this is *not* (for once) a post-Lucretian paradigm of poem-as-world, or world-as-poem, more a wasted opportunity in that direction, an uncreative flick of the wrist.

Meanwhile, Martial's oxymoronic book is a *libellus longus* which nevertheless does not satisfy (11.108, cf. 6.65). At 10.59, after sussing out his readers as lazy diners who prefer the short and sweet items in a book, he warns us that, in direct contradiction to earlier addresses, we are missing out on a sumptuous dinner containing ingredients from every market for a snatched canapé. Money is not an absolute measurement of value (6,000 sesterces can mean a little or a lot, depending on when and how it is given, as we learn in 6.30[42]). Neither is it a consolation, after all, that readers can make even the longer poems short, as many pennies add up to a bundle (*Disticha qui scribit, puto, vult brevitate placere. / quid prodest brevitas, dic mihi, si liber est?* 'He who writes distichs wishes, I suppose, to please by brevity. What use is brevity, tell me, if it's a book?' 8.29). 2.1 makes a similar point: after announcing the virtues of a compact little book, Martial sneers: *esse tibi tanta cautus brevitate videris? / ei mihi, quam multis sic quoque longus eris!* ('do you suppose you are protected by such brevity? Ah, how many will think you long even so!' 11–12). Poetry devoid of tragedy or epic bombast is not necessarily lightweight, and a slimline book doesn't necessarily make for quick and easy reading, as 2.6 advises: 'what good is it to me, a little book so skinny that it is no thicker than any roller stick, if it would take you three days to get through all of it?' (10–12).

the world. What he does not realise, Martial points out, is that there are any number of Naevias: *Naevia non una est*, 8); 5.49 also sees one person as many: 'when I chanced to see you the other day sitting all alone, Labienus, I thought there were three of you. The plurality of your bald head had me fooled. On each side you've got hair that might become a boy, but in the middle your scalp is naked.' This poem pairs up neatly with 2.52: Darius did the maths and charged Spatale three times to enter the baths – once for her head, and twice for her two enormous breasts. In contrast to 5.49, 5.38 divides instead of multiplies: Calliodorus and his brother both want to be knights, but only one of them has the qualifying fortune of 400,000 sesterces. 'Do you think two can sit on one horse?' Martial asks in line 4, referring to the original function of a knight, and then, playing further on the joke of two-in-one by mingling singular noun with plural verb and vice versa: *'unus cum sitis, duo, Calliodore, sedebis?'* ('Since you [plural] are one, will two of you [singular] sit down. Calliodorus?').

[41] At the risk of making another something out of nothing (or worse, nothing out of something, in the manner of Ponticus), could we also read echoes or reminders of *semen* and *uterus* in the verb *uteris* in line 2, and the repetition of *semel* in lines 5 and 6?

[42] In 6.30, Martial complains that if Paetus had lent him 6,000 sesterces immediately, it would have seemed an enormous amount and Martial would have felt indebted to the tune of 200,000. Yet Paetus coughed up after seven or nine months of being pestered, so that when Martial finally gets his 6,000, it feels like a paltry sum.

### THE ONE AND THE MANY

In Martial, small is the new big, and narrow pipes blast like tubas. To
illustrate this endemic point more closely, I want to turn now to poems 12–
14 of the *De Spectaculis*, a triptych describing the death of a pregnant sow
in the arena and the simultaneous birth of just one of her many piglets.[43]
We see here one of Martial's more intricate performances of the point that
restriction and amplification can go hand in hand within the same tight
space, or spaces:

> Inter Caesareae discrimina saeva Dianae
>     fixisset gravidam cum levis hasta suem,
> exiluit partus miserae de vulnere matris.
>     o Lucina ferox, hoc peperisse fuit?
> pluribus illa mori voluisset saucia telis,
>     omnibus ut natis triste pateret iter.
> quis negat esse satum materno funere Bacchum?
>     sic genitum numen credite: nata fera est.

> Amid the cruel perils of Caesar's hunt,
> a spear had pierced a pregnant sow, and one
> piglet leapt from the poor mother's wound.
> Savage Lucina, was this a birth?
> She would have liked to die by many more wounds,
> so to open sad paths for each one of her litter.
> Who denies that Bacchus was born from his mother's death?
> Believe it that a god was given life like this: so too a beast was born.
>
>                                                   *De Spect.* 12

> Icta gravi telo confossaque vulnere mater
>     sus pariter vitam perdidit atque dedit.
> o quam certa fuit librato dextera ferro!
>     hanc ego Lucinae credo fuisse manum.
> experta est numen moriens utriusque Dianae,
>     quaque soluta parens quaque perempta fera est.

> A mother sow, struck by a heavy weapon, her flesh gaping from the wound,
> lost her life and gave it simultaneously.
> How sure was the hand that balanced and aimed the steel!
> I believe it was the hand of Lucina herself.

---

[43] The poems are very reminiscent of *AP* 7.168 (Antipater), where Polyxo dies giving birth to triplets
('one god took life from her, and gave it to them,' 6), and *AP* 9.311 (Philippus), where a pregnant
dog gives birth to puppies by Caesarian section as her vagina has been sealed shut by a stab wound.
Also see *AP* 9.276 (Crinagoras): a washerwoman is swept off her feet by a wave and drowned, so 'in
one moment was released from both death and poverty'. See discussion in K. Coleman (1998) and
(2006, *ad loc.*).

As she died, the creature felt the power of both Dianas.
By one the parent was destroyed, by the other the beast was freed.

*De Spect.* 13

Sus fera iam gravior maturi pignora ventris
    emisit fetum, vulnere facta parens;
nec iacuit partus, sed matre cadente cucurrit.
    o quantum est subitis casibus ingenium!

A wild sow, heavily pregnant, sent forth her progeny,
product of her ripe womb, made mother by a wound.
Nor did the offspring lie still, but ran as its mother fell.
Oh how ingenious such coincidences are!

*De Spect.* 14

Together, this triplet of poems composed in elegiac couplets stages a series of clever games around the numbers one, two and three, and poses at least a couple of mathematical riddles. The pregnant sow giving birth and dying at the same time forms the central paradox and number trick: two events in one, or one beast (the pregnant sow) becoming two (sow and piglet). The spectacle is overseen by Diana, also called Lucina, who has two roles: she is the goddess of childbirth and of hunting, of birthing and of killing. Martial makes full use of the elegiac couplet to mark mirrorings and doublings in and between poems. His verse swings to the tune of contrast and comparison, especially in number two of the three poems: see for example 13.2: *sus pariter vitam perdidit atque dedit*; or 13.6: *quaque soluta parens quaque perempta fera est.* The first and second epigram seem natural twins: both end in the phrase *fera est*, and use much of the same vocabulary (*gravi telo/gravidam suem; suem/sus; matri/mater; Dianae/Dianae; mori/moriens*). The effortless violence of language merges heavy weapon and gravid sow, another case in which two become one (*gravidam suem*, 12.2; *gravi telo confossa*, 13.1).[44] Yet there are three poems, not two: *De Spectaculis* 14 is also born out of its two pregnant predecessors, tagging on to the couple to make a crowd. It begins with *sus fera*, the adjective taken from the last lines of 12 and 13; *vulnere* (14.2) repeats *vulnere* (12.3), *partus* (14.3) mirrors *partus* (12.3), and *parens* (14.2) picks up *parens* (13.6). Yet whilst Martial keeps adding versions of this same event, making it bigger and bigger, each poem in the triptych is smaller than the last by one couplet (8 lines become

---

[44] Interestingly, the spear that hits the sow in 12 is 'light' (*levis hasta*, 2), whereas 13.1 describes a 'heavy weapon'. How do we account for this? Is Martial describing the weapon in the second poem from the point of view of the sow, or emphasising that the spear sinks into and becomes part of the sow weighed down by her offspring?

6 become 4). We can't miss the paradox, either, that the sow seems more pregnant, heavier, in the last, smallest poem (*gravior* 14.1) than she did in the longest first epigram (*gravidam suem* 12.2), while at the same time we're reminded that this violent 'Caesarian section' is effectively a cruel reduction of many to one: only one piglet runs from the gaping wound, whilst the sow would have wished to suffer many more wounds in order to allow her other offspring to escape (12.5–6).

We weigh up this diminution against the ambitious expansiveness of this threesome, and are left grappling for answers to the remaining sums: if you subtract one from many, how many are left? How many more times could this same trick be replayed, or rather, how many wounds would it take to deliver the entire litter of baby pigs? And when we set Titus' ingenious two-spectacles-in-one against Martial's three-for-the-price-of-one performance, are they equal? Are many poems preferable to the single arena show? Or is there no upping the perfect, tragi-comic doubleness of the dying, birthing sow? *De Spectaculis* 12–14 push to the fore the subtle and energising doubling of, or competition between, performance and representation, the artistic direction of Titus on one hand and Martial on the other, that underlies the whole of this celebratory book. The programmatic number games we find here, which Martial goes on to make the classic domain of his, *Roman* epigram, get us thinking more generally about the relationship these poems envisage or imply between text and reality, and between poet and emperor. In one sense, we might say, the competitive edge to both these relationships can be fully integrated into the project of imperial encomium, as it is clearly important for the god-like emperor to be raised to the stars by an ingenious, *epic* epigrammatist producing ambitious, monumental(ising) compositions. In another (and this might go one of two ways), the entertaining *ludus* of epigram is geared up to toy seductively, in quickly forgotten, nugatory flashes, with expanding that dutiful service into a creative partnership, and even with turning the tables altogether, so that epigram's spectacles trump the real – the 'real', in Titus' arena, being already an aggressive trumping of outdated poetic fictions.

Crucially, the chiastic rapport between one and many has already played an important role in the introductory poems of the *De Spectaculis*, and later on in Martial's corpus it becomes core to our experience of reading successive books of epigrams. At 4.29.9–19, Martial thinks that despite their individual compactness, the sheer number of his poems might go against him, so urges his readers to think of each book as unique:

> tu quoque de nostris releges quemcumque libellis,
>    esse puta solum: sic tibi pluris erit.

> You too, whichever of my books you reread,
>    see it as the only one: that way you'll think more of it.

This is the magic of any epigram in a collection, let alone a lifework of multiple epigram books: each poem appears both as a single item and as a part of a whole made up of many interrelated parts, and on a larger scale, as Martial emphasizes here, each whole book can be read alone as well as in juxtaposition with its neighbours, and as part of a larger corpus. Yet 4.29 also confuses and jumbles 'one' and 'many', singular and plural. In the punchline above, one book seems 'more' (than one) when read by a reader pretending that it is Martial's only volume, while lines 3–4 give examples not of rare single things, but of rare multiples (first apples, winter roses),[45] and the contrast between one and many books in lines 7–8 is actually, in literal terms, a comparison of two singular nouns and texts: *saepius in libro numeratur Persius uno / quam levis in tota Marsus Amazonide* ('Persius scores more often in one book than trashy Marsus in his entire Amazoniad').[46]

The idea that Martial's epigrams are/represent *both* a crowd *and* a total-ising whole (which may be vast or tiny), both hundreds of little-big poems and a larger, singular frame (the book), is one that runs throughout his corpus. And symbolic oneness takes us, in typical Martial style, all the way from Callimachean rarities to epic universality, from humble down-scaling to global conquest. As Hardie discusses, the number one becomes symbolic of the entire epic project, since the 'agents in epic narrative are expansive, striving for a lonely pre-eminence and ultimate omnipotence'. The story of the singular, superlative hero, the synecdochic individual who comes to embody all his nation's hopes, aspirations and achievements, begins in the ancient world with Homer's *Odyssey*, whose first word is *andra* ('the man'), and continues through Vergil's Aeneas (in competition with the Latins' superman, Turnus), in a poem which looks towards the *unus homo* of Fabius Maximus ('the greatest') Cunctator[47] (*Aen.* 6.845–6)

---

[45] *rara iuvant: primis sic maior gratia pomis, / hibernae pretium sic meruere rosae* (4.29.3–4).

[46] Note what to us seems quite a strange use of the verb *numeror* here. Clearly this is another way in which Martial overlaps singular and plural: Persius gets lots of credit for a single book. Shackleton Bailey (1993, *ad loc.*) suggests that *numeror* is a term used in games, equivalent to 'to score' or 'notch up', and argues that this hypothesis also fits 3.6.1, 4.40.2 and 14.17.1. I have taken up his suggestion in my translation.

[47] Quintus Fabius Maximus Cunctator was the Roman general who after the disasters at Trasimene and Cannae saved the Romans from Hannibal by his delaying tactics, according to Livy 22, *passim*. Vergil at *Aen.* 6.845–6 alludes closely to Ennius *Ann.* 370, which also praises the general as an *unus*

and of course of Augustus, who is also Ovid's singular *princeps* at the end of the *Metamorphoses* (*Met.* 14.814, *unus erit quem tu tolles in caerula caeli*, 'there will be one whom you will raise to the blue skies').[48] In Roman epic, oneness becomes synonymous with autocracy, a figure split into two both by nostalgia for a Republic governed by a dyarchy of consuls, or by the relationship between twin brothers Romulus and Remus set deep into Rome's foundation myths, and by the trauma unravelled by memories of civil war, entailing the repetitive fragmentation of one into the chaos of many, the inevitable reduction of two, or three, into one. As Hardie points out, 'much of the hyperbole of Lucan's *Bellum Civile* is based on the "one against all" or "one for many" principle', while Statius' *Thebaid* and Silius Italicus' *Punica* further develop this rhetoric of one and many, and of violent, paradoxical duality, which now not only encompasses the most significant junctures in Roman epic, history and myth, but also parallels and re-presents some of the major imperial power struggles of first-century AD Rome: we think especially of Tiberius and Drusus, Gaius and Lucius, Nero and Britannicus, and Titus and Domitian.[49]

It is with this intimidating nexus of associations in mind that we turn back to the diminutive *De Spectaculis*. In the first three poems of his *munus* to Titus, Martial makes 'oneness' serve a variety of potentially contradictory functions. In poem 1, we trawl through a list of the great wonders of the world,[50] which are now usurped by the single magnificent achievement that is the Colosseum (as well as, suggestively, the *opus* of this book about it):

> Barbara pyramidum sileat miracula Memphis,
>    Assyrius iactet nec Babylona labor;
> nec Triviae templo molles laudentur Iones,
>    dissimulet Delon cornibus ara frequens;
> aëre nec vacuo pendentia Mausolea
>    laudibus inmodicis Cares in astra ferant.
> omnis Caesareo cedit labor Amphitheatro,
>    **unum pro cunctis Fama loquetur opus.**

> Let barbarian Memphis shut up about her wondrous pyramids,
> and Assyrian toil no longer boast of Babylon.

---

*homo* (*unus homo nobis cunctando restituit rem*). *Cunctator* means 'the delayer', but it is also tempting to see the adjective *cunctus* ('whole', 'altogether', 'entire') reinforcing *unus homo*.

[48] The words of Jupiter here famously quote Ennius *Ann.* 54–5. See discussion in Hinds (1998) 14–16.

[49] See P. Hardie (1993) 8–9.

[50] This poem seems much influenced by *AP* 9.58 (Antipater) which singles out the temple of Artemis at Ephesus as the grandest of the world's seven wonders.

> Nor should the soft Ionians get praised for Trivia's temple;
> And the altar of many horns should ignore Delos;
> Nor let the Carians heap extravagant praise on the Mausoleum
> poised in empty air, and raise it to the stars.
> All labour yields to Caesar's amphitheatre.
> Fame shall tell of one work in place of all.

As Fitzgerald points out, this final line is typical of Martial in that it can be read in two ways, a slippage perhaps encouraged by the notorious mischievousness of Fama's chattering tongue, which works against the Colosseum's power to silence the past in this poem: *unum pro cunctis* means 'one instead of all others', but also 'one on behalf of all others'.[51] The latter meaning is underlined by the epigram itself, which packages Titus' amphitheatre together with the Pyramids, the walls of Semiramis, the temple of Diana at Ephesus, and Apollo's altar of horns. The grandiosity of the Colosseum is always relative to other monuments, just as (and this is always the larger point, as spelt out in 4.29) the *opus* of this book may be said to be, or claims to be, epic vis-à-vis its epigrammatic predecessors. Oneness, then, is both singular, a bellicose obliteration of plural competitors, and a single amalgamation of plural elements whose relative smallness helps to show off the titanic scale of the whole – a whole which, paradoxically, is modest in size relative to what it symbolically represents and contains.

In poem 2 of the *De Spectaculis*, lines 2–4 use a similar formula to describe, this time, what used to stand on the site now occupied by the Colosseum, or rather on the area next to it: Nero's Domus Aurea (the Colosseum itself is built over Nero's lake, at the centre of his complex of gardens):

> Hic ubi sidereus propius videt astra colossus
>    et crescunt media pegmata celsa via,
> invidiosa feri radiabant atria regis
>    **unaque iam tota stabat in urbe domus.**

> Where the divine colossus sees the stars up close,
> and high scaffolding grows up mid-road,
> once gleamed the hateful halls of a cruel king,
> and in all the city stood a single house.

In Nero's Rome, there appeared to be just one house, an appropriation and conglomeration of all the houses not owned by the people of the city (*hic ubi miramur velocia munera thermas, / abstulerat miseris tecta superbus*

---

51  As Fitzgerald (2007) 38 points out.

*ager*, 'here where we admire the warm baths, a speedy gift, an arrogant plot
of land had robbed the poor of their dwellings,' 7–8). Here we see both
meanings of '*unum pro cunctis*' in play: whilst Nero and his Domus Aurea
stood for 'one in place of many', the Colosseum complex now stands
for 'one for the sake of many', or 'one for everybody'. Each and every
Roman can enjoy the amphitheatre shows, and wash in communal baths:
'the pleasures of a master now belong to the people' (*deliciae populi, quae
fuerant domini*, 12).

Yet what happens in grasping this point is that we end up reading
Neronian tyranny back into the imperial and literary ambition/eulogy of
*unum pro cunctis* at 1.8, one of whose meanings must be: 'one *instead*
of many'. One of the fascinating and provocative paradoxes of the *De
Spectaculis* is that it cleverly synthesises and overlays past and present whilst
at the same time marking the great gulf between Julio-Claudian (ending
with cruel Nero and the destruction of his golden palace) and Flavian
dynasties. Martial's collection seems to reflect and seek to play its own
messy part in Titus' and Vespasian's apparent desire to associate themselves
with the Julio-Claudian *gens*, especially Augustus and Claudius, whilst at
the same time distancing themselves from Neronian 'tyranny'. The image
of what lies beneath the foundations of the Colosseum stays with us, and
it is difficult to erase the idea we explored in chapter 2 of monument (and
epigram) as palimpsest, each new structure in some way absorbing as well
as covering up and cancelling out the old.

If we look closely, we can see that Martial pushes this idea to the fore
at several points in our manuscript of the *De Spectaculis*, repeating, for
example, phrases he has used to describe what the Colosseum suppresses
and replaces to describe events that happen during Titus' games. So the
silenced Mausoleum, *aëre nec vacuo pendentia* ('hanging in empty air',
1.5) becomes the clumsy flying bear caught in bird lime at 11.5: *deprendat vacuo venator in aëre praedam* ('let the hunter catch his prey in the
empty air'),[52] and we're reminded of Nero's lake when the Colosseum
is flooded for a sea battle in poem 28. Again, Martial claims that this
*naumachia* will 'silence' both Claudius' famous sea fight on lake Fuci-
nus in central Italy, and Nero's *stagna*, on which the emperor was also
known to stage such events: *hanc norint unam saecula naumachiam*, 'let
future generations know of only one sea fight' (28.12). Yet epigram's

---

[52] As K. Coleman notes (2006, *ad loc.*), 'the phrase "empty air" in connection with elevation above
the terrestrial plane or a physical obstacle is almost a cliché': cf. Horace, *Odes* 1.3.34, Vergil, *Georgics*
3.108–9.

wagging tongue, its basic trick of making many of one (a lot from a little, large spaces out of small, fortunes out of pennies) has just ensured that we cannot think of the one without remembering many others. The riddles of reshuffled formulae are part and parcel of the surprising (and again, potentially *flattering*) thrills of reading Martial's games. We need not assume, necessarily, that Martial's possible contradictions, aside from helping to frame the clever paradoxes of Titus' stage performances, are also designed to undercut or write over the laudatory purposes of this text. Yet certainly, this is not an uncomplicated and transparent celebration of Titus and his achievements, and there is the sense that part of the amusement (and lionisation) lies in Martial's hare-like twists and turns before the dignified, confident emperor.

In *De Spectaculis* 3, to complete the trio of variations on a single (double? ) theme, Martial turns to the audience taking their seats for the show that is about to begin. There is no race so remote or barbarous that it is not represented by a spectator in the Colosseum. Here we'll find the Rhodopeian, the Sarmatian, the Egyptian, Arab, Briton, Sabaean, Cilician, Sygambrian and Ethiopian, all unified in this one space, and all calling one emperor their *pater patriae* (11–12):

> **vox diversa sonat populorum, tum tamen una est,**
>     cum verus patriae diceris esse pater.

> The people all speak different tongues, and yet they speak as one
> when you are called true father of the fatherland.

The Colosseum has become a microcosm of empire, a place where many are united as one.[53] Here we seem to have an inclusive, generous, peaceful and democratic image of oneness, and the *vox diversa* of empire (a suggestive metaphor for epigrammatic miscellany, too) again rings out in contrast to the monumental silence of 1.1–7, and in support of Fama's loquaciousness at 1.8. Yet contrasts this sharp rarely hold their shape completely in this volume, or indeed in Martial's epigrams generally. *De Spectaculis* 3 contains a series of subtle pointers towards a different view of oneness again, a oneness that risks going *too far* in including and embracing the many – or rather, demonstrates the power of emperor and empire in much more literal and brutal terms. The first spectator mentioned is the farmer of Rhodope, who has come from *Orpheo Haemo*, Orphic Haemus, a mountain range in Thrace. Can we cancel out the connection with one of the most gory killings

---

[53] See also discussion in Fitzgerald (2007) 40–2.

of the arena, in *De Spectaculis* 24 (21), where a prisoner named Orpheus is torn apart by a bear in a perverse reconstruction of the beginning of Ovid *Metamorphoses* 11? Compare 3.3 (*venit ab Orpheo cultor Rhodopeius Haemo*) with 21.1–2 where the adjectival form *Orpheus* is also used:

> Quidquid in Orpheo Rhodope spectasse theatro
>   dicitur, exhibuit, Caesar, harena tibi.

> Whatever Rhodope is said to have watched on Orpheus' stage,
> the arena, Caesar, displayed to you.

*Rhodopeius*, the adjective used of the farmer in the audience at 3.3, is also another way of saying 'Orpheus'. The Sarmatian in the next line is 'fed on horses' blood' (*epoto pastus equo*, 4): this collection of barbarous people are meant to seem a bloodthirsty lot, and their bestial habits are emphasised in the verb used here, *pascor,* which belongs to the animal kingdom and strictly means 'to graze'.[54] In other words, as well as unifying and Romanising, Martial's language also works to separate barbarian from Roman.[55] Is this audience also already far too close to being blood*stained*, to becoming part of the spectacles they are about to watch, in an arena which unites everything (not just spectators from different lands, but spectators and victims, men and beasts)? Are there traces of blood and gore, too, in Haemus, the mountain range which alongside the blood-drinking Sarmatian evokes the Greek for blood, αἷμα? Or in the image of Cilicians sprayed, like the arena, with yellow-red saffron (which is what the *nimbi,* 'showers' imply in line 8)? Are *real* Romans already distancing themselves from these barbarians, with their dark skin, strange hairstyles and animal-like behaviour? Can we already see the Thracian country bumpkin being gored on the sand, the Sarmatian vomiting blood, the Briton being 'beaten' by waves (*quem supremae Tethyos una ferit,* 6), and the Egyptian drinking water (*bibit flumina,* 5), in a flooded arena? Is this what many-as-one amounts to? A collapse of the crucial boundary between spectators and spectated? Isn't this violence, after all, what the imperial Colosseum, and this *opus,* celebrate? Doesn't this epigram hint at everything that is to come in this

---

[54] See K. Coleman (2006, *ad loc.*) on the association of blood/milk drinking with nomads and barbarians in ancient ethnography and Latin poetry.

[55] Cf. Fitzgerald (2007) 40, who reads *De Spect.* 3 as follows: 'the third poem continues the process by moving from multiplicity to unity, and as it does so it erodes the distinction between foreign and Roman.' This is certainly what it claims to do, but in my view Martial finds ways of expressing the violent thrill of the games by manipulating an ongoing tension between merging and separation, and suggesting more than one perspective on unity.

book, giving us a taste of multiple violent episodes in a single programmatic gem?[56]

Poem 27, about the amazing gladiator Carpophorus, adds to this impression of the victimising coercion it takes to compress many into one. This prizewinning fighter is so formidable that he can subdue ten wild beasts at one time, giving him the edge on Hercules (*plus est / bis denas pariter perdomuisse feras*, 27.11–12). If he had been born in mythic times, the many-necked Hydra would have met a single death, and one stroke of his sword would have conquered the 'entire Chimaera' (*hoc armante manus hydrae mors una fuisset, / huic percussa foret tota Chimaera semel*, 27.5–6). The allusion in *De Spectaculis* 2.4 to Ovid's primordial chaos at the beginning of the *Metamorphoses* (*unaque iam tota stabat in urbe domus* 2.4, cf. *unus erat toto naturae vultus in orbe*, 'there was just one face of nature covering the whole globe,' *Met.* 1.6) should perhaps already have alerted us to the more disturbing possible aspects to universality or oneness.[57] We might also note that in *De Spectaculis* 24, the flooding of the arena for the *naumachia* deliberately recalls the flooding of the earth by Jupiter to punish brutal, iron-age man in Ovid *Metamorphoses* 1 (*dices, 'hic modo pontus erat'*, 'you will say, "just now this was all sea"', 24.6, cf. *omnia, pontus erat*, 'all was now sea', *Met.* 1.292; and *hic modo terra fuit*, 'just now, this was land', 24.4, cf. *dum terra fuit*, 'while it was still land', *Met.* 1.314).[58] In this all too present intertext, which itself contributes to undoing the singularity of Titus' punitive flood as vaunted in poem 28, Jupiter is intent on drowning precisely the kind of *barbarae gentes* that make up Martial's audience in *De Spectaculis* 3. His punishment of bloodthirsty man is itself, Martial knows, a violent *reduction* of many to one (or rather, to two ones). See *Met.* 1.325–6:

> et superesse virum de tot modo milibus unum,
> et superesse videt de tot modo milibus unam.

> He saw to it that just one male survived from what just now was thousands, and just one female survived from what just now was thousands.

---

[56] We're also reminded that, especially in poetry, singular can stand for plural and vice versa: in *De Spect.* 3 the singular nouns *cultor, Sarmata, Arabs*, etc. stand for groups of people, not for individuals (although miniaturising epigram pares down the crowd to one example of each nation), while the singular river Nile in line 5 becomes many rivers (*fulmina*). This poetic plural perhaps reminds us of the *end* of the Nile rather than, or as well as the beginning, when the river becomes a delta. See K. Coleman (2006), 45 and 267–9 on the apparent reference to the mysterious source of the Nile in this poem.

[57] For further discussion of Martial's use of Ovid *Metamorphoses* 1 in the *De Spectaculis*, see Rimell (forthcoming).

[58] Also see brief discussion in Hinds (2007).

The *De Spectaculis*, as I have read it here, becomes one of Martial's most sophisticated and engrossing displays of mathematical riddling, pushing us to see just how many twists and permutations can be wrung out of the simple contrast between one (two, three) and many. This book makes a big show of the paradoxical trope of one in/as many : many in/as one that is so basic to the poetics of epigram, and especially to the epigram book. Yet it also stages a constant dialogue with, overlapping of, and even competition between poetic and political strategies. It manages to capture in tiny pages the dynamics of cosmopolitan empire and 'Flavian spectacle', literary memories of cosmic chaos/ordering, and the oxymoron of remembering or forgetting past and present violence in an age of peace.

ALL THE TWOS: BOOK 2

In the final section of this chapter, I would like to look at a single book, *Epigrams* 2, in detail. It is only by homing in on the interactions of poems within a book, I would argue, that we really get to see how Martial makes enumeration central both to the poetics of epigram and to epigram's Rome. Book 2 is, literally, where Martial begins to count. It's where one becomes two, where *unus liber* begins to grow into the *turba* that will eventually require two hands to tally. Martial both retreats from and plunges into this incipient measuring, ending the book, as we've already seen, with the recommendation that this too can become another Book 1, or the only Book 1 (bearing in mind, though, that the book we've just read is, or will turn out to be, the longest volume of epigrams by Martial!). Regulus can simply remove one iota from its title (2.93):

> 'Primus ubi est' inquis 'cum sit liber iste secundus?'
>     quid faciam si plus ille pudoris habet?
> tu tamen hunc fieri si mavis, Regule, primum,
>     unum de titulo tollere iota potes.

> 'If this is the second book', you say, 'then where's the first?'
> What can I help it if the other is more modest?
> But Regulus, if you'd rather this one were the first,
> just knock off one iota from the title.

Stopping at one, this time *page* one, is precisely what Martial wants to avoid, however, in his epistolary preface to Book 2. This parodic *recusatio* announces that, after Decianus' objections, this book will not begin with a boring prose preface (which we're nevertheless reading). The epigrams are quite enough, and this is already excessive; yet Martial assures his readers that now he hasn't included a real prose preface, just Decianus' dull complaints, they won't come to the first page already worn out (*debebunt tibi si qui in hunc librum inciderint, quod ad primam paginam non lassi pervenient*, 2, Pref. 14–15).[59]

After the joke of (not) overdoing it before he's started, Martial makes his first epigram advertise all the advantages of a book that isn't 300 poems long. Here (2.1.3–8) he poses as schoolmaster poet, borrowing the 'Ovidian three-point system' from the textbook *Ars Amatoria*:

> at nunc succincti quae sint bona disce libelli.
>     hoc **primum** est, brevior quod mihi charta perit;
> **deinde**, quod haec una peragit librarius hora,
>     nec tantum nugis serviet ille meis;
> **tertia** res haec est, quod si cui forte legeris,
>     sis licet usque malus, non odiosus eris.

> Learn now what's good about a succinct little book.
> Number one, a short volume wastes less paper.
> Next lesson: the copyist gets through it in an hour
> and doesn't have to slave too much on my nothings;
> Number three's this: that if you happen to get read,
> you may be utterly bad, but at least you won't be a bore.

Compare Ovid, *Ars* 1.35–48:

> principio, quod amare velis, reperire labora,
>     qui nova nunc primum miles in arma venis.
> proximus huic labor est placitam exorare puellam:
>     tertius, ut longo tempore duret amor.

> To begin with, the soldier coming to battles new
> must first get to work finding someone to love.
> The next task is to seduce the girl you fancy:
> The third, to make that love endure.

---

[59] Sullivan (1991, 22–3) is not convinced, and would rather turn back to Book I, bored to tears by further enumerations: 'Book I, then, thanks perhaps to its re-editing, is an attractive and exemplary book as a specimen for Martial's abilities and interests. Book II is shorter and the perfunctory preface to Decianus is uninteresting . . . The analysis of the contents of the book is correspondingly simpler. Almost all, four-fifths of the book, are satirical epigrams; only six formal poems are addressed to possible patrons, including Domitian. Two epideictic epigrams describe Domitian's dining room and a trained lion who runs amuck (2.59; 79). Another half dozen are hortatory or moralistic . . . Conceivably, Martial had far too much poetic material to fit conveniently into one book of miscellaneous epigrams and therefore put together this shorter second book, then adding the book numbers, which prompted a mild joke with Regulus on the fact (2.93).' As Garthwaite reminds us (2001), Book 2 has until recently not attracted the analysis it deserves in part because of the influence of Friedländer's belief that the majority of poems in it are not topical but rather an assortment of older material.

2.1 begins by reminding this book of the risks involved in bloating out to 300,[60] and puts its money where its mouth is by knocking off two noughts and only counting to three. Martial also promises that if the book is short, the scribe in charge of making many copies of the one original might be able to avoid working too much (*nec tantum*, 6) and pare down that figure to one – a 'single hour' (5). Yet in the second half of the epigram, numbers begin to pile up again as we work up to a doubling of the corny joke in the preface. The diner can read this short book to the end while his five measures of wine are mixed, before the first cup begins to cool – that is, in a very short time, represented by a higher number. As the last couplet confirms, five might look like a lot when getting to one in three easy steps is the ideal. It's all relative: short can look long; even Book 2 can become too much. In other words, there are teasing subtexts to all this dull number-crunching (this book has a wicked tongue, *mala lingua*). Counting can be quite alluring, as Martial hints in his nod towards Ovid's boring-exciting love manual, in his coy *tenuis puella* of a book, already with its skirts hitched up, showing off its wares: this is the other meaning of *succinctus*, usually just translated as 'short', in line 3. Of course, the other thing about a book whose dress is tucked up is that she can always let it down again. Short can become long, if the mood takes her, if the reader doesn't touch her right, just like that. Here, Martial steals all he can from the overlapping sexual-literary worlds of Catullus, Horace, Ovid and Petronius, conjuring up bare legs, petite girls you could fit in your pocket, and dinner parties in which sweet nothings are painted in wine.

Martial's lessons in adding up *are* enticing, and contagious, it seems. He gets us counting with him and talking in numbers (How many poems are there in this book again? Vis-à-vis Book 1? What is the right length for a book? How many poems have we read when we begin to tire of it?). Williams' recent commentary on Book 2 gets us in the spirit from the outset, explaining all the ways epigrams can be enumerated. He focuses first on the structure of individual poems, then their length, before totting up metres, and finally syllables:

Another renowned trait of Martial's epigrams is their bipartite structure, and various ways of describing the two halves have been proposed. Among the most influential has been Lessing's division into an *Erwartung*, or 'expectation', created by the opening and the *Aufschluss*, or 'information' conveyed at the end; later

[60] Not a random number, as C. Williams suggests (2004, *ad loc.*), because 'the ideal limit for Martial is clearly 100 epigrams per book' (cf. 1.118). All Martial's surviving books, with the exception of the *Xenia* and the *Apophoreta*, come in at around this limit, ranging from 82 poems in Book 8 to 118 in Book 1.

variations have included Kruuse's distinction between *exposition* and *conclusion*, and Barwick's division (taken up by Laurens) into an *objective* and a *subjective* half; Marion Lausberg suggests *Bericht* ('report') and *Kommentar* ('commentary'); Siedschlag proposes *Ereignis* ('event') and *Kommentar*; in English, we might speak of *situation* and *response*. It is worth emphasizing, however, that . . . a bipartite structure hardly characterizes every poem in Martial's corpus. Kruuse 1941 observes, for example, that in some cases it is best to speak of a one-unit (*unicellulaire*) structure; in others, of a tripartite structure.

The epigrams of Book II are characteristic with respect to poem length, ranging from one (2.73) to twenty-three lines (2.41), the average length being about six verses per poem. The number of meters they use is limited, and in this too they are typical of Martial's overall practice. There is a noticeable preponderance of elegiac couplets (seventy out of ninety-three poems): otherwise, there are seventeen poems in hendecasyllables, five in scazons (choliambics), and one in pure hexameters. Martial's metrical techniques are essentially traditional, one exception being the relaxation of the earlier, especially Ovidian tendency to end pentameters of elegiac couplets with disyllabic words: Martial's pentameters not infrequently end in three-, four-, or even five-syllable words, and not just in the case of intractable proper names.[61]

But Martial shows us in Book 2 that there are far more ways to count than this, that epigram can (make you) count everything, so that the readerly process of measuring Martial becomes a fundamental part of comprehending and finding one's place in Rome, as well as the other way around. There are as many types of calculations and perspectives on numbers on show here as there are poems, and whatever is counted (hours, steps, sexual practices, foods, payments, body parts, honours, children . . .) is often framed to trace (and vice versa) all the cleverly exposed reckonings that have gone into making this book.

Not least, the excessive two-ness of this volume (which could easily return to, or become autocratic one-ness, with a flick of your pen) is splattered all over its epigrams – especially the ones composed in couplets, naturally. Together, they make a list duty-bound to make you yawn. 2.4 and 2.5, first of all, muck around with doubling up the twos: mother and daughter call themselves sister and brother in 2.4, and in 2.5 Martial walks two miles there and two miles back to (not) see Decianus, thus achieving a grand sum of zero: *duo* and *quattuor* are lined up in two hexameters and two pentameters, along with night and day (1–2) and seeing/not seeing (7–8). In 2.6, Severus has hardly read two pages of the book before he begins to yawn. We picture Postumus' two lips in 2.10 and 2.22; two possibilities

[61] C. Williams (2004) 9–10.

remain for Sextillus' sexual proclivities in 2.28, just as in 2.47 a husband does two things: *irrumat aut futuit*; Martial dares to add three noughts to two when he asks for a loan of 20,000 sesterces in 2.30; Caecilianus steals a woodcock meant for two people at a dinner party at 2.37; to be free, Maximus must be prepared, among other things, to go with a two-pence prostitute in 2.53 (this epigram, Scherf suggests, forms a 'thematic pair' with 2.18, also addressed to Maximus).[62] Two slave boys, compared to twins Romulus and Remus, are killed by a lion whilst raking the arena at 2.75, and, returning us to more important calculations, Martial makes a case about relative epigram length at 2.77 by pointing out that Marsus and Pedo often cover a single item in two pages (*saepe duplex unum pagina tractat opus*, 6), whilst at 2.71, he has only to recite a few couplets of his own work before Caecilianus starts quoting Catullus at him.

Even from this simplified catalogue, moreover, we can get the sense that the two-ness of Book 2 is not entirely stable, and might not add up to the right solution, for Martial or for his easily bored readers. First of all, we can arrive at number two by many different calculations, and Martial is often keen to show off his workings out: two is two ones, it is half of four, it is one less than three, it can be multiplied to make much larger numbers. For example, Martial mentions Sextus three times in two lines in poem 2.3, offering various 3 × 2s to make up the identity of a man marked by the number 6:

> **Sexte**, nihil debes, nil debes, **Sexte**, fatemur.
> debet enim, si quis solvere, **Sexte**, potest.

> You owe nothing, Sextus, we admit it Sextus, nothing.
> For only a man who can pay up has debts, Sextus.

This lesson in multiplication, after the didactic intro of 2.1, follows some (in a sense) more basic samples of addition in 2.2. This poem may be marked by two twos, but it follows the three-idea scheme of its predecessor, shaping three couplets, or 2 × 3 lines, which build up to a commemoration of one of Domitian's earliest military accomplishments, the AD 83 campaign against the German Chatti, for which the emperor added the cognomen Germanicus to his name:

> Creta dedit magnum, maius dedit Africa nomen,
>     Scipio quod victor quodque Metellus habet;
> nobilius domito tribuit Germania Rheno,
>     et puer hoc dignus nomine, Caesar, eras.

[62] Scherf (2001) 41.

frater Idumaeos meruit cum patre triumphos,
    quae datur ex Chattis laurea, tota tua est.

Crete gave a great name, Africa a greater,
borne by victorious Scipio and by Metellus.
Germany granted a nobler one when the Rhine was conquered,
a name you were worthy of, Caesar, even as a boy.
Your brother won Idumean triumphs along with your father,
but the laurel given for the Chatti is all yours.

The epigram begins by citing two famous historical exempla: proconsul Q. Caecilius Metellus succeeded in conquering Crete and made it a province, for which he was awarded the cognomen Creticus, while Scipio (probably the elder, *Maior*, hinted at in the adjective *maior* in line 1)[63] defeated Hannibal at Zama in 202 BC, and was thenceforth named Africanus. After the polyptoton *magnum maius* and the balancing act of *dedit . . . dedit* in line 1, we move onwards and upwards to Domitian's achievement (*nobilius*, 3), the third step. As Williams comments, this intensification is mirrored in the poem as a whole in the 'increasing geographical specificity' of *Germania* (line 3), *Rheno* (line 3) and *Chattis* (line 6).[64] Note also that the titles of these war heroes grow incrementally in size, mirroring Rome's, and epigram's, expansionist policies: Creta (5 letters), Africa (6 letters), Germania (8 letters). Domitian really is a step (or two) ahead in epigram, more than he would be if Martial had been writing in prose and could have afforded the longer Creticus (8 letters), Africanus (9 letters), Germanicus (10 letters). In the final couplet, Martial stresses that Domitian is (and stands out as) one of/over three, a fraction haunted by several other reductions of three to one etched into Rome's history books: the triumvirates of 60–40 BC, from which Caesar and Octavian emerge victors, and the 'three emperors' of 69, Galba, Otho and Vitellius, eventually all killed or defeated and replaced by Vespasian. Within the group of three, Domitian's brother Titus and father Vespasian are twinned by their AD 71 success in capturing Jerusalem, but Domitian is distinguished by his individual triumph. The poem itself, as Williams recognises, goes beyond and disrupts its own bipartite structure, a move mirrored in its content:[65] this second epigram gives us more than a

---

[63] Although Scipio is also clearly another (hidden) double, a blend of *maior* and *minor*, bigger and smaller, from which one can logically be struck off to make a single, greater man. The adopted grandson of P. Cornelius Scipio, one P. Cornelius Scipio Aemilianus, destroyed Carthage in 146 BC, and also won the cognomen Africanus, although he received the additional cognomen Numantinus in 132.

[64] C. Williams (2004) *ad loc.*

[65] C. Williams (2004) 28: 'The underlying thought can easily be described as bipartite: situation (Domitian has received the name Germanicus) and commentary (this is even more praiseworthy

simple exercise in doubles, adding up names, letters, places and triumphs to indicate how much larger numbers can be read into the more straightforward sums of $2 + 1 = 3$, and $3 - 2 = 1$. Martial doesn't miss a beat before beginning to perform the bullet-pointed conundrum of 2.1, in which even short can seem long, and small numbers seem equivalent to big. Too much and too little go hand in hand and are even the same thing in this book (see e.g. 2.36.4: *nolo virum nimium, Pannyche, nolo parum*; or 2.8.2: *sive obscura nimis sive Latina parum*).[66]

What's also interesting about *Epigrams* 2.2 is that it is clearly an epigrammatic double of a key passage from the *first* book of Ovid's *Fasti*, the poem on the Roman year which maps Roman time in numbers, of which Ovid completed only half (in other words, we're tempted to say that the sum $12 - 6 = 6$ shadows Martial's simpler suggested calculation of $II - I = I$ which frames this second book). *Fasti* 1.587–616 marks 13 January, the anniversary of the restoration of the Republic, and also the date on which Octavian received the title 'Augustus'. Martial takes from Ovid, without ever mentioning Augustus by name, the theme and etymology of that name, *augere*, 'to increase' (e.g. *Fasti* 1.613, *augeat imperium nostri ducis, augeat annos*, 'May [Jupiter] increase our prince's empire, and augment his years'). 'Caesar', in line 4, is as close as we get – this is the usual address for the emperor, but lest we forget, it was originally the cognomen of a branch of the *gens Iulia* and was taken by C. Octavius, later Augustus, when Julius Caesar adopted him in his will. Just as Martial multiplies honours, from Metellus' 'great' title (*magnum*, 1), to the greater name of Scipio Maior (as opposed to, but also perhaps including, Scipio Minor) in line 2, to Domitian's superlative achievement in Germany, so in Ovid's *Fasti* the conquest and titles of the Scipios (Africa, 593), of Publius Servilius Vatia and Quintus Caecilius Metellus (Isauricus and Creticus 593–4), of another Metellus (Numidicus), Manius Valerius Maximus (Messala), and Scipio the younger (Numantinus) in 595–6, of Drusus (Germanicus 597), of Pompey (Magnus) and Caesar (Maior 603–4), and finally of the incomparable Fabius Maximus (605–6), all lead up to the crescendo of Augustus, whose name implies infinite and unstoppable conquest or

than the triumphs of his father and brother because it was achieved alone). But the poem's structure does not fall so easily into two parts, as there is already some commentary in 3 (*nobilius*), while 5 adds further factual information. The absence of such a clear-cut division may be related to the epigram's very nature: panegyric requires an intricate blend of objective and subjective, of fact and praise.'
[66] Cf. 2.10.3 (subtracting = *maius munus*).

growth.[67] Martial lifts Ovid's *magnus /maior* build-up to aggrandise Domitian as the new Augustus (and also as the new Drusus, who is also given the name Germanicus, and is also remembered for being one of two famous brothers). Yet there are no superlatives in this epigram (and no analogies with Jupiter – see *Fasti* 1.607–8), only comparatives: Martial stresses, paradoxically, both the relativity and singularity of Domitian's triumphs and titles (just as he emphasises that this book is both the second in a series, and, if you want it to be, unique). While Domitian is graced with the longest, greatest title, Germanicus, and while his victory is associated with no fewer than three different labels (Germania, Rheno, Chattis), the poem ends by describing his primacy as a separate singular, at the same time replacing Ovidian floridity with epigrammatic spareness: *quae datur ex Chattis laurea, tota tua est* ('but the laurel given for the Chatti is all yours,' 6). Yet this *tota tua est* also picks up the abundance, *tot*, of Augustus' titles vis-à-vis his predecessors ('If Caesar took his titles from the vanquished, then he must assume as many (*tot*) names as there are tribes in the world!' *Fasti* 1.599–600).

*Epigram* 2.2 expands and contracts repeatedly as we read it, mirroring this book's tension between progressive ambition and the drive to shrink back to the more bashful identity of its forerunner – a singularity which at the same time contains the ideas of originality and autocracy. Not for the last time in this book, this oscillation is fuelled and framed by an Ovidian intertext (so that we compare and contrast not only Books 1 and 2, in the light of Book 2's comments on Book 1, but also poem and 'model'), and refers also (through the *Fasti*'s calendars) to historical time. Domitian is and is not 'Caesar', is and is not Augustus,[68] just as our passage from *Fasti* 1 and the anniversary of the Ides of January is both about remembrance or restoration, and about prophecy and the future growth of empire into *orbis*.

The numbers one, two and three are added together, multiplied, subtracted from and played off each other throughout *Epigrams* 2, helping frame the point that we are to see *Epigrams* I as a predecessor to *Epigrams* II:

---

[67] As Hardie puts it (1993, 5), '"Greatest" marks a limit in size, but the expansiveness of the name "Augustus" is freed from the rules of grammatical degree.' On the play with degrees of Magnus in Vergil see Feeney (1986) 12–13, 24 n. 90. On Ovid's rhetorical amplification of the greatness of Augustus in *Fasti* 587–616, see Henderson (1997) 126–8.

[68] The identification of Domitian with the title Germanicus, together with the allusion to Ovid's *Fasti*, also reminds us of his Augustan reorderings of and control over time: he renamed September and October Germanicus and Domitianus respectively (Mart. *Epigr.* 9.1, Plut. *Num.* 19.4, Suet. *Dom.* 13.3, Dio Cass. 67.4.4).

we can just as easily put them together (I + II = III) as knock one iota off II to return us to, or remake, I. In 2.6, it would take Severus three days to wade through one *libellus*. Maximilla has three teeth in 2.41, and three (in opposition to one) is the chosen figure at 2.34, where Galla has spent her entire dowry buying slave Phileros (lust-lover), whilst her three children starve to death. And we are prepared for the suggested calculation of 2.93 by the two poems on Martial's request for the *ius trium liberorum*, which granted various legal privileges to parents of three or more legitimate children. Even though Martial doesn't strictly qualify, he asks Domitian to grant him the right anyway, if he has enjoyed reading his little books of epigrams. Martial seems to be suggesting (after Ovid in *Tristia* 3.1, appealing to *his* emperor?) that his books *are* his children, even that *liberi* ('children') are close enough to *libri* ('books') for Domitian to turn a blind eye. In this way, these two poems offer themselves as a possibile triptych, linking up with 2.93 (a perfect 91, 92, 93 sequence). Indeed, poem 2.52 has already made us practise this game:

> Novit loturos Dasius numerare: poposcit
> mammosam Spatalen pro tribus: illa dedit.

> Dasius knows how to count the bathers. He asked
> big-boobed Spatale for three: she gave it.

This division of one into 2 + 1 = 3 has prompted much discussion over sums. On line 2, *pro tribus*, Williams notes:

The number has been the occasion of some dispute, not to say hairsplitting. Following Collesso, Friedlaender explains that Spatale is so big-breasted that she is as big as three ordinary women . . . Housman 1907: 234 harshly criticises Friedlaender . . . as 'not merely wrong but obviously and perversely wrong, and wrong where earlier interpreters were right': he has 'missed the force of *tribus*', which is that Spatale and her two breasts occupy the space of one normal woman *each*. Greenwood 1990, while agreeing that the point of Martial's joke is that 'her breasts are charged separately, as it were', defends Friedlaender: he understood the joke, but the 'conservatism of a German scholar of the – albeit late – nineteenth century led him to omit explicit reference to the woman's breasts'.[69]

The number paradox that equates one woman to three is nuanced by *mammosa*, 'big-bosomed', a singular adjective referring pointedly to *two* breasts, and by the double meaning inherent in the punchline of the poem, *illa dedit*, meaning 'she coughed up the cash', and 'she gave him it' (or, we imagine, *them*), that is, she paid in sexual favours.

[69] C. Williams (2004) 182.

In 2.52, we're building up to the point that, in translating the poetic maths of Book 2 into real-life socio-political relations, Martial makes numbers *physical*. Lurking behind all this, apart from the practical point that body parts (namely fingers) are the most obvious counting tools, must surely be Catullus' eroticisation of counting in poems 5 and 7, where he promises Lesbia hundreds and thousands of sweet kisses which both serve as markers for, and escape the solid boundaries of, his neatly counted metrics. Catullan erotics combine an ironic sympathy for the plebeian art of calculation with a seductive, immaterial world of magic, fantasy, infinity and non-knowledge.[70] The poet, part accountant, part dreamer, has one foot in both these universes. In Book 2, Martial blends sardonic allusions to Catullus' numbered kisses and fluid, self-perpetuating orality with reminiscences of some of the most tantalising scenes from Ovidian love elegy. This is a book comparatively lacking in *pudor* (2.93.2), stuffed into the pockets of readers (2.6.7) and rubbing up against palms and thighs. Suggestive and sordid tongues chatter and lick their way through the volume, fulfilling everything that the *mala lingua* of the preface seemed to promise. Are these wicked tongues bound to look 'dirty', after poem 2.61, in which an *improba lingua* gravitates compulsively towards 'male middles' and a *noxia lingua* is 'stuck to groins' (2.6.2, 7)? As this poem shows, there is a degree of correspondence between a sharp tongue and a filthy one.

Centrally, the Postumus poems at 2.10, 12, and 21–3, together with the epigram about not kissing Philaenis at 2.33, replace Catullus' ever-open and sensual mouth with the pursed and puckered lips of epigram. In 2.10, Postumus give Martial kisses with half his lips, so Martial asks that he do him a favour and subtract half from that too, hence not kissing him at all:

> Basia dimidio quod das mihi, Postume, labro,
>     laudo: licet demas hinc quoque dimidium.
> vis dare maius adhuc et inenarrabile munus?
>     hoc tibi habe totum, Postume, dimidium.

> You give me kisses with half your lips, Postumus.
> Excellent! You can subtract half from that too.
> Wanna do me an even bigger favour, one beyond description?
> Keep this whole half for yourself, Postumus.

The poem itself mouths the message for Postumus to lip-read. Its shape consists of two lips, couplets offered up to Postumus in place of the real

---

[70] See Janan (1994) 58–62, and Henderson (1999b).

thing. The inexplicable (*inenarrabile*) turns out to be not a mind-boggling accumulation of kisses, in the style of Catullus 5 and 7, but the withdrawal of a mere fraction of a kiss. Unlike Martial though, who suggests just two poems later (2.12) that Postumus' perfume is disguising the *os impurum* of a filthy *fellator*, we're lured into examining these lips more closely. Postumus' 'half lip' in 2.10.1 seems to mean 'half your lips', which would in turn imply a singular, 'half your mouth'. But is this right? Would it be possible to kiss with half of one lip (taking *dimidio labro* literally), and if Postumus is offering 'half his lips', which half are we to imagine? All of one lip, top or bottom, or, more likely, one side of the mouth brushing Martial's cheek (= literally, two halves of two lips)? The bottom 'lip' of this poem presents a second mathematical riddle: Postumus is to do Martial a favour and subtract half (*dimidium*) from his *dimidium labrum*. If you halve a whole (or two wholes) and then subtract half from that, what are you left with? The joke hinges, in both lines, on what *dimidium* refers to, as well as on the paradox of *totum dimidium*, 'a whole half'. In addition, of course, Martial is also rehearsing his own instructions on the cutting in half of two books in the similarly shaped 2.93. If we want Book 2 to become the first, and to become as modest (relatively speaking) as Book 1, we can knock off one iota, and also, with Martial, cut out Postumus' dirty kisses. The power to subtract, for Martial, is the key to a satisfied readership.

Yet in intertextual terms, the transformation or switch from second book to first also marks a return to as well as departure from 'sexy' poetry, while Martial's key word for the bored reader (*lassus*, Pref. 15, 2.6.14) gets stained with Ovidian connotations of pleasant, post-coital fatigue. Most obviously, 2.12.1, the first line of the second poem in the Postumus cycle, quotes the first line of the second poem in the first book of Ovid's *Amores*, where Ovid announces that he has fallen in lust. Compare the two passages:

> **Esse quid hoc dicam** quod olent tua basia murram
>    quodque tibi est numquam non alienus odor?

> What am I to make of it that your kisses smell of myrrh,
>    and that you always transmit some whiff that's not your own?
>                                                              2.12.1

> **Esse quid hoc dicam**, quod tam mihi dura videntur
>    strata, neque in lecto pallia nostra sedent,
> et vacuus somno noctem, quam longa, peregi,
>    lassaque versati corporis ossa dolent?

What am I to make of it that my bed seems so hard,
that the covers won't stay in place, that
I while away long nights deprived of sleep,
that my bones ache as I toss and turn?
                                    Ovid *Am.* 1.2.1–4

As Siedschlag notes, allusions in first verses of Martial's epigrams quite often refer to phrases found in the first verse of the earlier text.[71] But here, Martial plays off ones and twos with even greater accuracy. This second book contains a first, he emphasises, prodding readers who have stopped counting. Yet he also suggests, perhaps, that the second poem in *Amores* I should *really* be the first: in a book of love poetry, this is the true beginning. The epigrammatic imagination, with its irrepressible drive to reduce and compact, would subtract Ovid's clever behind-the-scenes performance of the machinery of erotic elegy, and cut right to the chase. Ovid's bones are (already? About time . . .) 'weary' in his second poem, like/unlike Martial's readers, (not) *lassi* at the end of the first page: *debebunt tibi si qui in hunc librum inciderint, quod ad primam paginam non lassi pervenient, Pref.* 14–15). But that's not all: the end poem of the Postumus 'cycle', 2.22 (all the twos), quotes, in its first line, the first line of the second book of Ovid's *Tristia*:[72]

> **Quid mihi vobiscum est**, o Phoebe novemque sorores?
>     ecce nocet vati Musa iocosa suo.
> dimidio nobis dare Postumus ante solebat
>     basia, nunc labro coepit utroque dare.

> What do I want with you, o Phoebus and nine sisters?
> Look, the playful Muse harms her poet.
> Postumus used to kiss me with half his lips,
> and now he's started doing it with both.

Ovid begins his *Tristia* II by wondering why he is torturing himself with a second book, when one punishment is surely enough (whether this refers to the *Ars Amatoria*, his guilty *carmen*, or to the 'torture' of the first book of *Tristia*):

> **Quid mihi vobiscum est,** infelix cura, libelli,
>     ingenio perii qui miser ipse meo?
> cur modo damnatas repeto, mea crimina, Musas?
>     an semel est poenam commeruisse parum?

---

[71] Siedschlag (1977) 116–17. Examples include Martial 1.15.1 (Ov. *Tr.* 1.5.1), 1.70.1 (Ov. *Tr.* 3.7.1), 1.108.1 (Ov. *Tr.* 1.10.1), 8.23.1 (*A.L.* 431 Riese).
[72] Casali (2005) 30–3, also discusses this allusion, in terms of 'la fissazione marzialiana sul modello "biografico" ovidiano come matrice dell'autorappresentazione della propria carriera poetica'.

> Why do I bother with you, little books, when you're a curse,
> and I'm a wretched casualty of my own artistic talent?
> Why do I keep coming back to the Muses I have damned?
> Or is it not enough to have deserved my punishment just once?

The echo of Ovid's 'excessive' second book in exile gives new life, once more, to Martial's fear of appearing *nimium*, 'too much'. Like Ovid, Martial is punished by his own poetic wit. These parallel literary doublings are incarnated now in Postumus' disgusting mouth: whereas at the beginning of this cycle of poems, he kisses with half his lip/s, now he's 'started doing it with both'.[73] Yet of course, Martial shows here that, compared to Ovid, he is far from verbose: Postumus' kisses in 2.12 and 2.22 take us in a flash from *Amores* 1.2 to its 'mirror' (in numbers) at the end of Ovid's writing career, *Tristia* 2.1. As Hinds puts it, 'these two not-widely separated epigrams *could* be read as debasing the entire story of Ovid's erotic elegiac career, from *Amores* to exile, into the mini-narrative of a Martialian encounter with an *os impurum*.'[74]

However, while Martial hints that the reader of epigrams might start Ovid's *Amores* at poem 1.2, Ovid also creates a *third* beginning to the book at 1.5, where after much deliberate procrastination he finally introduces his muse and object of his affections, Corinna. By comparison, *Amores* 1.2 looks like a tantalising false start, a maddening second deferral full of premature aches. Martial works this alternative first book beginning into the background of poem 2.6, where for the third time in this volume he confronts a bored reader who is already yawning after scanning two pages:

> I nunc, edere me iube libellos.
> lectis vix tibi paginis duabus
> spectas eschatocollion, Severe,
> et longas trahis oscitationes.
> haec sunt, quae relegente me solebas
> rapta exscribere, sed Vitellianis,
> haec sunt singula quae sinu ferebas
> per convivia cuncta, per theatra;
> haec sunt, aut meliora si qua nescis.
> quid prodest mihi tam macer libellus,
> nullo crassior ut sit umbilico,
> si totus tibi triduo legatur?
> numquam deliciae supiniores.

---

[73] Martial also recalls the *Tristia* when he apologises for his 'obscure or doubtful Latin', blaming it on the hurried, mercenary copyist, at 2.8.1–4. See *Tr.* 3.1.17 (*si qua videbuntur casu non dicta latine . . .*).
[74] Hinds (2007).

lassus tam cito deficit viator,
et cum currere debeas Bovillas,
interiungere quaeris ad Camenas?
i nunc, edere me iube libellos.

Go ahead, order me to publish my booklets!
You've hardly read two pages, Severus,
and already you're skipping to the end
and drawing out long yawns.
These are the poems you used to grab and copy down
as I was reading them through,
on Vitellian tablets too!
These are the books you liked to carry in your pocket,
one at a time, to every dinner, every play.
These are the very same, or even better ones
you've yet to read.
What good to me is a book so skinny it's
no thicker than a roller stick,
if it takes you three days to read?
I've never seen a lazier aesthete!
Does the traveller flag so quickly?
When you have to make a trip to Bovillae,
do you want to swap horses at the Camenae?
Go ahead, order me to publish my booklets!

Thus Martial bemoans the death of Severus' erotic relationship with his *libelli*. He used to 'seize' them like women (*rapta*, 6), carry them around in his 'lap' (*sinus*, 7), copy them onto Vitellian tablets (which were often used for love messages). We're reminded here of Ovid's advice to women in *Ars Amatoria* 3 to let a slave-girl deliver their love letters in secret by concealing them in her bra (compare *Ars* 3.621–2).[75] Moreover, the same line of 2.6, *haec sunt, singula quae sinu ferebas,* recalls one of Ovid's most famous couplets, dissected and revisited at points throughout his erotic works (*Am.* 1.5.23–4):

singula quid referam? nil non laudabile vidi
    et nudam pressi corpus ad usque meum.

Why tell you every detail? I saw nothing undeserving of praise,
and clasped her naked body to my own.

Whereas Ovid at the last minute throws a veil over Corinna's bodily charms, Martial wants to thrust the individual works Severus *used* to clasp to his

---

[75] *conscia cum possit scriptas portare tabellas, / quas tegat in tepido fascia lata sinu.*

body like *puellae* in front of his nose, repeating 'Here they are! Here they are!' (*haec sunt . . . haec sunt . . . haec sunt*, 5, 7, 9). This reader-lover is knackered already and wants to change horses – another nod towards Ovidian metaphors for sex, and to the tired hero-lover who still, in Ovid, makes an effort to carry on, at the end of *Ars Amatoria* 2.[76] Martial uses the premature (non-)ending of *Ars* 2, before the turn to (for men) more tantalising *Ars* 3, to reinforce his point about Severus' lazy reading: 'Hey, you've only just begun and you think you're at the end? Think again!' Sex and reading overlap again in the line *numquam deliciae supiniores* (13), which is usually translated metaphorically (as something like 'never was an aesthete so lazy').[77] But *deliciae* is often used in Roman love poetry to mean, more abstractly, 'alluring delights', 'darling' or 'favourite', and is famously employed by Catullus in the phrase '*deliciae meae puellae*' in his second poem, referring to Lesbia's sparrow, which Martial naughtily spells out for what it *really* is at 7.14 and 11.6. In this epigram, Catullan *deliciae* don't hop around in *anyone's* lap: Severus has lost his lust for reading, dismounting even before he's reached the Camenae, just outside the Porta Capena.[78]

As if to prove Severus wrong, we do, if we read on, get to the third book of Ovid's *Ars* in *Epigrams* 2, though not until (yawn) poem 41, where for the first and only time in his entire corpus, Martial mentions Ovid by name (2.41.1–2):

> 'Ride, si sapis, o puella, ride'
> Paelignus, puto, dixerat poeta.
>
> It was the Paelignian poet, I believe, who said,
> 'laugh if you've any sense girl, laugh.'

The first line seems to 'quote' a line from Ovid which can't be found in his extant works, but is close to, even paraphrases, two lines from *Ars Amatoria* 3 (*quis credat? discunt etiam ridere puellae*, 'who'd think it? Girls even *learn* how to laugh,' 3.281; *spectantem specta, ridenti mollia ride*, 'look at him looking at you, and when he smiles, smile sweetly back,' 3.513), and is followed by what must be a paraphrase of *Ars* 3.435 (*sed non dixerat omnibus puellis, / verum ut dixerit omnibus puellis, / non dixit tibi*, 'but he didn't say that to all the girls. However, supposing he did say that to all the girls, he sure didn't say it to you,' 2.41.3–5; cf. *quae vobis dicunt, dixerunt mille*

---

[76] Martial 11.29 also plays on the end of *Ars* 2. For discussion, see Hinds (2007).
[77] This is Shackleton Bailey's translation (1993).
[78] Ovid uses horse riding as a metaphor for sex. See e.g. *Ars* 3.777–86. Also see *Ars* 3.810 for the image of unyoking/ending a book.

*puellis*, 'what they say to you, they've said to a thousand girls,' *Ars* 3.435).
There's a possibility, of course, that Ovid did publish a poem containing
this line in hendecasyllables, even an epigram. But it's much more tempting
to side with Hinds' recent analysis, which imagines Martial quoting (or
misquoting – he only *thinks, puto*, he's remembering it right) 'a line of
Ovid as it emerges, imperfectly, from the hendecasyllabic memory of a
hendecasyllabic poet'.[79] Again, we're reminded, Martial counts *differently*
from Ovid – although, from another perspective, this could just be Martial's
perversely literal reading of Ovid's own claim to 'sing to the lyre in elevens' at
*Amores* 1.1.30. This poem uses Ovid's satiric passage on women's defects, and
specifically, on women advised not to laugh lest they expose their horsy or
blackened teeth (*Ars* 3.279–87), to paint a Juvenalian portrait of Maximina
(after Ovid's *maxima damna*, the 'big damage' suffered by ugly women
who laugh at *Ars* 3.280).[80] Whereas Ovid cautioned moderate laughter
and the pleasing, controlled half-smile, especially for the orthodontically
challenged ('let the mouth be slightly opened, with just small dimples on
either side, and the bottom of the lip should cover the top of the teeth,'
3.283–4), Martial advises poor Maximina, who has just *three*, pitch-black
teeth to match the *third* book remembered here, to adopt the closed-lipped
countenance of Andromache in mourning. If she has any sense, she'll weep
like a widow (*plora, si sapis, o puella, plora*, 2.41.23), another reference to
Ovid's advice in *Ars* 3 ('what's not artified these days? They learn to weep
prettily, and can turn on the waterworks how and when they choose,'
291–2)[81] – though in Martial's world she should cry out of sheer despair
and desperation, not because it's a seductive ploy.[82]

This is Martial's excessive Book 3, then, in a volume in which even
two is pushing it (for Severus, anyway). Read on, he shows, and you'll
get to the girls. Except this is epigram, and you may well be disappointed
if you came looking for smooth, Ovidian seductions, or perfect beauties
(which we also missed out on, incidentally, in 2.6's brush with the heat of
*Amores* 1.5). Or rather, what we get here, as Hinds suggests, is Martial's
cunning extraction of the most 'epigrammatic' section of the delightful *Ars*
3, where we get to peek misogynistically at women's hideous and barely

---

[79] Hinds (2007). Also see C. Williams (2004) *ad loc.*, and discussion in C. Williams (2006), who
looks in particular at the 'tease' of *puto*, and concludes: 'this epigram exemplifies the combination
of bluntness, self-awareness and unexpected complexity which marks so much of Martial's poetry.'
[80] This is a point made by Hinds (2007).
[81] Martial doesn't believe in prettiness: 2.7 is another case in point.
[82] For further allusions to Ovid in this poem, not just to the *Ars Amatoria* but also to the *Amores* and
*Medicamina*, see C. Williams (2004) *ad loc.*

disguised flaws.[83] In poetry which lays it all on the table – details, prices,
cavities and all – deferral can be more of a bore than a turn-on, and two, or
one, or even none, can be preferable to three. In this book, when mouths
open in random but connected acts of communication (gossiping, kissing,
licking, laughing), they are told to clamp themselves shut – even though,
arguably, they have already done their damage. Those *malae linguae* are
hard to check: just look at the example in 2.82 ('why do you cut off your
slave's tongue before you crucify him, Ponticus? Don't you know that
what he does not say everyone says?'). Old Maximina should wear *vultus
severos* (2.41.13), and practise this when she looks in the mirror, which in
turn reflects back the grim-faced *Severus* in 2.6. There shall be no loose-
mouthed Catullan wit in these restrained verses. Yet there it is, cackling
away in lines 17–18 of 2.41, [*vita . . .*] *et quidquid lepida procacitate / laxat
perspicuo labella risu* ('[avoid . . .] anything witty or rude that loosens the
lips in revealing laughter').[84] Try saying *lepida procacitate* without showing
your teeth.

   As much as it repeats that simple beat, then, this book blatantly exceeds
its two-ness, and we come to the end wearied of the notion that there is
no escaping the job of counting up the world, a task that must begin with
epigram. Like Ovid's *Amores* 1.1, which takes us backstage to tell us how
a book begins, *Epigrams* 2 draws us into the pragmatics and genius of the
epigrammatic imagination, so that we seem to rediscover the mechanics
of writing, and of reading, in every negotiation, greeting, dinner party,
accident, journey and triumph that takes place in the infinitude of Rome.
In his analysis of the 'complex structural design' of Book 2, Garthwaite
wants to 'ignore the more apparent arrangements based on metre and length
of poems', in order to concentrate 'on the less noticeable interplay of themes
and their significance'.[85] One of the things I have been suggesting here,
however, is the extent to which those categories become interactive and
inseparable. Martial hints both at how his surroundings are full of poetic
inspirations, reusable figures and rhythms, and at how the inhabitants
of Rome are all, if only they knew it, involved in quasi-poetic processes

---

[83] Hinds (2007): 'it is exactly what one would expect Martial to do with the body of the elegiac woman,
   debasing her for the lower genre of epigram, and programmatically disavowing both beauty and
   mythic preciosity in favour of the robust imperfections of real life.'

[84] *Lepidus* being a buzzword for neoteric wit.

[85] Garthwaite (2001) 52. His reading complicates the discussions of Scherf (2001) 50 and Barwick (1958)
   299ff. on 'cycles' of poems in Book 2: instead, Garthwaite highlights interacting motifs, personalities
   and themes, and goes some way towards understanding the overlap of categories – sexual, social and
   literary – in Martial.

of composition, arrangement and interaction. Similarly, readers join in composing this collection, help do the poet's work of creating this book by sketching patterns and measuring up. At the same time, we're warned at 2.86 that Martial doesn't do fancy metrics (complicated counting), and that 'it's so unclassy to make simple poems complex, and silly to get in a sweat over little nothings' (2.86.9–10). Martial is referring here to the unsuitability of metrical frills for his down-to-earth, streetwise epigrams. But having reprimanded Severus for not having enough stamina to read Book 2 through, does this comment also serve as a caution to readers putting in too much work, trying to join the dots between epigrams, and puzzling over what look like increasingly complex mathematical riddles? *Epigrams* 2 also has the potential to become a grand satire on reading. For critics worrying that the 1, 2, 3s of this book look a little too ABC, that's one more way of making Martial's numbers count.

# CHAPTER 4

# Mundus inversus: *Martial's Saturnalia*

*sed quid agam potius madidis, Saturne, diebus,*
*quos tibi pro caelo filius ipse dedit?*
*Ep.* 14.1.9–10

Martial's association of his work with festivals, especially the Saturnalia and Floralia, the games and the *convivium*, is one of the most immediate ways in which epigram inhabits and sinks into the world of Rome, a *turba* amongst *turbae*. The *Epigrams* are holiday poems – sweet and bitter titbits to enjoy when the sun goes down, when candles and torches are lit, at parties, at the theatre and amphitheatre, with friends, food and wine. In Book 5, for example, the *libellus* is itself a 'dinner guest or reveller' (*conviva est comissatorque libellus*, 5.16.9), is consumed while the drinks are being mixed in 2.1, and comes giggling, naughty and drunk at 11.15. The *De Spectaculis* is a *munus* ('gift', 'show') that is small enough to be carried to the games themselves, enjoyed in parallel with, before or after, or in place of the real spectacles, while *Epigrams* 1 is a display of theatre (*theatrum meum*, Pref. 15–16) aimed at those who also enjoy Floralia's games.

The main holiday of the year by the early empire, and the focus of this chapter, was the Saturnalia ('the best of days' according to Catullus, at 14.15). Six of Martial's books lay claim, all in different ways, to being 'Saturnalian' (as well as 13 and 14, the *Xenia* and *Apophoreta*, we have books 7, 11 and probably also 4 and 5).[1] The festival took place in mid-December, lasting at least three days in imperial times,[2] and was celebrated by a public sacrifice and *convivium* before the temple of Saturn, at which senators swapped their togas for the casual *synthesis*, and by private parties and feasts at which gambling was permitted and the wine flowed freely. The Saturnalia, our sources tell us, was a blast of liberation, abundance,

---

[1] See Citroni's discussion (1989) on whether Books 4 and 5 are Saturnalian.
[2] In Cicero's day the festival lasted seven days; Augustus reduced it to three, but from the reigns of Gaius and Claudius it was extended again to five.

and role-play or inversion, a flashback to the primitive plenitude of the Golden Age and the rule of the benevolent, just king Saturn (or the Greek Cronos).[3] Under Cronos' rule, Hesiod writes, men lived like gods, free from sorrow and grief, unburdened by work, enjoying constant feasting and merrymaking.[4] Starting wars and punishing criminals was considered sinful during carnival time, and slaves were 'freed' for these few days, allowed to dine and joke with their masters, who wore that symbolic status in the form of the *pilleum*, a cap donned by all new freedmen.[5] Children had time off school, and gifts were distributed and exchanged.

The Saturnalia is *the* setting for Martial's occasional verse, and its creative, mischievous vibe can be felt drumming throughout the corpus of epigrams, not just in the books that declare themselves Saturnalian. Through the *Epigrams*, the *mundus inversus* of carnival becomes almost synonymous with Martial's poetics: in this world made of words, most things can be turned on their head, or can change shape from different perspectives and according to various juxtapositions, keeping readers and critics on their toes and extending each poem's shelf life. As we've seen, Martial finds ways of making the minute huge, the tight loose, the serious funny, the deadly vibrant and vice versa. He specialises in inverting literary tropes, probing the flipsides of familiar images, figures, principles and orders. Read through the lens of Saturnalian sport, the epigrams are especially (conscious of being) difficult to read: the fiction of a temporary suspension of rules can make Martial's politics opaque, and expose readers to all manner of dirty tricks. Moreover, the reversals and paradoxes of carnival and epigram are set off, Martial knows, by the predictable but creatively compelling contradiction of what Statius calls *Saturnalia principis*, 'the emperor's Saturnalia' (*Silvae* 1.6.82).[6] This is in part what makes this Roman festival such a fascinating stage for Martial's ambitious poetics of full immersion. Bounded/metamorphic, gossipy/silenced, conservative/naughty, stuffed/starved epigram is perfectly poised to re-create and comment on the artifices of controlled, timetabled carnival, a loaded gift from autocrat to plebs during which liberties are carefully measured, and relaxed rules also serve to recarve and freshen up

---

[3] As Leary notes (2001, 4), Saturn's early function seems to have been agricultural, and the Saturnalia features in Numa's calendar (17 December) between the festivals of the Consualia (in honour of Consus, god of the corn bin) and the Opalia (in honour of Ops, a personification of abundance).

[4] Hesiod, *Works and Days* 111–120.

[5] On the idea that slaves were made equal to or even superior to their masters during the Saturnalia, see Acc. ap. Macr. 1.7.37, Macr. 1.10.22, 1.11.1, 1.12.7, Athen. 14.639B, Dio Cass. 60.19.3, Lucian *Sat.* 5, Hor. *Sat.* 2.7.4, Mart. 14.79.

[6] See Newlands (2002) 227–59.

the status quo. The Saturnalia, Martial recognises, is a politically loaded occasion, prime time for imperial image-making and propaganda, and *the* symbolic site, more than ever, for testing out creative freedom and poetic autonomy.

As I have been discussing throughout this book, these are issues that bubble through the *Epigrams* – poetry so conscious of being trapped in, as well as 'creating', the bustle of Rome, and so nostalgic for the interior, protected spaces and permanent *otium* of Augustan literary culture, as safe-guarded by 'ideal' patrons like Maecenas. In the Saturnalian books, I'll be suggesting here, we see Martial experimenting with, and pushing the limits of, the expansive relationship he envisages between epigram and world. Carnival, with all its connotations of liberation and looseness, becomes a privileged space for investigating tensions between past and present, nostalgia and novelty, between the suffocating smallness and symbolic vastness of the city. This is where we're challenged to question just how absorbed Martial, epigram and epigram readers are, or want to be, in the organised randomness of imperial Rome.

Domitian, whose reign spans the bulk of Martial's books, marks his personal regulation of popular liberty by moving the festival start date back from around 14 December to the Kalends: as Newlands puts it, 'the first day of the last month of the year could be seen then to open with Domitian, as the first day of the new year opened with the emperor involved in the inaugural ceremonies of office, often indeed in the role of consul.'[7] In *Silvae* 1.6.83–4, Statius cleverly highlights Domitian's management of Saturnalian licence with the lines: 'they call for their Lord with sweet affection. This liberty alone did Caesar forbid them' (*et dulci dominum favore clamant: / hoc solum vetuit licere Caesar*). The oxymoronic *vetuit licere*, literally 'he forbade to allow', itself forms a tightly packed slogan for imperial carnival. In the back of our minds, too, lurks Tacitus' tale in *Annals* 13.15.2–3 of Britannicus' misjudgement of Saturnalian free speech under Nero (he is murdered for bemoaning his exclusion from the throne in front of the emperor), and the bitter comment at the start of the *Agricola*, in the wake of Domitian's murder and *damnatio memoriae*: 'just as former generations witnessed the ultimate in liberty, so we have seen the worst of slavery' (*sicut vetus aetas vidit quid ultimum in libertate esset, ita nos in servitute*, *Agr.* 2.3). We also remember Ovid's lament in *Tristia* 2.491–4 that he was 'caught out' by the notion that nobody had ever been 'ruined'

---

[7] Newlands (2002) 236.

for 'playful verses written in smoky December', and had not expected to suffer such a dire punishment (*tristis poena*, 494) for verses that were 'not at all serious' (*non tristia*, 493). Of course, there can be no such thing as an absolute, temporary upturning of socio-political hierarchies, or the licensing of free speech without limits – at least, not without complete chaos: the blurring of norms and rules during the Saturnalia might make it *more* difficult to judge the point to which those limits have stretched, with potentially dangerous consequences, despite the tricky defence tactic of satiric humour.

Indeed, despite the influence of Bakhtin's theories of carnival (and paradigmatically, of the Roman Saturnalia) as popular defiance of social, political and legal norms, its energies containing all the potential for liberation and revolution,[8] many critics have thought differently: for René Girard, there is always a 'mimetic violence' underlying carnival rites which exposes societal tensions,[9] while others have suggested that the festival is best characterised as alternating and mixing up constraints and freedom.[10] We might remember that Saturn himself is a rather mysterious god, 'one of the most puzzling in the Roman cult',[11] who in the Italian version of his legend, as told in Vergil's *Aeneid*, takes refuge in Latium as an exile, 'in flight from Jupiter in arms' (*Aen.* 8.320), and is honoured for his didactic role in 'giving laws' to the primitive and uneducated nomads he hides among.[12] Saturn is a ruler and lawgiver: he imposes fair restrictions in order to civilise, contain and preserve the liberties of his subjects. At the same time, Vergil's phrase *arma Iovis fugiens* at *Aen.* 8.320 picks up the twisted narrative leading up to this role – the resonating myth in which Saturn castrates his father and jealously devours his own children (except Jupiter, who tricks him into eating a stone instead) so that his power cannot be threatened, only to later regurgitate and be overcome by them in a violent struggle.[13] In some part of this story, Zeus takes his revenge by putting his father in chains, from which Saturn then escapes or is freed, as celebrated by the Saturnalia (he is *compede exsoluta*, 'set free from his shackles', at *Silvae* 1.6.4). At the beginning of the *Apophoreta* (14.1.9–10), Zeus gives father Saturn 'tipsy

---

[8] See Bakhtin (1968). On the modern longing for the cathartic energy of the Saturnalia, see Bernstein (1992) 34–7.

[9] Girard (1977) esp. 118–42.

[10] Kerenyi (1962) 49–70, and Turner (1969) ch. 5. For discussion of critical attitudes to Bakhtin's theory of carnival, see esp. Stallybrass and White (1986) 1–31, and Bernstein (1992) 17–18, 34–5.

[11] I quote Scheid's entry on Saturnus in the *Oxford Classical Dictionary* (3rd edition, 1996).

[12] *is genus indocile ac dispersum montibus altis / composuit legesque dedit, Latiumque vocari / maluit, his quoniam latuisset tutus in oris* (*Aen.* 8.321–3). Also see *Geo.* 2.538, *Aen.* 6.792–5, 7.202–4.

[13] For fuller discussion of Saturn's myth, see Panofsky (1939).

days' in exchange for (rule of) the heavens: carnival itself is a trade-off, a few days of fun in exchange for the long-term surrender of power.[14] The temporariness of Saturn's liberty, and the contraposition of freedom and imprisonment, of the powerful and enslaved god, appears in awkward tension with the never-ending physical and mental freedoms of Golden Age man that constitute the utopian imperial model for *pax romana*. Saturn's myth is a mind-boggling tangle of tyranny, envy, cruelty, concealment and retribution on one hand, and peaceful, open rule and utopian fantasy on the other. In other words, disturbing and surreal Saturnalian inversions are, if you want to look, already defining aspects of Saturn's biography.[15] As we will see, awkward partnerships, layered and latent narratives, unpalatable and equivocal shards in apparently slick and reassuring wholes, are also the hallmark of Martial's remakings of Saturnalian fun.

### COLD CARNIVAL: THE *XENIA*

By the time Martial corners the market, Latin literature has already claimed the Saturnalia as prime imaginary space for satire, lampoon and experimental *sermones*, and by the Flavian period Saturnalian catalogue poetry had become a well-established tradition. Yet the epigrammatist finds his niche by scribbling and sending off exactly the rotten, irreverent gifts listed with spite in Catullus 14 and Statius *Silvae* 4.9,[16] and while Horace retreats to his Sabine farm to escape the excitement of the festivities in *Sat* 2.3 and 2.7, Martial instead dives right in, serving up and exposing himself to all the worst seasonal jokes, offering his versicles as surprise packages and canapés. Sardonically, given that in Vergil the people of Saturn's golden age are succeeded by and opposed to a 'worse race' of warmongers plagued by *amor habendi*,[17] in Martial the gift-giving rituals of December condense and lay bare the consumerist culture and pressured politics of exchange rampant in epigram's Rome. It's the economic value of gifts that counts in these poems, and the Saturnalia, like the modern Christmas, marks the season for commercial gain (the city is now even more attuned to the relative value of commodities, and the oppressive weight of debts) – though

---

[14] 14.1.9–10: *sed quid agam potius madidis, Saturne, diebus / quod tibi pro caelo filius ipse dedit?*

[15] On Saturn's 'characteristically contradictory aims and correspondingly doubled (destructive/restorative) tropes' see Bernstein (1992) 35–8.

[16] In poem 14, Catullus addresses Calvus, who has sent him a terrible collection of poetry as a hoax gift, and promises to take revenge, while in *Silvae* 4.9, Statius rebukes Plotius Grypus for giving him an unworthy present of a cheap, moth-eaten, mouldy book in return for a fine one. See discussion of Martial's 'self-denigration', in relation to Catullus 14, in Roman (2001) 130–1.

[17] See Vergil *Aen.* 8.325–7.

Martial, naturally, tends to home in on disappointing festive yields (see for example 4.88, where the poet receives no gifts at all, not even a tiny basket of shrivelled olives). Epigram itself, as we've seen, is sold as material product and brand (as well as a slave whose shackles are sometimes removed), which changes hands, rubs up against bodies and circulates in the restless city.

It is in the *Xenia* (Book 13), packed full of edibles, that Martial's vision of material, commodified poetry snapped up or spat out by a city of consumers, is most on show.[18] This is the first of two books written for the Saturnalia which consist of descriptions of gifts given by hosts to departing dinner party guests, published early in Martial's career between AD 83 and 85.[19] The *Apophoreta*, or 'take-aways' (Book 14), include all sorts of items from toothpaste to whips, seashells to dwarfs – a Plinian cornucopia of alternately precious and cheap objects. The *Xenia*, however, cover just foodstuffs, and the original-sounding title evokes the ζεινήια or guest-gifts which characterise the heroic code of hospitality in Homer, a connotation now superimposed onto Roman *amicitia*.[20] In Martial's numbered books, we'll find more than a few choice food metaphors – at 10.59, for example, he compares his book to a banquet, complaining that readers like to pick out the titbits and leave the staples, like bread, and punning on the verb *consumo*, meaning both to eat, and to use up (by writing or spending).[21] In retrospect, it is always tempting to read the *Xenia* as a literary programme in concentrate, a jolly trailer for the bitty, twelve-book *magnum opus* to follow.[22] Here, though, Catullan *nugae* hit rock bottom, and writing rubbish (just the kind of trash Catullus and Statius hated to receive come carnival time) is the new *novus sal*, Book 13's first quintessential Saturnalian twist. The muses are wasting good papyrus on this lowly opus, but at least dirty bookworms won't starve, and the paper can always

---

[18] Citroni (1989) argues that just such verses would have been circulated during the Saturnalia, and that the *Xenia* and *Apophoreta* model themselves explicitly on such collections. See also Leary (1998).

[19] On the dates of the *Xenia* and *Apophoreta*, see Leary (2001) 12–13, and Leary (1996) 9–12. For the *Xenia*, the use of the title Germanicus for Domitian at 13.4.1 provides a *terminus post quem* of AD 83.

[20] Leary (2001) 1. Leary also notes (2) that ξεινήιον can also be used of hospitable entertainment (e.g. Homer, *Iliad* 18.408).

[21] 10.59.1: *consumpta est uno si lemmata pagina* ('if a whole page is eaten up with one epigram . . .'): see Gowers (1993) 247–8. Also see Martial 9.81 (he caters to diners not cooks), or 7.25 (epigrams should be salt and vinegar flavoured).

[22] On the *Xenia* and *Apophoreta*, Gold (2003) 604 writes: 'We are prepared by them for a rather seamless transition into Books 1–12, where gifts, gift-giving, money and patronage become . . . overriding concerns, not just in relation to [Martial] himself but in larger compass for the entire social and cultural system of Flavian Rome.'

be reused for take-away tuna and olives (13.1.1–3).[23] Martial puts it up
front in poem 2 that the spiteful critic shouldn't waste his time taking him
down a few pegs, as even if his nose is so large he is practically all nose
(a pantomime, sky-sized hooter, 13.2.1–3[24]), he couldn't possibly say more
against the poet than he has said himself. Here, the sharp, rhinoceros beak
of Martial's addressee,[25] intent on malice, contrasts with the enchanted,
flared nostrils of Catullus' Fabullus,[26] who will want the gods to make him
one gigantic nose once he smells Lesbia's real or metaphorical perfume.
Both poverty-stricken poets are offering comic dinners in which verbal wit
replaces real food and wine, but whereas Catullus lures Fabullus to his own
home with tantalising promises of poetry and womanly perfume, Martial
gives his discerning guests the finger in public, promising not ambrosial
scent, but little scraps of almost nothing. Symbolically, Martial turns Catullus' world inside-out, making the point that Flavian epigram happens
*out there,* in the midst of the unforgiving city, among the gamblers and
revellers. Yet we can't help but note that *unguentum,* the tease of Catullus
13, is presented as a possible gift in the matching, penultimate poem of
Book 13, 126.[27] Again, Catullus' generous stinginess (no money, no food,
but so much more) opposes itself to Martial's plain, materialistic stinginess:
13.126 is a non-gift ('Perfume: never leave perfume or wine to your heir.
Let him have the cash, but give these all to yourself'). Martial continues in
13.2.5–10:

> quid dentem dente iuvabit
> rodere? carne opus est, si satur esse velis.
> ne perdas operam: qui se mirantur, in illos
> virus habe, nos haec novimus esse nihil.
> non tamen hoc nimium nihil est, si candidus aure
> nec matutina si mihi fronte venis.

[23] The idea of poetry as wastepaper begins in Latin literature with the famous image at Catullus 95.8, where the *Annales* of Volusius *scombris saepe dabunt tunicas* ('will often give tunics to mackerel'). See also Horace, *Epist.* 2.1.269–70, which possibly contains a dig at Catullus (see Barchiesi (2005a) 328). Horace's reference to the sheets of bad poetry used to wrap frankincense, perfumes and pepper (*tus et odores / et piper et quidquid chartis amicitur ineptis,* 269–70) is also picked up, Barchiesi notes, in the first two items of the *Xenia, tus* and *piper.*
[24] I.e., 'a nose so big Atlas would not want to carry it if asked'.
[25] On critics with rhinoceros noses, also see Martial 1.3 (*iuvenesque senesque / et pueri nasum rhinocerotis habent,* 5–6).
[26] *nam unguentum dabo, quod meae puellae / donarunt Veneres Cupidinesque, / quod tu cum olfacies, deos rogabis, / totum ut te faciant, Fabulle, nasum* (Cat. 13.11–14), cf. Martial 13.2.1: *nasutus sis usque licet, sis denique nasus . . .*
[27] As Ferguson (1963) and Leary (1996) note, Martial 14.206 also alludes to Cat. 13 (compare *meros amores* 14.206.1/Cat. 13.9).

Why gnaw tooth against tooth?
You need meat if you want to feel full.
Don't waste your energy: keep your spite for narcissists –
I know full well these things of mine are nothing.
But they're not too much nothing, if you come to me
with a friendly ear and not a morning face.

In a sense this is the escape, the holiday, that Martial offers his readers in the *Xenia*. He promises relief from the toil of concentration and scrutiny in reading, from the job of playing *ingeniosus lector*: just for the Saturnalia, poetry can be lighter than light – you won't get a headache like you do trying to work out what Horace's deft puppeteering of Davus means in *Satire* 2.7. Here we can pick and mix like gamblers at a party (but without losing anything: *alea nec damnum nec facit ista lucrum* ('such gambling brings neither loss nor gain,' 13.1.8)), treat this like a Schott's Miscellany to scan at leisure, or to pick over in snippets over someone else's shoulder. And to a point, modern readers will be especially rewarded if they take Martial's advice – we can happen upon weird and exotic Roman recipes, and some delightful bites of cultural history and myth: Flamingo tongue or milk-filled udders, anyone (13.71, 13.44)? The Capitol saved by a goose (13.74)? A pet gazelle for the kids (13.99)?

Yet whilst Martial seems to let us off the hook, giving us a taste of true permissiveness in an age of restricted tolerance, it's hard to separate private reading from public partying, the literary from the material, or poetic gifts from the symbolism of nasty, disappointing, meaningful *munera* which we find elsewhere in the *Epigrams*.[28] After claiming in 13.1 to be one step removed from the material pressures of real gambling (*alea nec damnum nec facit ista **lucrum***), Martial then stages a bartering scene with readers, spelling out the extent to which this project is all about who pays up and who gains, and replacing naughty festive gambling with mundane haggling on a street corner: *quattuor est nimium? poterit constare duobus, / et faciet **lucrum** bybliopola Tryphon* ('Is four too much? It could cost you two, and bookseller Tryphon would still make a profit,' 13.3.3–4). There are still lingering hints at the potential separation of poetry and material world, of Martial's and Domitian's Saturnalia: for example, we might want to say that Catullus' private hedonistic world and invitations *inside* haunt as well as contrast with Martial's sharp public sales pitch and fending off of

---

[28] For an introduction to gift-giving in Martial see Spisak (1998). On the tension between autonomy and social determination in the *Xenia* and *Apophoreta*, I want to extend but also complicate Roman's impressive analysis (2001, 130–8).

attackers in 13.2 and 3. And gift 7, the cheap, unluxurious *Faba* ('Beans'),[29] presents readers and diners with an opt-out clause, the chance to retreat into pre-imperial rusticity, and to decline the invitations of sophisticates (such as Catullus in poem 13):

> Faba
> Si spumet rubra conchis tibi pallida testa,
>     lautorum cenis saepe negare potes.
>
> If you've got pale beans boiling in a red clay pot,
> you can afford to turn down elegant dinners.

This nostalgic gift harks back to the modest, philosophical contentment of Horace in his *Odes* (especially *Odes* 1.31, where he prays to be happy with what he has, and wants to live on a simple vegetarian diet of olives, endives and marrows, 15–20). Clearly, the *Xenia* open up a range of imbricating perspectives on the relationship between epigram and world: on one hand the work is presented as a practical guide and accompaniment to the Saturnalian feast:[30] here you'll find gift ideas for the most awkward of friends and relatives. Yet these poems can also replace real gifts (*haec licet hospitibus pro munere disticha mittas*, 'you can send these couplets to your guests instead of a gift,' 13.3.5). The *'pro'* here is as double-edged as it is in the introductory poem to the *De Spectaculis* (*unum pro cunctis Fama loquetur opus, De Spect.* 1.8), as I discussed in chapter 3: the *Xenia* are to be used instead of gifts, but also *as* gifts. You can cut up the book and distribute the distichs at a dinner party, or take it along in your pocket for entertainment and ready jokes, but the *Xenia* is also a literary representation of the Saturnalia that can stand in for actual festivities – it lets you experience carnival (again) from the privacy of your own home (at any time of the day or year, not just when the calendar allows[31]), and lets Martial claim to rise above the material, preserve the nostalgia of poetic autonomy and self-sufficiency.[32]

---

[29] As Leary notes (2001, *ad loc.*), beans were the traditional gift of the poor, lowly and miserly. Cf. also Juvenal 3.293, 14.131, Mart. 7.78.

[30] Some critics have supposed that Martial intended Books 13 and 14 to be used as directories to help the unimaginative to choose presents. See e.g. Lindsay (1903, 37): 'the use of title headings was a necessity, in order that a donor might find without difficulty the couplet which would suit the present he thought of giving.'

[31] Cf. Seneca in *Ep.* 18.1, who comments, as he observes revellers in the street outside, that the carnival season never seems to end these days. According to a character in Petronius' *Cena Trimalchionis* (44.4), the 'big jaws' celebrate the Saturnalia all year round; Seneca's *Apocolocyntosis* turns Claudius' reign into a perpetual Saturnalia (see esp. 8.2, 12.2).

[32] See most recently Stroup (2006), who argues that the joke of the *Xenia* is precisely 'that ephemeral poetry can not only replace but even subordinate a real-life banquet' (311).

In 5.18, similarly, Martial implies that poems which he gives out at the Saturnalia are not gifts in the true sense of the word (they are not spiky hooks, they are nothings, *nihil*, 5.18.9): the poet claims to operate *outside* the prickly conventions of gift-exchange, in part because insubstantial epigrams barely register. Yet verses can also drip with venom (e.g. 7.72): we know full well that Martial's nothings are never just nothings, and that commodified poetry is fully implicated in Rome's subtle politics of trade and reciprocity. When we read Martial, we learn that gifts are like hooks (*imitantur hamos dona*, 5.18.7), and that many a fish has been caught by a juicy, dangling fly (7–8). Whoever gives a lot always wants much in return (5.59.3), and the use of *munus* ('gift') to refer to the violent amphitheatre games (Martial published his *De Spectaculis* just a few years previously in AD 80) tints other gift-giving in Martial with deadly connotations (e.g. 8.27: 'You are rich, Gaurus, and old. Whoever gives you presents says, if you have the wit to understand: Die!'). To what extent can we, and the *Xenia*, ever really evade the oppressive, bitter-tasting social exchanges that characterise epigram's Rome?

Similarly, the line between real food, and poetry as metaphorical food, is more difficult to maintain once we encounter the image of paper coming into close contact with or 'clothing' greasy foodstuffs (13.1), and Martial hints throughout not only that the gifts he lists are *literary*, but that his little poems *are* material gifts, able to integrate seamlessly into, or mill around in, the 'exterior' environment of the city in December. In Book 14, as Barchiesi discusses, it's no accident that the dinner party lots (*sortes alternae*, 14.1.5) evoke Ovidian jargon for elegiac couplets,[33] or that *synthesis*, the casual dress worn at the Saturnalia which in the ablative plural is the first word of the *Apophoreta*, is also the Greek (σύνθεσις) for any 'combination, collection, series of matching items' – in other words, a neat introductory label for this miscellaneous book. *Toga*, the second word of the *Xenia*,[34] is the Saturnalian alternative to *synthesis*, another 'prescription for casual dress, as well as for loose, laid-back poetic entertainment'.[35] The *Xenia*, as *togae*, can participate directly in the celebrations, or at least in Martial's epigrammatic, worm's-eye view of a Saturnalian feast. The poems make up a crowd of party-goers (*turba* 13.3.1), mirrored by, or metamorphosed

---

[33] *Alternus* is used of elegiac couplets at Ovid *Fast.* 2.121, *Trist.* 3.1.11, 3.1.56, 3.7.10.

[34] Some scholars have argued that the first two poems of the *Xenia* are later imports (see. e.g. Leary 2001, 37), though I agree with Stroup (2006, 303) that the view that they are original seems more persuasive, given that they both take food as their topic, and contain compelling parallels to the introductory poem of the *Apophoreta*.

[35] Barchiesi (2005a) 327–8.

into, the *maxima turba* of prawns at 13.83, as well as the large number of
guests Nepos doesn't drink with at 13.124 (*non ponit turbae*, 2), and the
amphitheatre audience waving *their togae*, at 13.99, under the gift marked
Dorcas (Gazelle). The *Xenia* slip easily from table to arena, book to crowd
(13.99):[36]

> Delicium parvo donabis dorcada nato:
> iactatis solet hanc mittere turba togis.

> You'll give the gazelle as a pet to your small son:
> The crowd usually lets her go by waving their gowns.

Yet whether the *Xenia* accompany an 'actual' dinner, or make up a clever
literary feast to be enjoyed any place, anywhere, what kind of Saturnalia
do they imply, or gift us? One of the first things we notice, which has
been much discussed in recent criticism,[37] is the fact that the book begins
and ends with a bow to imperial rule and to quasi-divine imperial power,
reminding us again of Statius' paradox of the *Saturnalia principis*. Poem
4, the first gift of *Tus* (incense), is given to Jupiter in the hope that *serus
ut aetheriae Germanicus imperet aulae* ('Germanicus may rule the heavenly
palaces late in time'), while at 13.127 *coronae rosae* close the collection
with an Alexandrian flourish (Meleager's anthology begins and ends with a
reference to *stephanoi*),[38] and translate Saturnalian liberty under Domitian
as quasi-divine control over and manipulation of nature: *dat festinatas,
Caesar, tibi bruma coronas. / quondam veris erat, nunc tua facta rosa est*
('winter gives you forced garlands, Caesar. The rose used to belong to
spring, but now it is yours'). At the same time, as several critics have noticed,
the artifice of winter roses inverts in more (Saturnalian) ways than one the
message of Horace's end poem to *Odes* I, 1.38. While Martial addresses
the emperor, Horace addressed his *puer*, and while Martial celebrates the
out-of-season rose, Horace rejected the pretension of seeking out late-
flowering roses, preferring the simple myrtle (Callimachus' plant) for his
closural garland. Martial's 'hurried', epigrammatic gift to Domitian cheers
on oriental luxury and celebrates the transcendence of natural limits, while
at the same time reinforcing the emperor's prerogative to bend the rules,
at the expense of anything or anyone.

---

[36] As Stroup puts it in her subtle discussion, the *Xenia* are presented as poetic 'embodiments' of the
physical world (2006, 307).

[37] See Roman (2001), Barchiesi (2005a), Leary (2001, *ad loc.*).

[38] The idea of literary closure here is emphasised further by the use of the word *festinatus* in the
hexameter, which is used elsewhere to refer to Martial's 'hurried' books. See discussion in Barchiesi
(2005a) 325.

Indeed, one of the 'jokes' of the *Xenia* is the extent to which it is peppered with restrictions and dampers on sexual pleasure – even more so because the escapist seductions of Republican Catullus (don't) flavour the opening dishes. As Martial warns in 13.2, this is epigram, so don't expect to get *satur* (this word is heavy with allusions to Roman satire and its constant play on satiety versus restraint).[39] In literal terms you can't get fat on representations of food, but epigram doesn't offer you metaphorical fullness either. The Saturnalian feast was traditionally characterised by exuberant gorgings on food and sex, and excessive drinking (at 13.1.4, Martial says his collection is inspired by *ebria bruma*, drunken midwinter).[40] And there *are* expansive, or expanding gifts for the picking here: the moon-sized cheese at 13.30 that will feed a thousand boys, the small bird with the giant's name (Porphyrions, 78), the turbot bigger than any dish (81), foods that seem to swell or 'grow' (*lacte papilla tumet*, 'the udder swells with milk,' 44.2; *Ceres crescit*, 'bread grows,' 47.1; *tumeat magno iecur ansere maius*, 'may the liver swell larger than the big goose,' 58.1). Yet the book also includes many anaphrodisiacs, or gifts which promise sensual delights whilst at the same time polluting our imaginations and dampening our desires (as Leary notes, too, the number of rude poems in this book is surprisingly low![41]). For example, 13.67 is a good bit of advice, but a pretty useless gift for the Saturnalia: it advises us not to consume ring doves, which 'slow down and depress the loins – anyone who wants to be salacious (*salax*) should not eat this bird.' Here the gift frustrates expectations aroused by the label, as doves were kissing birds and had erotic connotations. Compare 66 (*Columbinae*), which warns the reader initiated into Venus' mysteries not to eat doves, traditional lovers' gifts,[42] because the birds were sacred to her. At 18, if you eat this gift of *Porri sectivi*, a poor man's dish, you won't be doing any French kissing: 'when you have eaten the strong-smelling shoots of Tarentine leek, give your kisses closed (*oscula clusa dato*).' Sampling these foods will ensure fellow diners keep their distance and avoid physical or sexual contact, suggesting the opposite of *con-vivium*.

Martial's prescriptions to avoid the contagion inherent in Saturnalian mingling and promiscuity only serve to magnify the almost pathological concern with infection and decay which pervades the epigrams. Implicitly, as Martial hints elsewhere (e.g. 7.37 and 7.95), the threat of disease and

---

[39] *Satura* is frequently linked to *satur* ('full'), but Horace (in his *Satires*) and Seneca (in *Thyestes*) in particular also play on its resemblance to the word *satis* ('enough'). See e.g. Gowers (2005) and Schiesaro (2003).

[40] Also see 14.1.9, 11.6.1, 11.15.5, Statius *Silv.* 1.6.5, 95–7.    [41] Leary (2001) 77.

[42] See e.g. Theocritus 5.96 and 133.

infection is especially imminent in December, when everyone has coughs and colds. For the poet who claims to have to kiss arse constantly to make a living, the Saturnalia is a nightmare social season, every encounter a stomach-churning close-up of frozen hands and dripping noses. As I discussed in chapter 1, the Martial epigram is highly conscious of its tight boundaries and self-containment, shrinking back from (as well as re-creating, and amplifying) the disorder of the city, yet never letting us forget that the poet struggles in vain to maintain immunity from the filth. In reading the *Xenia* within the privacy of our own homes, we may be escaping the actual Saturnalian feast, and no real food may ever pass our lips, yet the book we are holding, Martial reminds us, is a material thing that has already lingered in some crummy bookstall in the heart of Rome, and may already be partly consumed by the 'unclean bookworm'. Who knows where it has been, whose chin has rubbed this papyrus? The familiar image of the bad poem as wrapping for mackerel or other cheap fish (13.1) becomes in Martial far more than an index of epigram's 'sub-literary' status: the carnival epigram book, already infected with an image of its own consumption (13.1.2), condenses the stifling anxieties germane to living and writing in Flavian Rome, where the poet struggles to exert his autonomy, and even to find space to breathe.

Other items in the *Xenia* look tasty, but come with an off-putting sell-by date (Martial has already hinted that some gifts may turn our stomachs: we are told in 13.3.8, *praetereas, si quid non facit ad stomachum* ('if something's not to your taste, just skip it')). 13.55 is a fresh-cured ham: but hurry, Martial warns, 'don't put your dear friends off – I want nothing to do with an aged ham.' The problem with this kind of meat was that it went bad very quickly. Diners are made all too aware that the sensual enjoyment of the Saturnalia is limited, that the clock is ticking (the imperative *propera* in line 1 perhaps reminds us in retrospect of Domitian's *festinatae rosae* at 13.127, and here it is the diners who are forced to hurry to please *amici*, just as roses are forced to do the bidding of the emperor).[43] The line *nam mihi cum vetulo sit petasone nihil* ('because I want nothing to do with an aged ham', 55.2) is reminiscent of epigram 3.32, when an old, sexually abhorrent woman is rejected as good as dead (*vetulus* is usually used of people or wine, and is probably uniquely applied to meat at 13.55):

> 'Non possum vetulam?' quaeris, Matrinia: possum
> et vetulam, sed tu mortua, non vetula es.

---

[43] Another shortlasting, unstable gift, or label for a gift is the *lalisio* at 97 (the foal of a wild ass doesn't have this name for long: *sed breve nomen habet*).

You grumble I can't do old ladies Matrinia? Well,
I *can* do old, too, but you're not old, you're dead.

3.32.1–2[44]

The idea that *petaso* conjures up female flesh which is *already beginning to rot* is continued in the next gift, 13.56, where, as if confirming the disgust at the *vetula* of poem 55, Martial asks, 'perhaps a womb from a virgin pig might take your fancy more?' An old woman is a terrible turn-off for her husband at 13.34, too, the gift of Onions:

> Bulbi
> Cum sit anus coniunx et sint tibi mortua membra,
>     nil aliud bulbis quam satur esse potes.

> Onions
> Since your wife's an old lady and your dick lifeless,
> all you can do is get stuffed on onions.

Martial's twisted Satur-nalia doles out a vegetable that is a traditional aphrodisiac (the idea is that they might help with impotence), yet will also, especially after we have read 13.18, result in very unappealing breath.[45] Perhaps part of the joke is that even if the husband does succeed in tricking his *membra* into action, having overcome both the unpalatable plate of onions and his off-putting wife, she will not be compliant on account of his stinky mouth. This taste of forced desire and closed-mouth sex still lingers when we're given 13.64: sexual pleasure is frustrated again when the hen succumbs in vain (*frustra*) to her neutered 'husband', the cockerel of 63. Compare and contrast the gorgeous *faciles puellae* at the crowd's disposal in Statius' Saturnalia at *Silvae* 1.6.67.

As the introductory poems of the *Xenia* confirm, guarding against excess is a basic (unsaturnalian) principle of epigram: *nimium* becomes a kind of token of carnival largesse, as well as the very thing epigram must guard against. The book must not cost 'too much' (*quattuor est nimium?*) in 13.3, picking up the thread of *non tamen hoc nimium nihil est*, 'these things of mine are not altogether nothing' (13.2.9), where the oxymoronic *nimium nihil* (too much nothing) becomes Martial's slogan for the paradoxes of epigrammatic and imperial carnival. *Nimium* is also used in poems 26 and 116, gesturing again towards the overlap of material book and material gift:

> Sorba
> Sorba sumus, molles nimium tendentia ventres:
> aptius haec puero quam tibi poma dabis.

[44] Old women (*vetulae*) are also the subject of 3.76 and 8.79.
[45] In Xenophon's *Symposium*, for example, Niceratus is accused of eating onions to cover up the fact that he has been indulging in some adulterous snogging.

Sorb apples
We are sorb apples, tightening too loose bellies:
Best give this fruit to your boy, not eat it yourself.

Signinum
Potabis liquidum Signina morantia ventrem?
ne nimium sistas, sit tibi parca sitis.

Signine wine
Will you drink Signine, that delays loose bowels?
So you don't repress them too much, just drink a little.

In the first of these two poems, sexual pleasure from the passive *puer*, or
*cinaedus*, is still the promise, yet this thrill is prefaced by the implication
that looseness might actually prevent such Saturnalian activity (this is the
hidden risk now in 13.29, the gift of laxative prunes[46]), and more generally
by the idea of tightening up any festive laxity. We might compare and
contrast Trimalchio's debauched Saturnalian feast in Petronius' *Satyricon*,
in which the host tells the guests to relax bowels and bladders in the spirit
of Saturnalian liberty (*Sat.* 49). Signine wine has the same effect as sorb
apples, but here Martial goes further, warning against immoderation even
in *correcting* excess. Similarly, you can find 'tipsy midwinter' in this book,
but you'll also find its foil: 22 lists a grape which is useless to Bacchus as
it can't be drunk (though if you *don't* drink it, says the riddle, it 'will be
nectar to you'), and 39 features a goat which likes to destroy Bacchus' wines,
presumably by eating them. The Saturnalian ethos of protecting the fruit
of Bacchus is introduced, ironically, by the image of Bacchus under threat,
and is tainted by the promise of violence: the lascivious goat, an animal
often associated in Roman poetry with lack of sexual inhibition,[47] is to be
punished, *det poenas* (13.39.2). The *deus* in line 2 of this epigram perhaps
also hints at imperial authority, especially in the light of Statius *Silvae*
4.3, which claims that Domitian sought to restore a 'sober countryside', a
reference to his vine edict, which according to historical sources decreed,
during a season in which a glut of wine coincided with a shortage of corn,
that no more vines were to be planted in Italy, and that vineyards in the
provinces were to be cut down. However, in Suetonius (*Dom.* 14.2) we are
told that Domitian dropped the proposal after a poem compared him to
a vine-eating goat. This little gift, then, is potentially full of satiric twists:

---

[46] These plums are *carie rugosa senectae*, 'wrinkled by the dry rot of old age', making loosening up
sound so unsexy.

[47] R. Coleman (1977) at Verg. *Ecl.* 2.64: *florentem cytisum sequitur lasciva capella*, and Ovid *Met.* 13.791,
*tenero lascivior haedo. OLD* s.v. *lascivus*, 1.

punishment of the goat's 'wantonness' at the same time goes *against* another god's drive for sobriety, another encoded version of the *nimium nihil* riddle that launched this collection.[48]

Yet isn't all this precisely what we expect from epigrammatic miscellany – a blend of *mala*, *bona* and *mediocria*, a satiric hotchpotch of cheap and expensive, generous and stingy, delicious and disgusting gifts? Unwelcome, surprising, bad or ironic gifts are typical Saturnalian fare, as were 'lucky dips of unequal presents':[49] we can just sit back and read the *Xenia* literally as an extended Saturnalian prank, and metapoetically as a pared-down demonstration of the 'bad' epigram book in which you're lucky to find a handful of hidden jewels. The game is that you win some, you lose some, and Martial claims to make the game very simple: reading is a controlled gamble, as if a poem isn't to your taste, you can just pass it by, weed out the *nice* ones. Reading the book through (or, as I've just been doing, picking out the 'un-fun' poems) is the pedantic and masochistic act of the foolishly sober, snobby reader attacked by Martial in 13.2. You choose whether or not to enter into the spirit of the occasion, and of epigram, and the joke's on you if you refuse to party. As 13.2 hints, there are (at least) two versions of carnival on sale here: one for the venomous critic, the other for the friendly, fun-loving reader. Take your pick.

At the same time, of course, these gifts are not discrete entities: the reader who skips distasteful poems is liable to make a fool of himself by misreading, and can fall victim to unseen juxtapositions. As Martial puts it in 10.59.5–6, readers risk missing out on a banquet if they handpick dainties from a book, instead of filling up on carbohydrates – although typically, even indiscriminate appetites are couched here in terms of guarding against excess:

> non opus est nobis nimium lectore guloso;
> hunc volo, non fiat qui sine pane satur.

> I don't need a reader who's too much of a gourmet;
> I'd rather one who never feels full without bread.

Poem 75 of the *Xenia* also seems to highlight this very issue.

> Grues
> Turbabis versus nec littera tota volabit,
> unam perdideris si Palamedis avem.

---

[48] Other encapsulations of epigrammatic paradox in the *Xenia* include 13.59 (the dormouse is fatter during hibernation when it does not eat).
[49] Gowers (1993) 27.

Cranes
You'll confuse the lines and the writing won't fly complete,
if you waste one of Palamedes' birds.

Palamedes invented the alphabet, and 'discovered' the sign *v* (*u*) by observing the flights of cranes in formation. If you miss one of the birds, then, the letter *v*/*u* will be incomplete, and the poem, which has four *v*s/*u*s, might become illegible. To what extent does the same rule apply to the book as a whole? Epigram teaches us to read the small print. How free are we, really, to read this book any way we want? How structured and bound is epigram's Saturnalia? Martial does seem to offer us (escape) routes for alternative orderings: while the book seems to be arranged according to food-type and courses,[50] and a great many of the *Xenia* reinforce principles of hierarchy and measuring (truffles are 'second only to mushrooms', 13.50; heathcocks rank first among fowl, 13.61; partridge costs more because it tastes better than woodcock, 13.76), there is also room for debate (92, 'among birds the thrush, if anything I decide is certain, is the prime delicacy . . .'), and hints at possible reshuffles: 14, *Lactucae* ('Lettuces') used to be served at the end of meals, but now they are eaten as a starter; olives (13.36) can either begin or end a dinner; the Goby, a small fish located towards the end of the *Xenia,* is generally eaten as an hors d'oeuvre (13.88); cheap sausage meat suggestively poking white porridge makes a satiric final garland (and a welcome one, *grata corona,* 13.35.2) to rival the strict, official *festinatae coronae* that crown this book at 13.127; while 13.51 sees Martial asserting his personal taste for a *corona turdis,* 'a garland made of thrushes', rather than of roses or rich nard. Again, epigram neatly performs the contradiction of ordered disorder, or disordered order that epitomises the Saturnalia. We too, with Martial, can exercise quasi-imperial power to manipulate and relabel: Domitian can transfer roses from spring to winter, while we can fastforward to any point in this collection, and return to Martial's literary carnival time in any season. If we get really impatient with the fiction of Book 13's lottery, we can even, as empowered consumers, take matters into our own hands entirely: see gift number 6, *Alica* ('Spelt', or 'gruel'), which

---

[50] See Leary (2001) 10–11 and Sullivan (1991) 12–13 on the order of epigrams in the *Xenia*. To summarise, poems 6–60 are starters, 61–78 deal with fowl, 79–91 with seafood, 92–100 with game, and 106–125, reflecting the *comisatio*, are concerned with wine. 13.5 links up with 101–5 (seasoners and sweeteners), a loose chiastic device, while there are sub-groupings within the main sections (e.g. salad or vegetables within the starters), pairings (e.g. 35 and 36 both refer to Picene products), and hierarchies (most noticeably in 92–100, starting with the hare, *prima mattea*, progressing through an alternation of fierce and docile animals, and ending in 97–100 where the young and grown wild asses frame the roe deer and gazelle).

anticipates the recipient's disappointment at not getting mead instead. *Nos alicam, poterit mulsum tibi mittere dives. / si tibi noluerit mittere dives, emes!* ('I can send you spelt water, though a rich man will be able to send you mead. If a rich man won't send it, then go out and buy!)

But what does the carnival reader miss? Or what can he not avoid? We are unlikely to have a taste for 56 after 55 – a rotten gift can kill an appetite even for honeyed poetry, and more often than not, we don't know poems/foods are off-putting, or about restraint, rules and anti-pleasure, until we read them, by which time it's too late (you only realise the Egyptian bean at 13.57 is a joke when you read the pentameter about its fibrous strands getting stuck in your teeth, for instance). The much-used verb *sapere*, meaning both to taste and to understand, also captures this idea: you don't *know* until you taste/read. What's more, one result of epigrammatic shrinking, as we saw in chapter 1, is that the good and the bad can be crammed into a single poem/gift, so that if you skip it, you both get lucky *and* miss out:[51] see for example 13.52 (*Anates*, 'Ducks'), which looks like an encapsulation of Martial's '*praetereas, si quid non facit ad stomachum*' (13.3.8): 'let a duck be served whole, but it is tasty only in the breast and neck. Return the rest to the cook,' or 13.84 (*Scarus*, 'Parrot wrasse'): 'This parrot wrasse that came worn down by sea waves has delicious entrails, but the rest of it doesn't taste too good.' If carnival reading backfires, and we (are forced to) see the *Xenia* as a carefully crafted volume designed to be read in its entirety, then this becomes a much more equivocal, and potentially bitter Saturnalia. Should it become a counting game? How many depressing gifts do we have to 'ignore' or (pretend to) laugh at for this to add up to a decently entertaining holiday, a break from the norm? How free can this book (can epigram) make us feel? In a festival marked by twists, inversions and collapsed categories, what, if anything, can truly count as 'unsaturnalian', and how would we detect a poet bent on legislating against our fun? Can *anything* be passed off as irreverence, even (paradoxically) the enforcing of rules, or the suggestion of aggression, punishment and constraint?

As I mentioned at the beginning of this chapter, it was apparently considered sinful to begin wars or to punish criminals during the Saturnalia, despite the violence endemic in Saturn's myth.[52] Yet noticeably, many of the foods on offer in the *Xenia* come tagged with hints of torture and violence,

---

[51] A similar idea is that a gift may only be tasty if paired with others. E.g. 13.13: beet is flavourless unless you eat it with wine and pepper.
[52] Macrobius *Sat.* 1.10.1.

subtly flouting this prohibition. We might even say that a master's right
to exploit and brutalise his slaves is not so much suspended in Martial's
Saturnalia, as merely dressed up or displaced onto anthropomorphised
animals and foods. As well as the goat facing punishment at 13.39, in 86,
sea urchins line up in their armour, like soldiers in a tortoise formation,
and the diner fights back against their spears by penetrating the shell
and exposing the soft innards. This is followed by 87, the Murexes (a
species of large snail) which vaunt the fact that people wear cloaks (*lacernae*
were cloaks originally worn by soldiers) dyed in their blood. Rabbits are
captured despite their military skill in digging 'siege tunnels' at 13.60. 13.96
is a handsome stag which may have belonged to Silvia, thus recalling the
episode in *Aeneid* 7 when Ascanius killed Silvia's stag, an act which triggered
the war between Trojans and Latins (and launched Vergil's '*Iliad*'). Other
gifts recall the sadistic pleasures of the amphitheatre (again the echo of
*munus* as gift/amphitheatre games lingers): the oryx at 95 is the victim
of 'morning shows', though the elephant at 100 and the gazelle at 99 are
to be spared by the fickle crowd; we watch cheese being tortured in 33
(*commendat gratia duplex, / sive levi flamma sive domamur aqua,* 'we offer
a double appeal, whether we are subdued by light flame or by water'); the
awe-inspiring peacock (*Miraris, quotiens gemmantis explicat alas,* 'do you
admire him every time he spreads his jewelled wings?') is handed over to
the 'cruel cook', as if to an executioner, at 13.70. We watch fish die a slow
death in 79, 80 and 102: the live mullets, *mulli vivi*, are brought to the table
in glass vessels of sea water in 79, so that diners can watch their colours
change as they die of suffocation;[53] in 80, the eel is caught when its skin
is scorched by the sun, and it no longer has the strength to swim, and in
102, garum (*munera cara,* 2) is made from the 'first blood of a mackerel still
breathing its last'. Even if your slaves are nominally granted the right of
free speech for the Saturnalia, you can take comfort in the fact that dumb
mules can never talk back at 13.11 (the muleteer can keep the gift of barley
for himself, to sell on to the innkeeper, as his animals can't complain),[54]

---

[53] See Leary (2001) *ad loc.* and Pliny *NH* 9.66: *mullum expirantem versicolori quadam et numerosa
varietate spectari proceres gulae narrant, rubentium squamarum multiplici mutatione pallescentem,
utique si vitro spectetur inclusus.*

[54] The theme of silent or silenced animals continues at 77 (the swan chants its own death with dying
tongue) and 71 (the flamingo's tongue is cut out, a treat for epicures): yet in this case the flamingo
hits back, suggesting its tongue might be *garrula.* As Leary explains (2001, *ad loc.*), there is a double
entendre lurking here, which, implicitly, the flamingo's tongue is ready to tell: whilst red feathers
account for the flamingo's name, the adjective *rubens* also has other associations. The colour red was
associated with the Phoenicians, who were associated with a fondness for oral sex. *Gulosus* is from
*gula*, 'gullet', hinting that this diner is already all too fond of having things in his throat. The fact
that this bird's tongue has been cut out doesn't make it any less powerful, as it threatens to lash out
with dirty jokes, to pollute the diner's mouth and silence him in the most malicious way possible.

just as hens kept imprisoned in the dark and fattened up for slaughter
are passive and accommodating at 13.62 (*facilis gallina*, 1), while fruits are
'home-bred slaves' (*vernae*), plucked from suburban gardens at 13.43 – no
need for any 'liberating' rhetoric here.

   Is this another way, then, of offering two Saturnalia in one, a way
for slippery, multifaceted epigram to cater to all tastes, promising radical
freedoms, both creative and socio-political, whilst at the same time con-
solidating poetic and class structures? From the start, this is a 'double'
work, a plural *turba* rather than a singular *liber* that will look very different
depending on whether it attracts a kindly or spiteful readership. This idea
of fending off the wrong readers (the violently critical ones), of juxtapos-
ing two opposing experiences of cosy-cold December, is actually already
familiar to us from an author whose ghost haunts the *Xenia*, and much of
Martial's later books: Publius Ovidius Naso. Indeed, it is hardly surprising
that Martial carefully frames his first major carnival collection with poems
praising Domitian, given Ovid's unforeseen punishment for *his* unserious
'Saturnalian' *carmen*, and his miserable, freezing December spent sailing
into exile on the Black Sea (*gelido tremerem cum mense Decembri*, *Tr.* 1.11.3).
Like Ovid in the *Tristia*, Martial apologises for his sloppy poetry (the exile
poetry is a major, ironic model for the scrappy, unpolished epigrams), and
calls upon his reader to be *candidus* (*non tamen hoc nimium nihil est, si candidus aure / . . . venis*, 13.2.9–10). Compare Ovid's famous lines at *Tristia*
1.11.35–6:

> quo magis his debes ignoscere, candide lector,
>    si spe sint, ut sunt, inferiora tua.
>
> So, kind reader, if these verses should be (and they are),
>    poorer than you hoped, indulge me all the more.

Martial warps Catullus 13, warning off instead of seducing his addressee,
to trace (and in a sense pre-empt) the reversal of favour suffered by Ovid
in the *Tristia*, where he moans that Augustus and his allies, with whom he
could once joke and play (like a new Catullus, *Tr.* 2.427) have suddenly
turned against him. In *Tristia* 1.1, Ovid coaches his book not to defend
itself aggressively, even though it is 'bitten by words' (*quamvis mordebere
dictis*, 1.1.25), while Martial uses the same image of biting in 13.2.5–6 to
deal in advance with his own unfairly harsh critics, pointing out that there
is really nothing in epigram for them to get their teeth into (*quid den-
tem dente iuvabit / rodere?*). Might also Martial's instruction to readers
at 13.2.7–8 to keep their 'venom' for 'self-admirers' (*qui se mirantur, in*

*illos / virus habe*) allude to Ovid's obsessions with Narcissus and narcissism, which would later lead Martial's contemporary Quintilian to berate the poet as '*nimium amator ingenii sui*' ('too much in love with his own genius')? Incidentally, the next time that verb *miror* is used in the *Xenia* is in reference to the slaughtered peacock, an animal which symbolises narcissistic beauty in Ovid (and in many other authors from Aristotle on),[55] and whose gift alludes to just such an analogy in Ovid's *Medicamina*. Martial writes:

> Pavones
> Miraris, quotiens gemmantis explicat alas,
>  et potes hunc saevo tradere, dure, coco?
>                         13.70

> Peacocks
> Do you admire him, when he spreads his jewelled wings,
>  and can you hand him over, cruel man, to the callous cook?

In Ovid's *Medicamina* 31–4, men as much as women are pleasured by their own good looks, just as the peacock struts and spreads its wings, proud of its beauty (*laudatas homini volucris Iunonia pennas / explicat*), a line paralleled by *Ars Amatoria* 1.627 (*laudatas ostendit avis Iunonia pinnas*, 'Juno's bird shows off her much-admired wings'). Certainly, the point Martial seems to be making is that he is *not* guilty of Ovid's pre-exilic arrogance and Saturnalian misjudgement – not least because, although he writes in the same metre as the *Ars Amatoria*, this is epigram (too small to grasp, never *nimium* anything), and you won't find much overt celebration of sex in this volume. The question is, whether the vague backdrop of Ovidian culpability detracts from the pleasure even 'friendly' readers might find in the *Xenia*, whether a post-Ovidian, post-exilic literary Saturnalia under Domitian can ever really relax, and to what extent anti-pleasure can be packaged as epigrammatic trick-not-treating, rather than, say, bitter, unseasonal counterattack from a poet who, in the best Augustan traditions, would rather be (and feels safer being) one step removed from the city in December.

In *Tristia* 2, Ovid himself debates whether there might be two different kinds of Saturnalian poetry (as well as two different kinds of readers), whether how a work is presented and framed might determine its reception: he cannot understand why so much racy Roman poetry has gone, and still goes, uncensored and unpunished, whilst his fun-loving productions are

[55] See also Pliny *NH* 10.43: *gemmantes laudatas exponit colores*.

now deemed so criminally obscene. Among the examples of *opera* which got off scot-free, he includes what look in retrospect like summaries of the book Martial will later write: one 'lays down the rules for feasts and entertaining' (*his epulis leges hospitioque dedit*, 2.488), others 'tell of the arts of playing at dice' (*sunt aliis scriptae, quibus alea luditur, artes*, 2.471) – dice games being Martial's metaphor for composing the *Xenia* (13.1.7–8). Can it be, Ovid asks, referring to risqué mimes, that 'this type of writing is rendered safe by the stage to which it belongs?' (*an genus hoc scripti faciunt sua pulpita tutum?* 2.517). By bringing to life one of Ovid's 'safe' examples, Martial apparently does all he can to avoid Ovid's *carmen et error*.

However, as Ovid's cultivation of a *candidus lector* echoes weakly through the *Xenia*, Martial also shows us that during carnival time, there are no stable guarantees, that epigram must warily restrain its tongue and join the masses, even while it strains to free itself, and its readers, from the bounds of creative, social and political conventions. The Saturnalia, that winter festival of light, fertility and excess set in a season of gloom and disease, becomes the perfect arena for epigram to flex its core paradoxes, and to contemplate its relation to a 'golden' past. This oxymoronic book performs Domitian's Saturnalia as authorised licence, as constrained liberty, as a menu of delicious, disgusting cuisine. We could read the *Xenia* as a witty comment on the ironies of the *Saturnalia principis*, but not without some awareness of how implicated epigram is in imperial power games, how it re-creates for its readers the experience of being simultaneously let loose and inhibited. Both the casual, desultory reader and the critic who pores over every word and label are liable to be lampooned by this string of loaded *munera*: paradoxically, carnival licence ensures that it is difficult to escape the claustrophobic feeling of being watched, and laughed at. Through the Saturnalia, then, and through his readers, Martial in the *Xenia* finds new ways of showing off and testing out the relationship between book and city, poet and patron. The physical and temporal space of carnival is where the epigrams integrate most with *turbae* of party-goers, with the social dynamics that bring Rome to life: epigram has ambitions not only to commemorate and celebrate the Saturnalia, but also to make it, do it, become the party everyone remembers, and can come back to. Yet the conscious boundedness of Saturnalian licence, mirrored in epigram's own tight poetics, puts pressure on and satirises the pleasures of this full immersion. Epigram's totalising bid to *be* Rome, as we have been seeing throughout this book, is shot through with a competing sense of instability, risk and constraint.

## NERVA'S NEW AGE: BOOK II

In the second part of this chapter, I want to turn to the most patently 'Saturnalian' of Martial's numbered books, which is in many ways presented as Rome's, and epigram's, *real* carnival, a truly uninhibited tour de force after Domitian's 'forced' celebrations: Book 11. This collection was published in December 96, the same year as Nerva's accession. In other words, when we read the books as they are presented in numerical order, rather than according to publication date, Book 11 works as a kind of flashback after the ripple of Book 10 (edition two), published in 98 when Nerva had already died and his adopted son Trajan has taken his place as emperor. And indeed, in the spirit of Saturnalian nostalgia, Book 11 is all about contrasting present and past, reviving the 'golden ages' of Republican and Augustan Rome in a new age of liberality and sensible tolerance. In flicking backwards and forwards between Books 9, 10, 11 and 12, puzzling over the various metamorphoses that frame this period of political upheaval, we mime the movement (or the strain) between forward thinking and regression which characterises Books 10 and 11 in particular.[56] The ostensible idea in this book is that Nerva's reign, epitomised by as well as feted in his first Saturnalia, can unite (certain aspects of) different times, and iron out troubling paradoxes. So this will be the Republic all over again, with all the celebrity fathers of old (Camillus, Fabricius, Brutus, Sulla), yet without the conflict, without the resentment and civil war (see 11.5).[57] As Tacitus claims in his *Agricola*, 'from the very beginning of this happy era, Nerva has united things long incompatible, the principate and liberty' (*et quamquam primo statim beatissimi saeculi ortu Nerva Caesar res olim dissociabiles miscuerit, principatum ac libertatem, Agr.* 3). No longer shall Statius' '*Saturnalia principis*' seem a contradiction in terms. Coins of 96 celebrate the new *libertas publica*, and the words *libertas restituta* were inscribed on the Capitol on the very day of Nerva's accession, 18 September, echoed by Pliny in *Letters* 9.13.4, where he writes of 'restored liberty' after Domitian's murder (*ac primis quidem diebus redditae libertatis . . .*). And whereas, as we've seen, the *Xenia* is bound to disappoint readers hungry for dirty jokes and serious titillation, *Epigrams* 11 is easily the most risqué of Martial's productions: as Hinds discusses recently, most

---

[56] Although the Saturnalia is presented as a festival of nostalgia for the Golden Age of man, we are reminded that the myth of Saturn also involves symbolic distortions of time: Saturn eats the future in the form of his children and then regurgitates them.

[57] See Gowing (2005) on the memory of the Republic in Latin literature, esp. 102–31 on Flavian literature. Mentioning *Ep.* 11.5, and noting Martial's well-developed sense of the absurd here, Gowing suggests that the poem is typical of how references to the Republic appear less overtly political, more like window dressing, in later imperial literature (105–6).

of the instances of Martial's epigrammatic 'dirtying' or pornografication of Catullan and Ovidian erotic poetry are to be found here. Hinds even has the gall to suggest that this Priapic book veils a silent but irresistible pun on *Nerva* and *nervi* ('tendons', 'vigour', or 'penis').[58] So is this when Martial's *turba* of epigrams can truly be let loose to party, when epigram can finally burst out of its meagre confines, fearlessly encompass its imperial-urban landscape, and, in the eleventh book, make that last epic thrust to twelve-book greatness? Or is it all too late for that, especially as Martial is already an old man (*senex*, 10.96.2)?

Critics have generally discussed Book 11 in terms of what seems to be its distinguishing feature – 'epigrams of a very frank nature'[59] – and have stressed its 'unifying theme' of Saturnalian licence, writing without inhibitions. It's all here. As Fearnley sums it up, 'in this book Martial gives a representative list of topics typical of satire: adultery, pederasty, circumcision, masturbation, impotence, oral sex, ugly women, foul genitalia, frigidity, prostitution, nights of drunken revelry.'[60] Throughout the book, free poetic and political speech, associated with republican times, comes to be embodied in Catullus, in his 'impure mouth', 'oral' lyrics and numberless kisses.[61] Yet as I'll be stressing, it is also clear in Book 11 that it is not easy to revive the past while at the same time contrasting present and past – the book shows up just how messy and mixed up, as well as nuanced, the political (and poetic) strategy of modelling present on past, or integrating present with past, can be. Alongside the Catullan vibe of irreverent chatter and determined poetic autonomy, there is the strong sense, more than ever, that the imperial Saturnalia is a time of deft political manoeuvring and propaganda. The obscenity and let-it-all-out ethos of Martial's Nervan Saturnalia belies, to an extent, the poet's careful, step-by-step negotiation of his new position and opportunities in a period of immense change. There is much at stake here: he is still hoping for imperial patronage, and perhaps has more cause for optimism with Nerva, whom he lauds as 'the new Tibullus' at epigram 8.70. As I've hinted, the 'return' to AD 96 that we experience in reading Book 11 after Book 10 is in canny harmony with Nerva's politics of revival, and Martial drives this home in

---

[58] See Hinds (2007).   [59] Kay (1985) vii.   [60] Fearnley (2003) 623.

[61] Until Fitzgerald (2007) 167–86, the only extended treatment of Martial's use of Catullus, apart from Paukstadt's catalogue of references (1876) is Swann (1994, 1998), best read together with Batstone's critical review (1998). As I explore here, and as Fitzgerald has already stressed, there is much more to Martial's appropriation of Catullus than straightforward 'borrowing' from a fellow 'epigrammatist'. On numbers and innumerability in Catullus, see Henderson (1999b), and also Janan (1994) esp. 58–62, Newman (1990) 153.

his opening poems (*cum pia* **reddiderint** *Augustum numina terris,* 'since the pious gods have restored Augustus' divinity to earth', 11.3.9; *et qui purpureis iam tertia nomina fastis / Iane,* **refers** *Nervae,* 'and you Janus, who now bring back the name of Nerva to the purple annals for the third time', 11.4.5–6; *si* **redeant** *veteres . . . patres,* 'if the fathers of old were to return', 11.5.5; **revocatus** *. . . si Cato* **reddatur,** 'even if, recalled . . . Cato himself were to be returned to us', 11.5.13–14; *votis* **redditus** *ecce meis,* 'look, he is restored to my prayers', 11.36.2). Yet the concepts of return, revival and free expression are not straightforward or unrisky ones here, and the book reminds us of what has been lost to time, as well as of things which are uncomfortable or inconvenient to recall. Historical periods, and the literature belonging to them, live on in the imagination as nexuses of overlapping and incompatible associations that can be creatively encompassed in the disjointed order of a book of epigrams. *Epigrams* 11, like the *Xenia,* gestures towards all kinds of questions about the role and potential of Martial's poetry, and about how far epigram can, wants to, or should assert its expressive power under Nerva. Does the return of Saturnalian '*libertas*' in this book just amount to epigram's malleability, its ability to mould itself to any regime (epigram *is* Rome, whatever Rome wants to be . . .)? Does Martial dare, through Catullus, to revive a sense of resistance to social order?

The interacting components of Book 11 are engaged in the delicate balancing act of forging Nerva's, and Martial's, image. The new emperor is a reborn Augustus (11.3.9), a second Aeneas (11.4) – though at the same time Rome is of course still lacking an equivalent of Maecenas (11.3.10). *Otium,* meanwhile, looks like rather an anachronistic concept (as Martial puts it at 12.68.5–6, 'I am fond of leisure and sleep, which great Rome has denied me'), Vergil is long dead (his tomb tended only by Silius Italicus at 11.48 and 50), and the 'Venuses and Cupids' that are Lesbia's seductive perfume in Catullus are buried (*condita*) in 11.13.7–8 along with the once-gorgeous body of Paris, the *pantomimus* murdered by Domitian for apparently having an affair with his wife. Martial prays for Nerva's consulship with a 'pious mouth' (*ore pio,* 11.4.6), yet fills his book with the filthy gobs of Catullan fellators, while Nerva must be presented both as a progressive liberal (e.g. 11.2) and as a proponent of traditional Roman morality (under his rule, adulteress Paula 'can be Penelope', 11.7.5). The epigrammatist promises to give his boy 'Catullus' sparrow' in 11.6, setting an aggressive Phallic tone for the rest of the book, yet in 11.18 his new country property exhibits all the signs of a crudely comic programme for stingy, tight-lipped, Callimachean epigram: in this garden, after the giggling *libellus* at 11.15.3, figs don't have room to 'gape' (literally, 'to laugh', 11.18.16), suggestive cucumbers and snakes can't stretch out straight and erect (10–11), and there isn't space for even half a Priapus (*non est dimidio locus Priapo* 22).

Meanwhile, what is felt in Martial as an unstoppable intertextuality demonstrates the near impossibility of handpicking elements of the past without dredging up other ghosts. For example, Republican loudmouth Catullus, for whom the Saturnalia was famously 'the best of days',[62] may defy moralising officials with his uncountable *basia,* create an untouchable parody world of *otium,* of sex and/as poetry, yet for Martial, he must be read through the more recent past, not least (and not for the first time) through Ovid's 'mistaken' experiment in provocative, Saturnalian verse, and subsequent exile to the Black Sea. The first poem of the book, 11.1, begins with the much-borrowed trope of poet addressing personified book and sending it off to win over friendly readers, which is most familiar from Ovid's *Tristia*:[63]

> Quo tu, quo, liber otiose, tendis
> cultus Sidone non cotidiana?
> numquid Parthenium videre? certe:
> vadas et redeas inevolutus.
> libros non legit ille sed libellos;
> nec Musis vacat, aut suis vacaret.
> ecquid te satis aestimas beatum,
> contingunt tibi si manus minores?
> vicini pete porticum Quirini:
> turbam non habet otiosorem
> Pompeius vel Agenoris puella,
> vel primae dominus levis carinae.
> sunt illic duo tresve qui revolvant
> nostrarum tineas ineptiarum,
> sed cum sponsio fabulaeque lassae
> de Scorpo fuerint et Incitato.

> But where are you off to, lazy book,
> all dolled up in fancy purple?
> Is it to see Parthenius? Right:
> You'd go and come back unrolled.
> He doesn't read books, only *pamphlets*;

[62] Cat. 14.15.
[63] Horace *Epistles* 1.13 tells of a similar scenario: the poet instructs a messenger, Vinius, to carry a copy of his poems (probably the *Odes*) to Augustus, and jokily expresses anxieties about how the emperor will receive them. *Epistles* 1.20 also addresses a personified book, calling it (as in Martial's epigram) a *liber* in the first line.

He's no time for the Muses,
else he'd make time for his own.
Do you reckon you'll be satisfied
falling into lesser hands? Then
head for neighbour Quirinus' portico.
Not even Pompey, or Agenor's girl,
or the fickle captain of the first ship[64]
has a crowd lazier than this.
There are two or three there to unroll
the bookworms breeding in my versicles.
Though you'll have to wait till bets are closed
on Scorpus and Incitatus, and everyone's bored
of gossiping on the races.

Of course, Martial's epigram is in many ways a comic, Saturnalian inversion of Ovid's mournful *Tristia* 1.1: Ovid's slavish book wears the grey garb of exile, and purple covers are banned (*Tr.* 1.1.5–7), whilst Martial's book is all dressed up like a gent in Sunday-best 'Sidonian' and is deciding itself where it would like to go. Instead of trudging humbly to the Palatine to beg an audience with the emperor himself, this book is planning to swank off to Parthenius, Domitian's chamberlain who, according to Cassius Dio (67.17.1), played a key role in the last emperor's assassination. However, Martial predicts that it would 'go and return unrolled' (*vadas et redeas inevolutus*), suggesting a sort of acting out of the mental to-ing and fro-ing involved in remembering/forgetting Domitian in order to construct a contrasting present. This book will have to settle for a lesser audience – two or three guys who happen to be hanging out by the temple of Quirinus, who may possibly give it the time of day after they've finished betting on the races. Not for the first time, epigram hints slyly that, even if it wanted to, it is far too small and insignificant to offend. Ovid's self-deprecation in the exile poetry has nothing on Martial's.

The next poem, 11.2, begins with the word *triste*, another nod, perhaps, to the title of Ovid's letters from exile (except that in Martial, all 'gloominess' is definitely out), and ends with an allusion to *Tristia* 2.1. Lines 7–8:

lectores tetrici salebrosum ediscite Santram:
nil mihi vobiscum est: iste liber meus est.

You sour-faced readers learn jerky Santra off by heart:
I can't be bothered with you: this book is mine.

---

[64] References are respectively to the Porticus Pompeii, the Porticus Europae and the Porticus Argonautarum (the *levis dominus* is Jason, so called because of the way he treated Medea).

immediately evoke the opening phrase of *Tr.* 2.1[65] (typically – because after all, this is going to be another book that draws on the poetics of Catullan counting – Martial spans two books of Ovid in two short epigrams: 11.1 + 11.2 = *Tr.* 1.1 + 2.1):

> Quid mihi vobiscum est, infelix cura, libelli,
>    ingenio perii qui miser ipse meo?

> Why do I bother with you, little books, when you're a curse,
> and I'm a wretched casualty of my own artistic talent?

Here, then, Martial engineers another sharp reversal: whereas Ovid curses his verse for ruining his reputation and goes on to plead for clemency, Martial tells austere critics where to go, distancing himself from them, not from his book, with which he boldly identifies: *iste liber meus est.* In the ensuing 11.3, he again deflates the horrors and anxieties of Ovidian exile, boasting of how far we have come. The wild lands that were torture to banished Ovid are now easily encompassed and 'conquered' by Martial's bestselling books, which are 'thumbed by hard centurions alongside Mars' standards in Getic frosts' (*sed meus in Geticis ad Martia signa pruinis / a rigido teritur centurione liber,* 11.3.3–4).[66] Book 11 even suggests itself as a defence, or vindication, of the erroneous, 'Saturnalian' *carmen* that won Ovid a one-way ticket to the Black Sea. Poem 11.20 is a mocking exposure of Augustus' own naughty versicles, including an epigram which began something like: 'Because Antony fucks Glaphyra, Fulvia decided to punish me by making me fuck her as well' ('*quod futuit Glaphyran Antonius, hanc mihi poenam / Fulvia constituit, se quoque uti futuam,*' 11.20.3–4). As Casali stresses in a recent article, the *tristis* addressee of 11.20 (following on from the *triste supercilium* of 11.2.1) hints again at the *Tristia* and at the role of Augustus himself as harsh reader of Ovidian erotic poetry.[67] But Augustus *must* let Martial's witty little books off the hook, given that he too 'knows how to talk with Roman candour' (*qui scis Romana simplicitate loqui,* 10), an argument Ovid himself never used and presumably didn't dare to (just as Martial doesn't risk any overt *Nervi* puns), because it was too aggressive and inflammatory. Given that Martial spells out what Ovid could not, 11.20 can't help but remind us of the difference between addressing a dead emperor, and feeling one's way with a live, new one. Especially as 11.3 praises

---

[65] Compare Martial 2.22.1, which quotes *Tr.* 2.1.1, as I discussed in chapter 3.

[66] Compare also 11.53, a portrait of a chaste Roman matron who is actually a British lady, now fully integrated and a living symbol of how the empire has swallowed up and Romanised what a generation or two ago seemed exotic and mysteriously distant places.

[67] Casali (2005) 33–4. On 11.20 also see Fitzgerald (2007) 31.

Nerva directly as Augustus reborn, even while echoes of Ovid's banishment
and Augustus as punisher still linger from poems 1 and 2. Martial may be
a celebrity in the now not so far off lands of Ovidian exile, but this poem,
and the Saturnalia more generally, still want to take us back to the past,
and hint ever so obliquely at an unpredictable present. To what extent *will*
Nerva turn out to be a 'new Augustus'? This is carefree December, for
sure, and anything goes – but there are limits, and careful judgements to
be made, if not for now, then with future events and relationships in mind.

At the same time, the double-edged reference to Augustus' return in
11.3 mingles and competes with the blast from the past that is line 6 (*quid
prodest? nescit sacculus ista meus*, 'but what's the use? My purse knows
nothing of all that'), an allusion to Catullus' literal poverty and poetic
riches in Cat. 13, the dinner party invitation to Fabullus that also framed
the *Xenia*: Catullus' guest will only dine well if he brings the food, wine
and good humour himself, as the poet's 'purse is full of cobwebs' (*nam tui
Catulli plenus sacculus est aranearum*, Cat. 13.7–8). Throughout the book,
evocations of Catullus, and his defiance of moralising officials, pull against
what is constructed as a specifically post-Ovidian awareness of the political
risks of provocative poetry in imperial times. Epigram 11.15, and the line
'this little book does not have my morals' (*mores non habet hic meos libellus*,
13) will later recall Catullus' classic distinction between squeaky-clean poet
and sexed-up verses (16.5–6),[68] which Ovid reuses in a very different context
as part of his plea of innocence before Augustus in the *Tristia*.[69]

I want to look more closely now at the string of epigrams in Book 11
which blend Martial's cool take on the politics of (Republican) Catullan
and (imperial) Ovidian seductions, which often appear to be inseparable.
After the nod to Cat. 13 at 11.3, the phallic programme for Nerva's Saturnalia
is announced as explicitly (post-)Catullan at 11.6:

> Unctis falciferi senis diebus,
> regnator quibus inperat fritillus,
> versu ludere non laborioso
> permittis, puto, pilleata Roma.
> risisti; licet ergo, non vetamur.
> pallentes procul hinc abite curae;
> quidquid venerit obvium loquamur

---

[68] *Nam castum esse decet pium poetam / ipsum, versiculos nihil necesse est.*
[69] See *Tr.* 2.353–4: *crede mihi, distant mores a carmine nostri / vita verecunda est, Musa iocosa mea.*
Sullivan (1991) 106–7 remarks on the theme of the poet's apology for his work in the *Epigrams*, and
notes that this is a defence made by Ovid, who elaborates from Catullus. For Sullivan, 'Martial's
phrases stem rather from Ovid', yet one of the things Book 11 shows is just how bound up the two
defences, and these two poets, become in the epigrammatic imagination.

morosa sine cogitatione.
misce dimidios, puer, trientes,
quales Pythagoras dabat Neroni,
misce, Dindyme, sed frequentiores:
possum nil ego sobrius; bibenti
succurrent mihi quindecim poetae.
da nunc basia, sed Catulliana:
quae si tot fuerint quot ille dixit,
donabo tibi Passerem Catulli.

On the rich feast days of the old man with the Scythe,
over which the King of gambling rules,
I think you'll permit me, cap-clad Rome,
to have some fun with superficial poetry.
You smile: so I'm allowed then, not forbidden.
Away with you, pale-faced anxieties;
Whatever I encounter, let me speak of it –
no moody meditation.
Here boy, mix me halves, then thirds,
just like Pythagoras used to give to Nero;
Mix 'em, Dindymus, but keep 'em coming:
I'm useless when I'm sober; but when I've had a few
fifteen poets come to aid my inspiration.
Give me kisses, but make them Catullan.
If they're as many as he said there were,
I'll give *you* Catullus' sparrow.

Martial begins this poem by asking permission to indulge in some off-duty
versifying, and carefully measures the body language of Rome's response
before going ahead, even though he then resolves to open his mouth
without ever thinking about it (7–8): licence, in these times, is about
'not being forbidden' (*licet* = *[ergo] non vetamur*, 5). The mid-section
of the poem then trips along gaily to the tune of Catullus 5, the escapist
fantasy of countless kisses,[70] transformed in Martial into precisely measured
glasses of wine poured by Dindymus, which then fuel the demand for
real *basia Catulliana* in line 14. Yet whilst Catullan kisses in poems 5
and 7 were endless, an eternal foreplay, epigram's dirty version is not
interested in innumerability: the slave is ordered to serve wine in fractions
(*dimidios . . . trientes*), just like Nero's slave Pythagoras (which of course
is also the name of a very famous Greek mathematician); 'fifteen' is the
number chosen to indicate multiple inspirations at line 13 (*succurrent mihi
quindecim poetae*), and although Martial says he's operating without design

---

[70] Compare 11.6.9–11 with Cat. 7.7–9 (*da mi basia mille, deinde centum, / dein mille altera, dein secunda centum, / deinde usque altera mille, deinde centum . . .*).

(*sine cogitatione*, 8), his measured beginning and unsubtle weighing up of Dindymus' willingness to offer him much more than just kisses, speak otherwise.[71] Whereas the emphasis in Catullus 7 is on the uncertainty (*quot?* 'how many?' 1) of how many kisses are enough for the poet (answer: an infinity), Martial will settle for *tot* ('so many'), which all the time invite the graphic climax, the *ending*, of *Passer Catulli*.

Similarly, 11.26.3–6 is all for adding up, Catullan-style, but only if the end result is 'the *true* joys of Venus':

> basia da nobis vetulo, puer, uda Falerno,
>     pocula da labris facta minora tuis.
> addideris super haec Veneris si gaudia vera,
>     esse negem melius cum Ganymede Iovi.

> Give me kisses, boy, wet with old Falernian,
> give me cups made smaller by your lips.
> And if, above this, you add the proper joys of Venus,
> I'd say Jupiter had no better time with Ganymede.

Note also that in sharing a wine cup with his beloved in this epigram, Telesphorus' lips make the cup smaller (*minora*, 4), another hint at Martial's reining in of Catullus' mouthy expansiveness. As we saw in chapter 3, epigram's poetics ostensibly subtract and count down, more often than not.

After 11.7, which ponders whether adulterous Paula will change her habits under Nerva (she won't, she'll just be more honest about them), 11.8.11–14 returns to *basia Catulliana* in the shape, or smell, of a boyfriends' kisses. This is a well-developed motif in the Greek anthology, as well as reminding us of Catullus stealing a single ambrosia-scented kiss from Iuventius in poem 99:

> singula quid dicam? non sunt satis; omnia misce:
>     hoc fragrant pueri basia mane mei.
> scire cupis nomen? si propter basia, dicam.
>     iurasti. nimium scire, Sabine, cupis.

71 As C. Williams explains (2002b, 166–7), we're already thinking about far more than just kisses in line 10, when Martial asks for the kind of wine the emperor Nero received from his slaves. Pythagoras was no ordinary slave: ancient sources (e.g. Tac. *Ann.* 15.37.4, Dio 62.28.3) report that Nero got 'married' to a number of men, including the ex-slave Pythagoras, with the emperor, not the slave, playing the role of 'bride'. As Williams puts it (167), 'to a Roman readership familiar with this gossip, the image of the bridegroom Pythagoras "giving" something to Nero would have been quite piquant, particularly in view of the euphemistic use of the verb *dare* to signify the bestowal of sexual favours . . .' Williams reads this line in 11.6 as metaphorical (Dindymus is capable of giving Martial 'poetic inspiration' for his phallic epigrams), though Martial also seems to be flirting here with a quasi-Catullan vacillation between active and passive roles, as explored by Fitzgerald (1995, *passim*).

Why pin things down to this or that? They're not enough – blend all together,
and then you'll get the perfume of my boy's morning kisses.
You want to know his name? If it's because of the kisses, I'll tell.
You swear it. You want to know too much, Sabinus.

The allegories Martial can offer for the sweet scent of his boy's kisses are
individually not enough (*non sunt satis* 11), answering Catullus 7's *quaeris
quot sint satis,* and so are to be mixed together (*omnia misce* 11) in the manner
of 11.6's cocktails, which lead us back to the *basia Catulliana* of that poem.
11.8 also performs another kind of (epigrammatic) blending, mixing up
'endless' Catullan eroticism with Ovid's sexiest poem, *Amores* 1.5.[72] The
line *singula quid dicam?* almost repeats Ovid's *singula quid referam?* in the
following well-known passage (*Amores* 1.5.23–6):

> singula quid referam? nil non laudabile vidi
> et nudam pressi corpus ad usque meum.
> cetera quis nescit? lassi requievimus ambo.
> proveniant medii sic mihi saepe dies.
>
> Why spell out the details? I saw nothing I could not praise,
> and pressed her naked body onto mine.
> Who doesn't know the rest? We both lay back, exhausted.
> Here's hoping for many more such afternoons.

In posing this question, Martial in some ways recaptures the erotic tension of Ovid's poem, and spices up his account of his boy's kisses with
the memory of something more, the thing that leaves Ovid and his girl
exhausted in bed in the middle of the afternoon. When Martial then asks
his curious reader Sabinus whether he wants to know the boy's name (13),
only to swiftly withdraw the offer, he mimics the power games and seduction strategies of both *Amores* 1.5 and Catullus 5 and 7: we are allowed
a peep into the poet's private boudoir, and are teased by the promise of
revelation, only to have the door shut in our faces. The poem speaks of
insatiability, makes Sabinus desire in excess. At the same time, we might say
that this is a very tame poem compared to Corinna's glimpsed undressing
in *Amores* 1.5, and contains none of the passion and pain of Catullus 48
and 99, about Iuventius' sweet kisses. We get not even a fleeting look at
this boy's body, and the analogies for the scent of his kisses in lines 1–10 all
concern things that can be smelt, often from a distance, not touched and

---

[72] Note that *Ep.* 12.44.5–6 also, more directly, mixes up couples Lesbia–Catullus and Corinna–Ovid in
the same couplet (*Lesbia cum lepido te posset amare Catullo, / te post Nasonem blanda Corinna sequi*,
'Lesbia could have loved you along with witty Catullus, seductive Corinna might have pursued you
after Naso').

tasted with the mouth, unlike Iuventius' kiss in Catullus 99 (*dulci dulcius ambrosia*, 'sweeter than sweet ambrosia'). Martial's ideal kisses smell faded and far away, a bit like Catullan verse itself (perfume of 'tired' balsam in yesterday's vases in line 1, apples ripening in boxes, and so not yet edible, in line 3, a broken jar of expensive wine, yet far off, *longe*, in line 7). And whereas the *singula* flashes of Corinna's body were suggestive in *Amores* 1.5, leading on to sex scenes whose only limit is in readers' imaginations, in Martial the *singula* similes in lines 1–10 will simply be added together to make a satisfying whole, the singular *hoc* of line 12. In more ways than one, Martial assembles lots of ones, then mixes them together to make a single whole, in direct contrast to Catullus, who as we know always counts big – in hundreds and thousands, even hundreds of thousands in poem 48.

While it's undoubtedly the case, as Hinds stresses, that Book 11 often appears to be more graphic, consciously 'dirtier' than many of the erotic poems it incorporates, epigram's lowered tone often seems to come at the expense of seductiveness, and demands near-instant, measurable satisfaction. While Corinna seduces Ovid in the half light with her suggestively draped tunic in *Amores* 1.5, Martial's wife in 11.104 has no such luck: she overdoes the shyness, and he wants the lamps blazing and full nudity, quick (*at mihi nulla satis nuda puella iacet*, 'no girl lies naked enough for me,' 8). Ironically, being more 'loose-mouthed' involves imposing restrictions, bringing arousal to an end-point. Is being explicit a turn-off after all? we're left asking; is pornography ever erotic? There are two especially salient examples in Book 11 where hard-core language later becomes (or is held up to be?) disgusting: in 11.16, Martial advertises the arousing naughtiness of his book by saying that even a girl from Patavium (a town with a reputation for strict morals) will get 'soaking wet' (*uda*, 8) when she reads his *lusus*. But a few poems later, the obscene 11.21 paints a gross portrait of Lydia, whose vagina is so slack it is like 'an old shoe soaked in muddy water' (*vetus a crassa calceus **udus** aqua*, 4): here, the vocabulary of moistness is meant to express and evoke revulsion, and represents the very antithesis of sexual pleasure. The epigram ends: *hanc in piscina dicor futuisse marina. / nescio; piscinam me futuisse puto.* / 'I'm said to have fucked her in a marine fish-pond. Don't know about that: I think I fucked the fishpond' (11.21.11–12). Martial pulls a similar trick with the word *ulcus* in 11.60 and 11.98: first of all, 11.60 sets the scene with up-for-it Phlogis, every red-blooded male's fantasy fuck, minus the good body. For Phlogis has the *ulcus*, 'the itch', such that could rejuvenate ancient Priam and Pelias, an itch 'all men want

their girl to have' (5).[73] As if to emphasise her insatiability, Martial can't
repeat *ulcus* enough (it appears four times in twelve lines). Yet in the tirade
of 11.98, the same word means 'ulcer', of the nauseating type that afflicts
the menacing 'kissers' of Rome:

> Effugere non est, Flacce, basiatores.
> instant, morantur, persecuntur, occurrunt
> et hinc et illinc, usquequaque, quacumque.
> non **ulcus** acre pusulaeve lucentes,
> nec triste mentum sordidique lichenes,
> nec labra pingui delibuta cerato,
> nec congelati gutta proderit nasi.
> et aestuantem basiant et algentem,
> et nuptiale basium reservantem.
> non te cucullis adseret caput tectum,
> lectica nec te tuta pelle veloque,
> nec vindicabit sella saepius clusa:
> rimas per omnis basiator intrabit.
> non consulatus ipse, non tribunatus
> senive fasces nec superba clamosi
> lictoris abiget virga basiatorem:
> sedeas in alto tu licet tribunali
> et e curuli iura gentibus reddas,
> ascendet illa basiator atque illa.
> febricitantem basiabit et flentem,
> dabit oscitanti basium natantique,
> dabit cacanti. remedium mali solum est,
> facias amicum basiare quem nolis.

> Escaping kissers, Flaccus, is impossible.
> They push, they cling, they stalk you and bump into you,
> this side, that side, anywhere and everywhere.
> A weeping ulcer, shiny zits, a rotting chin, or
> filthy scabs or lips smeared thick with oily wax,
> or snot dripping from a frozen nose –
> absolutely nothing will get you off the hook.
> They'll kiss you when you're sweating in the
> heat, or shivering with cold, or when you're
> keeping a kiss for your new bride.
> Pulling a hood over your head won't set you free,
> nor will a litter screened by leather and veil,
> or a sedan chair barricaded for your privacy.

---

[73] The use of *ulcus* to mean what Martial has it mean here, a kind of perverse sexual insatiability, seems
to be rare in Latin (*OLD ulcus* 2 lists only this instance). The word usually means a sore or ulcer.

Not the consulship itself, nor the tribunate or six *fasces*,[74]
nor the proud rod of the loud-mouthed lictor
can drive away the kisser.
If you sit on a high tribunal and judge whole nations
from your curule chair, the kisser
will find a way to get to you.
He'll kiss you when you're feverish or weeping,
he'll kiss you when you're yawning, when you're swimming,
when you're taking a shit. The only cure for this malaise?
Befriend a man you would not wish to kiss.

The way in which the word *ulcus* and its different usages (genital itch, facial sore) link these two epigrams itself re-enacts the disturbing contact between mouth and genitals behind the punchline to 11.98,[75] the lengthiest in a series of poems in Book 11 centred on the disgust aroused in encountering the mouths of those who have indulged in oral sex (see especially 11.30, 61, 95, and more generally 11.25, 40, 46, 85). In this culminating epigram, the playful staccato rhythms of Catullan erotics morph into the incessant jabbing of Martial's filthy social kisser: compare for example Catullus' hopping sparrow (*sed circumsiliens modo huc modo illuc*, 3.9), and his endless demands for kisses (*da mi basia mille, deinde centum, / dein mille altera, dein secunda centum, / deinde usque altera mille, deinde centum . . .* 5.7–9) with Martial's *occurrunt / et hinc et illinc* (11.98.3), and his *febricitantem basiabit et flentem, / dabit oscitanti basium natantique, / dabit cacanti* (11.98.20–2). Whilst Catullus creates an escapist parody world where there are no borders and rules, where the delicious foreplay of kissing can go on forever, in Martial's Rome there is no escape or refuge from public spaces inhabited by men you would do anything to avoid touching with your mouth.[76]

Needless to say, the contamination of mouth with genitals ('pure' with 'dirty') is ever-present in Roman obscenity, not least in Catullus:[77] we think for instance of poem 97 (where Aemilius' mouth is less clean than his arse), 39 (where Egnatius brushes his teeth with urine), or the many threats of

---

[74] I.e. the six lictors who carried rods and axes for a praetor.

[75] The idea in the last line of 11.98, as Shackleton Bailey explains (1993, *ad loc.*), seems to be that the only way to avoid these kissers is to make friends with a *fellator*. As a favour to you he will then kiss back anyone who kisses you, and they will be so repulsed that in future they will leave you alone. See Henderson (1999b) 286 n. 55 on Cat. 97.2 and *osculum* ('kiss') as *os* + *culus* (mouth-arse).

[76] On the soiling effect of kisses, also see e.g. 6.66 (here Martial tells the story of how Gellianus kissed his slave-girl on the sale platform in an attempt to increase bidding. It had the opposite effect – she was now implicitly soiled merchandise – and all cash offers were swiftly withdrawn), and 10.22 (Martial goes out with a plaster on his chin and his lips painted white with lead to look as if he's (already) diseased, in order to avoid being kissed), cf. 7.95.

[77] See discussion in Fitzgerald (1995) 63–72, Richlin (1992) 144–56, and Dupont (1999) 141ff.

oral rape designed to silence Catullus' enemies (e.g. 28, 37, 74). Yet Martial hypes up these anxieties, and fills every corner of his city with the threat of pollution, brought alive in sordid poetic interactions. Excessive lust and aggressive moves (he wants his wife to be a Lais, or prostitute, in the bedroom in 11.104, he will fuck lovers and enemies alike in 11.6 and 11.58) appear nostalgic and in constant competition with their denial: his wife won't let him sodomise (*pedicare negas*, 11.104.17), echoing Catullus' self-defining *pedicabo vos* at Catullus 16, and Flaccus (like Martial himself in the similar 12.59[78]) is enslaved to Rome's kissers in 11.98.[79] It is difficult, too, not to bring the epitaph to Canace at 11.91 into this discussion.[80] Canace is a seven-year-old girl who has died of a hideous facial rot that 'settled on her tender mouth and ate her very kisses' (*horrida vultus / apstulit et tenero sedit in ore lues, / ipsaque crudeles ederunt oscula morbi*, 11.91.5–7).[81] Even an innocent child is not immune from the perversion of and clampdown on *basia Catulliana* that runs like a plague throughout this book:[82] this slave-girl is no more immune to disease than the 'enslaved' Flaccus in 11.98, even during the Saturnalia, when slaves are meant to be free. And whereas the kissing Catullus, as critics have often emphasised,[83] is also the lyric, *talking* Catullus, the oral 'corruption' (*lues*) that afflicts Canace and her kisses also 'closes down the channel of her sweet voice' (11), so that she cannot even beg the fates for mercy.[84]

Throughout the book, too, the use of the word *satis* continues to revive Lesbia's question in Catullus 7, *Quaeris, quot mihi basiationes / tuae, Lesbia, sint satis superque?* ('you ask, Lesbia, how many kisses are enough and more than enough for me?'), as well as Catullus' answer. But Martial's reply is consistently different to that of his insatiable predecessor: he's on the other side of the fence in 11.22, when he watches his boyfriend 'rub snow-white Galaesus' soft kisses' with his 'hard mouth', and 'lie with naked Ganymede', and declares it excessive: *hoc nimium est. sed sit satis* ('it's too much. But

---

[78] In 12.59, the idea that Rome's dirty kisses are Catullan is spelt out more literally. See lines 1–3: 'Rome gives you a quantity of kisses, now that you've returned after fifteen years, such as Lesbia never gave Catullus.'

[79] Note especially the use of the verb *adserere* in line 10 of this poem, meaning 'to free a slave' (*non te cucullis adseret caput tectum*).

[80] See also Fitzgerald (2007) 128–9, on the interesting juxtaposition of 11.90 and 11.91.

[81] Kay (1985 *ad loc.*) conjectures that Canace died of *noma* or *cancrum oris*, 'a gangrenous condition which occurs in poorly fed children and tends to complicate debilitating infections like TB'.

[82] Perhaps the reference here to kisses being 'eaten' (line 7) also makes us think back to Catullus' '*vale puella*' poem, where he reminisces about Lesbia 'biting' his lips (*cui labella mordebis?* 9.18).

[83] See e.g. Fitzgerald (1995) esp. 10–11, Henderson (1999b).

[84] In a strange repetition/reversal of this idea, in 11.102 Lydia is told to shut up because when she opens her mouth she 'spoils' her 'flesh' (*sed quotiens loqueris, carnem quoque, Lydia, perdis*, 5).

let it stop there'). At 11.41, Amyntas is guilty of overfeeding his animals (*indulget pecori nimium*, 1), a seasonal 'crime' for this Saturnalian book (the festival revolved around feasting and overeating), and kills himself by falling from the apple tree whose fruits he is shaking down: it would have been 'enough' (*satis*, 8) for him to just count his herd (*annumerare pecus*, 8), Martial comments, rather than being obsessed with fattening them up. We might also look at 11.52, the book's longest parody of Catullus 13, the dinner invitation to Fabullus:[85] Martial's opening promise, *Cenabis belle* ('you'll dine in style,' 11.52.1), immediately recalls the tune of *Cenabis bene* (Cat. 13.1). Yet the poem imagines the opposite of Catullus' sexy feast of witty poetry, laughter and gorgeous girls. Instead, there will be plenty of food, and a menu of *hors d'oeuvres* is listed in full (lettuce, sliced leeks, fish garnished with eggs and herbs, roasted eggs, cheese, and fancy Picene olives, 5–11).[86] As Kay notes, these dishes have all the humility (and we might add, sexlessness) of the spread offered up by rustic Baucis and Philemon in Ovid *Metamorphoses* 8.[87] When he has talked 'quite enough' of starters (*haec satis in gustu*, 12), Martial asks, *cetera nosse cupis?* ('do you want to know the rest?'), another distinctive nod, after 11.8, to the titillations of *Amores* 1.5.25: *cetera quis nescit?* ('Who doesn't know the rest?'), referring to Ovid's afternoon romp with Corinna, all the more exciting for being evoked, not described. In 11.52, however, not only is this dinner conspicuously devoid of sex, *puellae*, even noeteric poetry (Martial promises to sit through Julius' epic 'Giants', and recite nothing of his own verse), but all delicacies are spelt out, even though they may not exist (*mentiar, ut venias*, 'I'll say anything to make you come,' 13). Ovid gives us the starters, and leaves us to fill in the rest, but Martial has no qualms about fabricating the main courses, too. He sets boundaries, where Catullus overrides them. As a result, Book 11 is itself frustrating, as the end poem indicates, never enough for readers, who ask for more:[88] in the imagined exchange that follows, they are required to pay up if they want the poet

---

[85] Also see discussion in Fitzgerald (2007) 173–4: particularly interesting is the point that while Catullus draws on the language of aristocratic social relations to characterise his love affair with Lesbia, Martial returns these poems to the sphere of *amicitia*, as 11.52 exemplifies.

[86] Many of these are foods offered in the *Xenia*, which also plays on Cat. 13, arguably minus the seduction (lettuce at 13.14, sliced leeks at 13.18, Velabran smoked cheese at 13.32, Picene olives at 13.36).

[87] See Kay (1985) *ad loc.* Line 9 seems to allude to *Met.* 8.667, and the word *coacta* in line 10 picks up *Met.* 8.666.

[88] As Fitzgerald puts it in his discussion of Catullus (1995, 54), 'the innumerability topos is as much an expression of the fact that the audience can never quite be satisfied as it is of the boundlessness of Catullus' love for Lesbia.'

to continue, and when they don't, he cuts off contact by bidding them a gruff 'farewell' (*lector, solve. taces dissimulasque? vale*, 11.108.4).

This Saturnalian book makes us long for euphemism, for the freedom to imagine, while at the same time dampening and shutting down the fantasy that is evoked so often in the shape and scent of Corinna, Lesbia and Iuventius, in the irreducibility of *basia Catulliana*. So in 11.23, whilst Martial's boy slave will give him *lasciva basia* in front of Sila, if he marries her she will give him kisses only rarely, and only on request, in the manner not of a bride but of an elderly mother: *oscula rara dabis nobis et non dabis ultro, / nec quasi nupta dabis sed quasi mater anus* (11.23.13–14). Catullus' '*da mi basia mille*', and on and on to infinity, is turned on its head – and we can always say that this is all part of Saturnalian fun. In 11.24, following on from this, Martial complains that garrulous talk is in direct competition with his written books: the more he is forced to chat with Labullus, the less he writes, so that whilst Catullus, we recall, counted his verses, like his kisses, by the thousands (see e.g. Cat. 22), Martial has just a few books (*ut tibi tuorum / sit maior numerus togatulorum, / librorum mihi sit minor meorum?* 'so that the number of your little clients be larger, should the number of my books be smaller?' 11.24.10–12). At 11.97, similarly, his sexual boasting doesn't make it into double figures ('I can do it four times in one night, but I'm damned if I can do you once in four years, Telesilla').[89] In this literary climate, where Catullan and Augustan *otium* is but a distant dream, the epigrammatist can't afford to count in enormous numbers, and reckons every minute, every penny.[90]

Epigram 11.29 parodies Catullan enumeration in a slightly different way:

> Languida cum vetula tractare virilia dextra
>     coepisti, iugulor pollice, Phylli, tuo.
> iam cum me murem, cum me tua lumina dicis,
>     horis me refici vix puto posse decem.
> blanditias nescis: 'dabo' dic 'tibi milia centum
>     et dabo Setini iugera certa soli;
> accipe vina, domum, pueros, chrysendeta, mensas.'
>     nil opus est digitis: sic mihi, Phylli, frica.

> When you begin to maul my flaccid manhood with your
> ancient hand, Phyllis, I am slaughtered by your thumb.

---

[89] Compare fuck-counting in *AP* 11.30 (Philodemus): 'Yes, my dear Aphrodite, I who used to be able to do it five and nine times can hardly manage it once from dusk to dawn . . .' Cairns (1973) makes the link between this kind of enumeration (an 'Alexandrian theme') and Catullan kiss-counting.

[90] See also 11.36.7 (Martial counts to five, six, eight, not in hundreds and thousands); and cf. the limited number of kisses he wants (or doesn't want) in 9.93 or 2.10.

And when you call me your 'mouse', or 'light of my eyes',
I think I'll need ten hours plus recovery time.
You've no clue about seduction: say, 'I'll give you a 100K
and some reliable acres of Setine soil;
take wine, a house, some slaves, a dinner service, tables.'
No need for fingers: just rub me up the right way, Phyllis.

As Hinds discusses, Martial engages here in a rich dialogue with Ovid's
*Ars Amatoria*, from which the charmless Phyllis has failed to learn: she
knows nothing of the art of seduction (*blanditias nescis*, 5; cf. *nec blandae
voces iucundaque murmura cessent*, 'keep up the seductive whispers and
pleasing groans,' *Ars* 3.795), even though she tries hard to pull off the
manual stimulation Ovid recommends at the famously saucy finale to
*Ars* 2 (see 2.705–8). Neither Ovidian foreplay nor Catullan numbers are
working for Martial; the only thing that turns him on, and identifies him
in the process with the malicious, sexless accountants of Catullus 5 and 7,
will be promises of 'hundreds of thousands' in cash (5–6).[91] His parting
comment, *nil opus est digitis* (8), quotes two Ovid poems in one: *Ars* 1.137,
where he tells lovers they have no need for sign language when they can
signal across the table with nods and winks, and *Amores* 1.11.23, where he
tells Nape that Corinna need not tire her fingers by writing a whole letter,
just the instruction '*Veni!*' 'Come!' (recalled here, this instruction reads
neatly as an advertisement for epigram, whose motto is always 'why use
ten words, when one will do?'). According to Martial, then, who writes
over both these innocent references with the masturbation scenes of *Ars* 2,
there can be no talk of fingering that isn't rude. Yet the joke is also that
he adds one more (*non*-sexual) meaning to the phrase *nil opus est digitis*,
imagines one more (*non*-sexual) use of fingers: counting. Phyllis will be so
generous with her darling Martial that she'll not bother counting in small
amounts, using her fingers, only in sums so enormous they don't mean
much at all. Finally, he implies, he has found a way to profit from Catullan
innumerability.

　　At the same time, this epigram's pointed last line is a classic example of epigrammatic hyperallusivity, the packing in of multiple allusions,

---

[91] If we flick forward for a moment to 11.39, we find counting associated again with moralising elders
out to stop Martial's fun. This is the epigram about Charidemus, Martial's guardian who still won't
allow him to 'play' or 'love', and counts his drinks with a disapproving look, even though his boy is
now a grown man (see esp. line 13: *et numeras nostros adstricta fronte trientes*). Counting money is
also the subject of 11.62 (*cum futui vult, numerare solet*, 2), and large numbers are used for cash not
kisses at 11.70.1 and 11.76.

meanings and/or puns into one word or phrase, in a way that gets readers counting, and performs the many-as-oneness at the heart of Martial's
imperial poetics. Indeed, Catullus has already shown what a kick can be
got out of summing up many as one (see Cat. 5, *rumores senum seve-*
*riorum / omnes unius aestimemus assis!* 'Let's value at one penny all the
mutterings of stern old men!'), a technique Martial rehearses in 11.31, in
his exposure of cheap host Caecilius: guests are served 'so many' (*tot*,
21) courses at a banquet, yet all the food is actually made out of pump-
kin, cut into *mille partes* ('a thousand pieces', 3) which cost Caecilius
around 'one penny' (*unum assem*, 21). In 11.35, similarly (though here the
tables are turned) 300 guests at Fabullus' dinner party leave Martial feeling all alone, as he knows none of them (the name Fabullus, and the
number 300, evoke many Catullan poems in one four-line epigram).[92]
Almost by definition, as we saw at length in chapter 3, epigram must cram
large numbers into small spaces, work the ingenious paradox of less as
more.

It is this paradox, we have seen, which is also one of the defining features
of Martial's Saturnalia. What begins as a triumphant collection bent on
throwing out all that is *tristis* and putting liberality back into the epigram
*liber,* has become, in the reading, a difficult mixed bag that tests out the
*politics* of poetic miscellany. Martial's vibrant intertextual energy stirs up
contradictions at every turn, not least in a book which performs a tricky
juggling of past and present, remembering and forgetting, freedom and
restriction, satisfaction and frustration, excess and limit, showing us in the
process just how far those 'separate' elements are commingled, as much in
the jumbled-neat epigram book as in the Roman imagination. We've seen
how Martial buries Catullus and writes *basia Catulliana* to death whilst
also reviving, to a point, his ambitious orality, snappy wit and ever-shifting
position.[93] Similarly, we've looked at how he dredges up Ovidian longing,
and exile, whilst at the same time stamping out seduction and slipping
cannily between emperors' jaws, past and present. As we saw in 11.29, it's
not simply the case that Book 11 is a culminating exercise in exposing
'the coy language of erotic elegy to sexualisation':[94] it does often stain and
degrade, for sure, but as the phrase *nil opus est digitis* (11.29.8) exemplifies,
in the way it condenses allusions to writing, sex and counting, there is

---

[92] For Fabullus, see the invitation at Cat. 13; for '300' see Cat. 9 (Veraniolus is the best of 300 friends),
Cat. 11 (Lesbia can fuck 300 lovers), Cat. 12 (Catullus will send 300 hendecasyllables as a punishment)
and Cat. 48 (300 kisses).
[93] On the latter see especially Fitzgerald (1995).     [94] Hinds (2007).

always *more*. As ever, Martial makes it very difficult for us to neatly sum up his literary and political strategies. In a city in which all space for manoeuvre has been eradicated, especially during the social season, where foul-mouthed *basiatores* lurk on every corner, epigram manages both to represent Rome in all its dazzling, suffocating variety, and to offer readers a parallel world that is even more intense.

CHAPTER 5

# *The space of epigram*

*si tibi mens eadem, si nostri mutua cura est,*
*in quocumque loco Roma duobus erit.*

*Ep.* 10.13.9–10

In each chapter of this book, we have touched on the importance of the conception of space to Martial's poetic-global vision. These 'little' poems, and 'little' books (*libelli*) often boast of only occupying tiny spaces – which is presented partly as neo-Callimachean skill, and partly as a socially determined necessity that turns Callimachean aesthetics on its head: Martial's books are no less likely to present themselves as shoddy, unpolished scraps than as finely spun or filigreed creations. Moreover, spatially aware poetics appear to emerge from, and merge with, the 'realities' of the poet's existence and of life on the streets of Rome: pinched poems are composed in snippets of time, in cramped apartments, in a suffocating metropolis packed to bursting point with people – most willing to trample over one another to get what they want and go where they want to go. The *Epigrams* are born out of this vision of the Flavian city and its vicious, intense sociality; the books of upwards of 89 poems each are continually enacting, and become inseparable from, the buzz and webs of interaction that constitute modern Rome. I have also suggested that the playful and original way in which Martial tests out the relationship between poetry and city, private and public, imagination and the 'real' constantly invokes the paradoxes at the core of his aesthetic. As we've seen from various starting points in all the chapters so far, one of Martial's most obvious poetic strategies is to exploit the subjectivity and malleability of perception – of space, time and measures. He is the first poet, and certainly the first Roman poet, to concentrate exclusively on epigram and use it to build up a massive, monumental opus (12 books, and then some). He shows us how this diminutive, casual, throwaway poetic form, which nevertheless was originally meant to be carved onto stone and last forever, can become the (post-Ovidian,

181

and we're almost tempted to say *postmodern*) epic of its time, yet still be neat enough to be held in our hands, light enough to slip through our fingers. By experimenting in how far poetry can become material and fully immersed in the 'real life' of a city, Martial captures a Rome in minia-ture, an oxymoronic microcosm of monumental spaces made tight and constraining. At the same time he visualises the most minute and humble of poetic forms expanding to fill and become the greatest city on earth. Though – as I discussed in chapter 4 – this poetic expansionism is itself double-edged, and by no means drained of all anxieties, or regrets.

In this final chapter, I want to examine Martial's shifting and paradoxical figuring of space more directly, pulling together and filling out points I have picked up through the book. In particular, we will discuss in detail how the trope of exile is used in the epigrams, and look at what happens when, at various points in the twelve numbered books, the poet or his addressees leave Rome, and write or receive epigrams in places from which the city, the empire, and the writing of poetry, are perceived differently. This urbanocentric verse is constantly testing the relationship between Rome and 'outside-Rome' or 'not-Rome', offering a new, layered vision of imperial pastoral, and of the binaries inside/outside, town/country, centre/periphery which obsess the Roman poetic imagination.

## GOING PLACES

By the time Martial is writing, the idea of poem as journey is a much-worked metaphor, as is the trope of the personified poetry book leaving its master's study and being 'sent out' into the world as his representative (see especially Horace *Epistles* 1.20 and Ovid *Tristia* 1.1 and 3.1).[1] Yet never before has poetry been so *mobile*. Partly because of the convenience of the codex, and partly because epigram presents itself as the ultimate in light entertainment, Martial's poems really can go places. A *festinatus libellus* can be up and dressed, or only half-dressed but ready to leave, in no time at all. This speediness is implicitly what lets Book 8 head off on the tail of magistrate Arcanus, who is returning to his job in Narbo Paterna (now Narbonne), the capital of Gallia Narbonensis, in 8.72: in one of Martial's many flippant turn-arounds of Catullus' opening poem (all hairless and

---

[1] As Hinds suggests (2007), 'the *Tristia* stand among Martial's most significant intertexts . . . Martial's books are programmatically obsessed, especially in their openings and closings, with the book poetics of Ovid's exile, and especially with the personifications of the book in the balancing *Tristia* prefaces 1.1 and 3.1.' Also see Casali (2005) 19–36.

oiled up for our pleasure), this collection is *nondum murice cultus asperoque /
morsu pumicis aridi politus* / 'not yet decked in purple and polished by the
bite of dry pumice' (8.72.1–2), and has to move 'in a hurry' (*properas*, 3).

As well as weaving its way like a pro through the topography of Rome
(a handful of poems warp the model of Ovid's exilic begging letters navi-
gating the route to Augustus' palace on the Palatine in *Tristia* 1.1²), the
epigrams can go *ubicumque*, 'anywhere' (1.2.1), and *ubique*, 'everywhere'
(8.3.4), thanks to their portability and international fanbase of readers.
Martial is forever boasting that his books are thumbed worldwide, even
in the farthest, and until recently undiscovered, reaches of the empire:
they are pored over like dirty mags³ by homesick centurions in 'Getic
frosts',⁴ and sung by native Britons in 11.3; 'everyone' (old man, young
man, boy, even chaste young woman in front of her conservative husband)
reads him in Vienne, he hears in 7.88. Book 7 has itself just been shipped
off to 'Getic Peuce and prostrate Hister' (*ad Geticam Puecen Histrumque
iacentem*, 7.84.3), areas of Germany recently subjugated by Domitian in the
Sarmatian expedition of AD 92, which is celebrated at the start of *Epigrams*
7. In 8.61 he is 'scattered through all the nations under Rome's dominion'
(*spargor per omnes Roma quas tenet gentes*, 5), an image which captures both
the crumbling fragmentariness of Martial's bitty little books, and the sense
in which market-dominating epigram allies itself with and operates as a
tool for imperial conquest and Romanisation.

Just as a book (after Ovid's exile) can embody its author, in Martial poems
and books are fused, metaphorically and literally, with their thousands of
readers – clasped to chests, hugging hips and thighs in pockets (*haec sunt,
singula quae sinu ferebas / per convivia cuncta, per theatra*, 'these are what
you used to carry in your lap one at a time to every dinner party, every
theatre,' 2.6.7–8), and allowing Rome's bestselling poet not just to travel
the globe, but to be in multiple places simultaneously. This is epigram's
idiosyncratic, 'real-life' version of the Ennian ambition to 'live on in the
mouths of men' that reverberates through much of Latin poetry. It is also
just one of the ways in which epigram transcends its own distinctive poetics
of closure: the marked 'end' of Book 4, for example, a collection which 'was
already finished even on page one' (4.89.6), strains like an animal to keep
unrolling, galloping on and on to infinity and forcing the copyist to pull

---

² See e.g. 1.70, 5.6, 5.22, 10.20, 11.1.
³ I'm referring to the innuendo in 11.3.4: *a rigido teritur centurione liber.*
⁴ The adjective *geticus* is immediately evocative of Ovid's exile in Tomis, 'land of the Getae' (see e.g.
   *Ex Ponto* 1.7.2, 1.8.6).

on the reins: *tu procedere adhuc et ire quaeris, / nec summa potes in schida teneri*, 'you want to go further and keep going, there's no holding you at the final sheet' (4.89.3–4).

Martial makes us very aware that he is out to realise Ovid's dream in the epilogue to the *Metamorphoses* – to be read wherever Roman dominion extends. Yet as we saw in chapter 2, whereas the Augustan poets fantasise about fame after death, an existence beyond the spatial and temporal limits of the poet's person, the *Epigrams* visualise this achievement in the here and now, concretise the dream and space of empire in the present. In this, as we've also seen, Martial is much influenced by Ovid's conceptualisation of exile as a living death, as a means to imagine beyond the mortal frame, beyond Rome, and even beyond the boundaries of *imperium*. Yet while for Ovid, as Hardie puts it, 'the expectation of fame' and 'the power of the poet to transcend the limits that constrain the real world' are transmuted into 'a desperate desire to realise an epistolary presence in Rome',[5] in Martial, Rome is a much more flexible, moveable and inclusive concept, and the epigrams make mischief messing with what in retrospect appears as the limiting, almost unimaginative directionality of Ovidian ambition. Ovidian exile (which itself absorbs other literary endeavours from exile, not least Cicero's) frames every imperial move to send fleshy poetry books over long distances, from foreign places. What Martial does, in the course of (what amounts in the end to) his massive lifework, is to take the idea of that journey and to apply to it all the liberating genius and wit of epigrammatic miscellany – so that it splits, bends back, loosens up, loops the loop, is stretched and shrunk.[6]

He experiments, for example, in role-reversal: in Book 7, it is (provocatively?) the poet stationed in Rome who calls for and then celebrates Domitian's return from his campaign against the Sarmatians.[7] Elsewhere, instead of the poet posting his book from dismal far-off lands to the centre of the universe that is Rome, and the emperor, epigrams are packaged up and sent off from Rome to emperors and officials on campaign, or holidaying, abroad. For example, Book 5 begins:

> Hoc tibi, Palladiae seu collibus uteris Albae,
>     Caesar, et hinc Triviam prospicis, inde Thetin,
> seu tua veridicae discunt responsa sorores,
>     plana suburbani qua cubat unda freti,

---

[5] Hardie (2002) 284.
[6] See e.g. Fitzgerald (2007) 189, where he explains how Martial's books 'reverse the direction of Ovid's exile poetry'. I want to build on and complicate this discussion here.
[7] See 7.5–8, with Pitcher's comments (1998, 69–70).

seu placet Aeneae nutrix seu filia Solis
   sive salutiferis candidus Anxur aquis,
mittimus, o rerum felix tutela salusque,
   sospite quo gratum credimus esse Iovem.
tu tantum accipias: ego te legisse putabo
   et tumidus Galla credulitate fruar.

This I send you, Caesar, whether you're enjoying Alba's hills,
looking out at Trivia on one side and Thetis on the other,
or whether the truth-telling sisters are learning your replies,
where the flat sea sleeps on the town's edge,
or whether Aeneas' nurse, or the daughter of the sun,
or shining Anxur with her heath-giving waters please you,
o blessed protector and saviour of the world,
whose safety gives us faith in the gratitude of Jove.
I only hope you will accept it. I shall believe you've read it,
and bask proud in my Gallic gullibility.

Wherever Domitian happens to be, this book will reach him. In 7.80, similarly, instructions are given to Faustinus to send this book to Marcellinus, a general who has been campaigning in Dacia, recently conquered: he'll throw in the slave messenger as an extra bonus, and in return Faustinus will be sent a slave *captivo ab Histro*, 'from captive Hister' (11), who can be put to work feeding sheep at Tibur. And it is not only the poet himself and friends who disperse the *Epigrams* to all four corners of the rapidly expanding empire, to function as flags for Roman presence abroad, for conquest itself. Tourists (themselves retracing the steps taken by banished Romans) are constantly doing the same job, exporting multiple copies as souvenirs of their trip to the capital (see 8.3.7–8: *me tamen ora legent et secum plurimus hospes / ad patrias sedes carmina nostra feret*, 'they'll still read me, and many a stranger will carry my poems back to their homelands'). Meanwhile, Roman informers are punished in the Colosseum in *De Spectaculis* 4 and 5 by being sent into exile, the very fate they caused others to suffer. As Fitzgerald points out, this surprise twist is made even more effective by the fact that the poems follow *De Spectaculis* 3, where foreigners from as far afield as Northern Britain and Ethiopia move in the opposite direction as they flock to Rome for the great show.[8]

The reversal of Ovid's/the exile's transmission of poetry from foreign places *to* Rome is also felt too in a series of poems mapping the changing dialogue between city and country, or suburbs: the punchline to 7.31, 10.37 and 10.94, for example, is that gifts of meat, fish, fruit and vegetables,

[8] Fitzgerald (2007) 42–4.

which look so authentically organic, are actually recent purchases from
Rome's markets in the midst of the sweaty Subura (e.g. 10.37.19: *omnis
ab urbano venit ad mare cena macello*, 'every seaside dinner comes from
the city market').[9] Status-symbol country properties in the epigrams are
often barren, or uncultivated, so that when you meet Bassus near the Porta
Capena driving a cart laden with 'all the produce of a prosperous farm'
(3.47.6), and assume he's heading back to Rome, you'd be wrong: *urbem
petebat Bassus? immo rus ibat* ('was Bassus on the way to Rome? On the
contrary, he was off to the country,' 15). Martial picks up and runs with
the idea of *rus in urbe*, 'countryside in the town', of which we see further
permutations in, for example, 12.57, about Sparsus' mansion complete with
vineyard on the hills of Rome, in 8.68, where Entellus' grand townhouse
offers a rural idyll preferable to Alcinous' legendary orchards, or in 11.18,
where there is more *rus* in the window boxes of Martial's town apartment
than in the minuscule country property he has just been presented as a gift.

The *Epigrams* are themselves often composed from outside Rome –
Book 3 (the opening poems tell us) from Gaul, and Book 12 from Bilbilis
in Spain (we had already watched him leave Rome at the end of Book 10,
edition two). For the provincial Spaniard seeking fame and fortune in the
big city, poetry and poetic identity are fundamentally connected with place
and space. As he implies in 1.61, Catullus *is* Verona, Mantua is most famous
for producing Vergil, the land of Aponus bases its fame on the success of
Stella, Horace and Livy, the Paeligni resound with the name Ovid, and so
on. One of the most fascinating bits of trivia about Roman literary culture
is that until quite late, none of the great writers (the possible exception
being Julius Caesar) was born in Rome. In Book 10, as he announces his
departure for Spain, Martial appears to make a link between his desire
to return to his homeland and the fact that he often writes of 'extremely
far-off peoples' (10.96.1–4):

> Saepe loquar nimium gentes quod, Avite, remotas
>   miraris, Latia factus in urbe senex,
> auriferumque Tagum sitiam patriumque Salonem
>   et repetam saturae sordida rura casae.

> Do you wonder, Avitus, when I have grown old in Latium's city,
> why I often speak of far-off peoples,
> that I thirst for gold-rich Tagus and my native Salo,
> and return to the rough fields of a well-stocked cottage?

---

[9] Naturally, Martial is not entirely consistent in saying this. In 7.49, for example, he sends his friend
Severus the gift of eggs and fruit which were produced in his 'suburban garden' at Nomentum.

Martial arguably makes more of his provincial origins than any other imperial poet. Yet he also presents his foreignness or double identity as a multiplication of vantage points from which he can better exercise epigram's expatiating and all-encompassing ambitions. Epigram is to take a culminating and unique place in politico-literary explorations and markings of imperial territory which include all the great Roman epics, from Lucretius' poem-as-world to Virgil's *Aeneid*, Ovid's *Metamorphoses* and Lucan's *Bellum Civile* – 'poems of universal geography'[10] – as well as exilic poetry (Ovid and Seneca), Petronius' *Satyricon,* Tacitus' *Agricola* and *Germania* and Pliny's *Natural History*. The extent of imperial rule and the origins of Rome are bound up in the Roman cultural imagination, Martial knows, with the idea(l) of exile.[11] He uses all the multiformity and elasticity of epigram to unpack and play off the contrasting elements of the 'Roman dream' imagined in Latin literature from Virgil's fundamental epic onwards: Aeneas is the first exile, a brave refugee from Troy who sails to Italy and the future site of Rome, and the uprooting of this epic hero is previewed in Vergil's first *Eclogue*, where Meliboeus is forced to flee his homeland, and at the end of *Georgics* 4, where the old man cultivates his garden near Tarentum, having been displaced from his Cilician home. It also haunts Ovid's letters from exile (in *Tristia* 1.3, for instance, the poet's last night in Rome is compared to Aeneas' last night in Troy[12]), and Juvenal's third *Satire* (where the figure of Umbricius despises the city and resolves to leave it for good, just as Aeneas left Troy – a sardonic mirror image of Ovid's all-consuming desire to return). In the *Epigrams*, refugee-immigrant Aeneas shadows the exiled informers in *De Spectaculis* 4 (the *delator* is *Ausonia profugus ab urbe*, 'a fugitive in exile from the Ausonian city', at line 5 of this poem, after Aeneas, *fato profugus*, at *Aen.* 1.2), and in 10.58, a poem I mentioned in chapter 2, the poet himself is 'tossed on the city's ocean' (*iactamur in alto / urbis*, 7–8), recalling the third line of Vergil's *Aeneid, terris iactatus et alto*. We can trace a long tradition of exiled writers and of literary responses to exile in Roman history,[13] which together span pain, punishment, isolation, identity crises, artistic loss, love for and

---

[10]  As Barchiesi puts it (2005b, 404).

[11]  As Edwards puts it, 'exile, alienation, displacement were associated with Rome from the beginning of the city's history' (1996, 12).

[12]  See parallels discussed in Videau-Delibes (1991) 29–49.

[13]  See overview in Edwards (1996) 110–33, and see especially Cicero *Tusc.* 5.106–9, on arguments to console the exile, echoed by Livy's Camillus (cf. Ogilvie (1970) *ad* Livy 5.54), and by Ovid (cf. Nagle (1980) 35). Seneca in Corsica seems to have consoled himself by reading Ovid (see Griffin (1976) 62).

resentment of Rome, as well as innovation-in-change, heroism, nostalgia, hope, and refoundation.

While Ovid's *Tristia* emerge as the most palpable model for Martial's experiments in distance-writing, and the threat of punishment at the hands of an unpredictable emperor certainly scaffolds the deft, slippery and some-times provocative epigrams about or addressed to Domitian in particular,[14] the epigrams use the metaphor of exile in ambitious and *ground-breaking* ways. Although exile is sometimes presented as based on constraint (Mar-tial writes Book 3 from Gaul as he claims not to be able to afford to live in Rome), it is, for the poet at least, a crank for the imagination, representing the freedom to flit where he wants, take up the literary position he desires, view Rome from any angle. The exilic pose, for which the flag is usually the 'sending off' of personified book (*vade liber . . . . ibis in urbem . . .*), often becomes now a platform for vaunting literary self-confidence and one-upmanship: Martial has *learnt from Ovid*, and is not about to make the same mistakes, although he sometimes has us relish the drama of tread-ing that line.[15] Any trips *he* takes to exotic places will be voluntary leisure breaks, opportunities for 'book tours', visiting family and friends, or just for a change of scene and some fresh air. Gone is Ovid's black psychological isolation, emotional rollercoastering, and air of desperation.

There is the strong sense in Martial that as Romanisation and technolo-gies advance, the world *seems* smaller, and less frightening, because it is more easily encompassed by the imagination. Indeed, this idea goes right to the core of epigram's magnifying/miniaturising project. Since the early empire, Roman interest in geography and graphic representations of the world had exploded, culminating in texts like Pliny's *Natural History* and Tacitus' *Agricola*, where the British Isles – the most mysterious and north-ern region of the empire – are finally mapped, visualised and catalogued after 100 years of campaigning.[16] As Tacitus writes, *ita quae priores nondum comperta eloquentia percoluere, rerum fide tradentur* (whereas earlier writers

---

[14] As Casali puts it in his discussion of the preface to *Epigrams* 1 (2005, 23), 'Come per Ovidio l'insistenza ossessiva del discorso dell'esilio sull'*Ars* non ha alla fine altro effetto che non quello di *rivendicare* l'*Ars* e la sua potenza, così per Marziale le movenze dell'esilio ovidiano servono più a sottolineare, e a rivendicare, la "pericolosità" delle proprie scelte poetiche che non a cautelarsi davvero.'

[15] As Pitcher (1998) 61 puts it, 'in Ovid he discovers how to approach an emperor, mindful of the need to avoid giving offence.' Pitcher also discusses Martial's comparison of Domitian to Jupiter in e.g. epigrams 4.1, 6.10, 7.56, 7.99, 8.24, 8.36, setting this flattery against the backdrop of Ovid's imagery of Augustus as Jupiter in the exile poetry. Also see the discussion in Fitzgerald (2007) 186–90.

[16] See discussion in Evans (2003).

had to conjure up the undiscovered with rhetoric, I'll be telling you the plain facts,' *Agricola* 10.1). 'The News' in Flavian Rome is now truly international, as 9.35 sets out to show: dinner-party gossip Philomusus knows 'what Pacorus is deliberating in his Arsacian palace', the number of 'Rhenish and Sarmatian hosts', what the 'Dacian chief' writes in his letters, 'how many times dark Syene is drenched by Pharian rain . . . how many ships leave the Libyan shore . . .' (3–8), and still fails to impress. And in 11.53, Britain is so Romanised and fully integrated into the known world that Claudia Rufina ('little red-head'), born of the 'blue Brits' (so called as they painted themselves with woad), passes as the ultimate *matrona Romana*![17]

So it comes as little surprise that, as Pitcher discusses, the opening poems of Book 3 (especially 3.2, 3.4 and 3.5) clearly allude to but also work in opposition to *Tristia* 1.1:[18] whereas Ovid is holed up at 'the edge of the world, a land far removed from my own' (*nobis habitabitur orbis / ultimus, a terra terra remota mea*, *Tr.* 1.1.127–8), Martial is biding his time in Roman Gaul (as he reminds readers in 3.1.2, it's named after the Roman *toga*[19]). Although it is quite a distance from Rome itself (*longinquis mittit ab oris*, 3.1.1), the town Forum Cornelii (3.4.4) is a well-known colony easy to find on a map: so much so that you can almost point to it down the road ('if Rome asks where you came from, say from the direction of the Aemilian way,' 3.4.1–2). Epigram, naturally, splices *Tristia* 1.1 into bits, and cuts a long (implicitly rather tedious) story short: *breviter tu multa fatere* (3.4.5). And while Ovid's title-less book-in-mourning casts round for, not even a patron, but a sympathetic ear, anyone who'll be prepared to vouch for the poet's innocence (*Tr.* 1.1.27–30), Martial's *libellus* already has a rich, friendly protector lined up in the shape of Faustinus, who'll allow it to swank around in purple, oiled with cedar, its bosses painted, its 'title blushing scarlet' (3.2.7–11). No begging or self-justification is required, the book is simply to announce 'Marcus sends his greetings', *et satis est*, 'and this is enough' (3.5.11).[20] Epigram confidently whizzes around and dominates Roman territory, making huge steps look small.

---

[17] Claudia's name also reminds us of Claudius, and hence of Britain's subjugation. She is 'named territory', marked by conquest, but at the same time imperial-sounding.

[18] See Pitcher (1998) 59–60. Also see Fusi (2006) 47–51 and *ad loc.*

[19] *Gallia Cisalpina* was also called *Gallia togata*, because of its adoption of the toga. See Fusi (2006) *ad loc.*

[20] Roman (2001, 124): 'In general, Martial adapts motifs formed in the context of "poetry in exile" and rewrites them in terms of "poetry as usual".'

### RETURN AND REVERSAL: BOOK 12

Book 12, written from Bilbilis in Spain, also begins with a nod to *Tristia*
1.1, and Martial's metamorphosis is in a similar vein: like Ovid, Martial is a
foreigner now (*nunc peregrine liber*, 12.2.2; cf. *venias magnam peregrinus in
urbem*, 'may you enter the great city a foreigner,' *Tr.* 1.1.59), posting off a
title-less volume from abroad to Rome, rather than vice versa (3.2.1–4). Yet
unlike Ovid, he already has a powerful and empathetic patron in Stella, and
while Ovid's book lacks a title because it is (under-)dressed[21] (thus risking
being taken for the criminal *Ars Amatoria*, *Tr.* 1.1.65–8), Martial's dispenses
with titles, and any notion of guilt, as he is so well-known and loved: *quid
titulum poscis? versus duo tresve legantur, / clamabunt omnes te, liber, esse
meum. /* 'Why do you ask for a title? Just let them read two or three verses,
and everyone, book, will shout out that you are mine' (12.2.17–18). The
'brothers' of Ovid's book are found on his own private shelves, whereas
Martial's are lodged in Domitian's public library, *tot* ('so many', 12.2.6)
compared to Ovid's numbered volumes.[22] Later in the book, Martial is at
pains to stress that at the end of their journey, his poems will be welcomed
by the 'mildest' of emperors, Nerva (12.6.1), and that the 'terrors' of past
tyrants (meaning Domitian, but inevitably hinting, too, at Augustus' punishment of Ovid and rejection of leniency to the end) 'have turned tail and
gone' (*longi terga dedere metus*, 12.6.4). Moreover, Book 12 as we have it
kicks off with an epistolary preface addressed to Terentius Priscus, in which
the poet announces a forthcoming *cena adventoria* in Gaul for his friend,
where he will be presented with a copy of this book, *before* it is sent off
to Rome in 12.2. In other words, Martial has already performed a familiar
volte-face: this book 'in exile' first has its important readers come *to it*,
rather than the other way around. However, the preface to *Epigrams* 12 also
imagines a confusion as well as reversal of directions: Martial left all the
pleasures of the city of his own accord (*reliquimus*, 13), though it seems now
that it was they who withdrew from him (*quasi destituti*, 14). 12.8 reverses
perspectives once more, imagining Rome at Trajan's succession addressing
foreign tribes, the nobles of Parthia, chieftains of Seres, Thracians, Sarmatians, Getans and Britons, and willing them to come to Rome (*venite*,
10) to set eyes on their new Caesar. Trajan was himself born in Spain, at
Italica, near Seville, and in the following epigram addressed to him, 12.9,
the 'foreign' Spanish are 'our Iberians' (*nostros Hiberos*, 1), while the adjective *peregrinus*, used so conspicuously at the start of 12.2 to describe this

---

[21] *Ut titulo careas . . . (Tr.* 1.1.61).     [22] See discussion in Pitcher (1998) 62–4.

'foreign' book (*peregrine liber*, 12.2.2), is readopted to partner the noun *pax* in 12.9:

> Palma regit nostros, mitissime Caesar, Hiberos,
>   et placido fruitur Pax peregrina iugo.
> ergo agimus laeti tanto pro munere grates:
>   misisti mores in loca nostra tuos.

> Palma governs our Iberians, most gentle Caesar,
> and Peace overseas enjoys her placid power.
> Happily, we thank you for so great a gift:
> You've exported your *mores* to our lands.

*Peregrina Pax*, then, is exported *Roman* peace, yet under the authority of a 'foreign', Spanish-born Roman emperor (who was himself away from Rome, on the Danube, when he became princeps, returning to the capital only about eighteen months into his reign, when Martial had already left for Spain[23]) – just as this volume is the 'foreign' book of a Spanish-born author who has lived all his adult life in Rome. In the last line of this epigram, there is again a certain ambiguity of direction: does *misisti mores in loca nostra tuos*, 'you have sent your manners to our land' (4), refer to the influence of a Spanish-born Roman emperor on his native lands, or to Trajan's noble Spanish influence on Rome or Roman Italy? Where are *nostra loca*, given that for Martial both Rome and Bilbilis count as 'home'? Is this a Spanish or Spanish-Roman book? What is it to write a poem sent to Rome from abroad to an emperor who not only hails from the same location, but also may not even be in Rome at the time, stationed in some other region of a vast empire?

*Epigrams* 12 is a difficult and puzzling book for several reasons. As a concluding *nostos*[24] and finale to a would-be twelve-book epic before Martial's death in 103 or 104,[25] it looks melancholy, fractured, anticlimactic, making us very aware of the gap of three years (according to the epistolary preface) between this and the last numbered volume (which was probably the second edition of Book 10, published in AD 98 after Book 11 came out two years before that). It is usually dated October 101 or 102, but includes epigrams addressed to Nerva and Parthenius (who would in that case have

---

[23] Trajan was an experienced military man, and was said to have taken personal charge on campaign, marching on foot in the front line. His reign was marked by two great wars of conquest, in Dacia and Parthia, meaning that he would have spent large chunks of time absent from Rome.

[24] As e.g. Holzberg (2002, 35–9) and Lorenz (2002, 228–31, 233) see it.

[25] Pliny tells a friend of Martial's recent death in *Epist.* 3.21, helping us to date it to 103 or 104. See Sherwin-White (1966) 263.

been long dead), as well as to Trajan, and a poem reporting a new shorter anthology of selected epigrams from Books 10 and 11 (12.4), which has been read as an actual, out-of-place preface to that collection, which does not survive.[26] It concludes sharply with a prayer for the new governor of Spain, Instantius Rufus. Sullivan and Shackleton Bailey[27] take literally Martial's very familiar, and of course potentially metaphorical, reference to a *brevis libellus* (12.1.3), composed in *paucissimis diebus* (*Pref.* 21), which leads them to conclude that the basic framework of this Spanish book was then padded out with old epigrams which seemed to fit, either by Martial himself or by an editor gathering up errant scraps of poetry after Martial's death, even as late as 104. Arguments in this vein (as well as opposing ones, like those of Lorenz) are stoked by the discrepancy between manuscript families γ and β: the former is missing poems 4, 5, 6, 11, 15, 28, 29, 36, 47, all of which are transmitted in the latter. It has been suggested either that the shorter volume is the more 'original' one, with the longer volume appearing after Martial's death, or the other way around.[28]

It is difficult to be convinced either way. It does seem a cop-out, however, to just decide that the book was probably (a) not compiled by Martial and (b) is therefore a random hotchpotch littered with strays, in which context and position have little significance. For sure, this is an odd book (much about Martial is odd). But it's worth remembering that Books 10–12 together are also a strange trio,[29] taking us backwards and forwards in time and space, and having footholds in two or rather multiple worlds. In other words, the puzzle of why Book 12 includes 'poems from the past' might conceivably be seen as part and parcel of poetic reflections on spatial/temporal/cultural hybridity and dislocation, rather than simply as an accident of fate – although it's of course perfectly possible, in theory, that the collection was sewn together by a later editor who had no such thoughts in mind.

When we read the book through, we encounter multiple versions of a kind of culminating epigrammatic schizophrenia about identity and geography. We have already begun to see how Martial's post-Ovidian 'exile'

---

[26] 12.4 is cited by White (1974) as evidence that private *libelli* were the main means of presenting poems to patrons. See reaction of Fowler (1995, 41), who argues that the poem plays a distinctive role in Book 12, together with Fitzgerald's recent discussion (2007, 158–9).

[27] See summary in Lorenz (2002) 234, with n. 106. Sullivan (1991) 52–3, Shackleton Bailey (1993) *ad loc.*

[28] For this view see Lorenz (2002) 234–8.

[29] Holzberg (2002, esp. 221) makes much of this possible three-book structure (his views are much more rigid than mine), and even argues that Books 10, 11 and 12 work in parallel with the triad *Tristia* 1–3. Also see Hinds (2007) on the major constellation of '*Tristia* motifs' in Book 12.

to Spain and the rise of a Spanish-born emperor create the framework for an epigrammatic collapse of as well as contrast of spaces and times. Hence this book risks becoming Spanish and not just Spanish-Roman (*Pref.* 26–7): the 'exile' both leaves Rome and is left by it (*Pref.* 13–14); Martial welcomes his audience from Rome (*ab urbe*, *Pref.* 19) as well as sending his poems to Rome; the trek to far-off lands is itself a return, although it also makes the poet long for a return to Rome.[30] Moreover Spain, or rather viewing Rome from Spain, a forward-looking move towards the end of Martial's oeuvre and his life, is also the site for nostalgia: in 12.3, Priscus is the new Maecenas, and through the *Tristia*, Nerva and Trajan are and are not Augustus reborn (as well as being the opposite of Domitian: see 12.5, 12.15); 12.8 looks *back* (from presumed time of publication) to Trajan's succession, a time when Rome was looking to a new *future* (*Traiani . . . cum futuros / tot per saecula conputaret annos*, 3–4).

The conjuring of Bilbilis as a rural idyll in 12.18 and 12.31 is a pivot for a broader kind of pastoral nostalgia, but again, comparisons between Martial's regressive, 'golden age' homeland and the filthy noise of modern Rome are typically unstraightforward and tend to overlap or infiltrate one another. The lengthy 12.18 is addressed (almost certainly) to the contemporary poet Juvenal, who began publishing his *Satires* around AD 100:[31]

> Dum tu forsitan inquietus erras
> clamosa, Iuvenalis, in Subura
> aut collem dominae teris Dianae;
> dum per limina te potentiorum
> sudatrix toga ventilet vagumque
> maior Caelius et minor fatigant:
> me multos repetita post Decembres
> accepit mea rusticumque fecit
> **auro Bilbilis et superba ferro.**
> hic pigri colimus labore dulci
> Boterdum Plateamque – Celtiberis
> haec sunt nomina crassiora terris – :
> ingenti fruor inproboque somno
> quem nec tertia saepe rumpit hora
> et totum mihi nunc repono quidquid
> ter denos vigilaveram per annos.

[30] The paradox of going as returning and vice versa is also mirrored in the carrying-back-as-bringing theme of 12.28, where, after Catullus' napkin thief Asinius at poem 12, Hermogenes 'never brought (*attulit*) a napkin *to* dinner but always carried a napkin back (*rettulit*) *from* dinner' (21–2).
[31] Watson and Watson (2003) 143–50 comment at length on this poem. Juvenal the satirist also features in 7.24 and 7.91.

ignota est toga, sed datur petenti
rupta proxima vestis a cathedra.
surgentem focus excipit superba
vicini strue cultus iliceti,
multa vilica quem coronat olla.
venator sequitur, sed ille quem tu
secreta cupias habere silva;
dispensat pueris rogatque longos
levis ponere vilicus capillos.
sic me vivere, sic iuvat perire.

While you, Juvenal, might be wandering
restless in the noisy Subura,
or treading mistress Diana's hill,
your sweaty gown flapping as
you cross those VIP doorways, worn out
trudging big and small Caelian,
I'm here in Bilbilis, the town proud of her
iron and gold, revisited after many a December:
it's welcomed me and made of me a rustic.
In my idleness I make the pleasant trek
to nearby Boterdus and Platea – such are the
uncouth names in Celtiberia.
I enjoy sleep marathons, often opening my eyes
past the third hour of the day, and
reward myself in full for thirty
years of wakefulness.
The toga is unknown round here, but when I ask
I'm handed the nearest garment from a broken chair.
When I rise, a fireplace warms me, piled proud
with oak from a nearby wood and crowned with pots
courtesy of the bailiff's wife.
The huntsman comes in next, one you'd rather fancy
hanging out with in a secret grove.
The soft-skinned bailiff gives my boys their rations
and asks me permission to cut his long hair.
I want to live and die like this.

This is Martial's take on a familiar literary theme – the superiority of country to city living – which recalls such poems as Tibullus 1.1, Horace's second *Epode*, *Epistles* 2.2 or *Satire* 2.6, and Vergil's second *Georgic* (the topos originated in Hellenistic bucolic poetry). It's possible that it also plays heavily on Juvenal's famous third satire, where Umbricius, who has decided to withdraw from Rome to the peaceful isolation of Cumae, rants about how much he despises the city. As I've mentioned, both Martial and Juvenal in *Satire* 3 work the same imperial irony of the urbanite who traces Aeneas' foundational journey to Rome in reverse. In *Satire* 3, clear contrasts are tainted beyond redemption when degenerate Umbricius heads for Cumae, gateway to the choice seaside resort of Baiae on the bay of Naples which is otherwise famous for being the entrance to the Underworld (where Aeneas retraces *his* steps as well as glimpsing the future in *Aeneid* 6). Umbricius, the poem hints, leaves one hell for another, firing up dirty, urbanocentric satire in the process. Similarly, the overt praise of country life in Horace *Epode* 2 is undercut when the voice of reason is exposed as that of Alfius, a hypocritical, rapacious moneylender born and bred for cut-throat city living. Predictably, there are pointers towards a satirical messing up of discrete ideals throughout 12.18, too: first of all, as Lindsay and Patricia Watson note, whereas words connoting plenty and luxury are applied pejoratively to city life in the rural fantasies of say, Tibullus 1.1 or *Georgics* 2, Martial (like Statius in the *Silvae*[32]) 'imports' urban riches to his country pad, integrating them into an image of simple rustic abundance.[33] So a 'proud pile' of logs welcomes him when he gets up (19); the hearth is stocked (*cultus*) from a nearby wood, *cultus* being a buzzword, after Ovid, for *urban* sophistication.[34] Bilbilis, like the pile of logs, is *superba*, 'proud' of her natural resources of gold and iron in line 9,[35] yet that same adjective *superbus* has been used of the tyrant Domitian, again in connection with gold, just three poems back in 12.15 (an epigram which, remember, does not appear in the γ manuscript family). Here Martial is describing how Nerva or Trajan moved the treasures from Domitian's palaces into temples, where the public could see them (12.15.3–5):

> miratur Scythicas virentis auri
> flammas Iuppiter et stupet **superbi**
> regis delicias gravesque lusus.

> Jupiter marvels at the Scythian flames
> of vibrant gold, and looks amazed at the whims
> and oppressive playthings of a proud king.

Next to 12.15, Martial's nostalgic rural paradise in Bilbilis is reminiscent of another blast from Rome's past – Domitianic tyranny, echoing back all the way to Tarquinius *Superbus*, Rome's last king. Meanwhile, Martial makes

---

[32] See discussion of *Silvae* 1.3 and 2.2 in Newlands (2002) 119–153.
[33] Watson and Watson (2003) *ad loc.*   [34] See e.g. Ovid *Medicamina* 1–7.
[35] Martial seems to talk here not just from the perspective of the proud native, but as a coloniser, reporting back what Spain is good for – gold, iron, pottery, etc.

*Martial's Rome*

a joke in 12.18 of living the simple life of a pauper and 'rustic' (8) from the perspective of a gent spoiled by urban seductions: in the country, the toga is 'unknown', yet he has someone else to hand him his clothes from a 'broken chair', a comic prop indicating dire poverty in the mould of Callimachus' Hecale, or of Ovid's Baucis and Philemon; he goes on day trips to Boterdus and Platea, but apologises snobbily for their 'uncouth' names; and he sees to it that his bailiff is a smooth-skinned honey, the kind you'd like to frolic with in a 'secret grove' – a sophisticated, post-Ovidian *locus amoenus* redolent of pubescent beauties like Narcissus and Hermaphroditus.

Indeed, in 12.21, Martial is back yearning like a love-sick elegist for his 'mistress Rome' (*dominae urbis*, 12.21.9). Fortunately, his desires are somewhat satisfied, as well as deferred, by his Spanish patron Marcella, who is so genteel she is more Roman than Roman, even though (that key word again) she is the product of a **peregrini** *partus* ('foreign birth', 7):

> Municipem rigidi quis te, Marcella, Salonis
>     et genitam nostris quis putet esse locis?
> tam rarum, tam dulce sapis. Palatia dicent,
>     audierint si te vel semel, esse suam;
> nulla nec in media certabit nata Subura
>     nec Capitolini collis alumna tibi;
> nec cito ridebit **peregrini** gloria **partus**
>     Romanam deceat quam magis esse nurum.
> tu desiderium dominae mihi mitius urbis
>     esse iubes: Romam tu mihi sola facis.

> Who would think that you, Marcella, were a citizen
> of ice-cold Salo, born right here in my native lands?
> You have so rare and sweet a quality. If the Palatine
> hears you speak just once, it will say you are its own.
> No woman born in the heart of the Subura, no daughter
> of the Capitol can rival you; no time soon will a foreign birth
> produce another treasure who makes a better Roman bride.
> You ask that I stop pining for my mistress city:
> But you alone make Rome for me.

In the final couplet, Marcella and Rome are one: a desirable woman, an irresistible 'can't live with her, can't live without her' *domina*. This is a term laden with all the erotic thrills and power games of Roman love elegy, and is repeated to refer specifically to Marcella at 12.31.7 (*munera sunt dominae*), when Martial reflects on the idyllic house and gardens she has given him. This idea is not a new one: Ovid's exile poetry also elides woman (wife) and city as the lost object of love.[36] As Edwards discusses, the image also has a long history in European thought: in the sixteenth century, for example, Du Bellay envisages Rome as a seductive mistress luring him away from France, his legitimate wife, while Goethe in his *Roman Elegies* makes Rome the setting for a series of erotic encounters, so that sexual consummation becomes the dominant metaphor for intellectual, spiritual and emotional intimacy with the city.[37]

In 12.18, however, the vision of female patron as embodying both Rome and not-Rome, as well as the idea that one may not be able to perceive the difference between true Roman and foreigner, stages the collapsibility and shiftability of spaces and identities in the epigrammatic imagination. This is a book of small places, where the world can be shrunk down by virtue of it being known and encompassed by the name of empire. In the preface to this 'short' volume, Martial calls Bilbilis a *pusillus locus* ('tiny location', *Pref.* 15–16); poem 12.4 shows off how even diminutive collections can be 'compressed' and 'filed down' further; Martial's estate in Bilbilis is his *parva regna* ('small kingdom') in 12.31.8, his land at Nomentum *parva rura* in 12.57.1. Paradoxically, such a 'brief' collection can condense not just many different occasions but many different sites, covering a vast geographical area, because of the way (it showcases the idea that) 'Rome' extends not just to the 'commuter belt' of green suburbs and seaside resorts, but even as far as Spain. The preface to Book 12, which maps out the pros and cons of Rome/provincial life, and seems painfully drawn between the two, introduces a volume that – as we might expect – flits anxiously between roles and locations. We find ourselves juggling (polluted) pastoral fantasies against 'homesick' visions of the pleasures of Rome, against the harsh realities of farm life (e.g. 12.72), against bitter memories/experiences of oppressive life in the city (see e.g. 12.82, or 12.59, where someone returns to Rome only to find himself attacked from all quarters by *basiatores*, making him regret his decision). Epigram 12.57, where we skip back to Martial's other house near Rome at Nomentum, takes us closer and closer (back) to the city via Sparsus' symbolic *rus in urbe*, the 'country house' with all the trimmings on the hills (proving that there is Rome, and then there is Rome . . .). Here, location counts, yet Rome is also wherever Marcella is (12.21). Bilbilis, too, does a great impression of Rome in 12.62 and 12.68: 12.62 celebrates Priscus' return from Rome to Spain on the Saturnalia (itself a 'return' of Saturn's days, 16), and the whole town will be decked out in gifts for the people, 'just like an Ausonian market' (*Ausonio similis*

---

[36] Ovid *Tr.* 1.3.62–4.    [37] Edwards (1996) 130–1.

*macello*, 9), while in 12.68 the morning clients Martial left Rome to avoid are bugging him abroad, too, and he resolves to 'return' (*redeo*)[38] if he loses any more sleep. Similarly, we're reminded of urban spectacles, and the violence of the arena (not least, from the *De Spectaculis* and Book 1) in 12.14's picture of a treacherous hare hunt: *non derit qui tanta tibi spectacula praestet* ('there will always be someone to provide you with such spectacles') says Martial in line 7, referring to Priscus' propensity to push his horse too far and get thrown off. We revisit the shows for real in 12.28, when we spy Hermogenes stealing napkins in the theatre (*spectacula*, 15).

Conversely, Rome itself is full of foreigners and foreign produce. Crystal cups are imported from the Nile in 12.74,[39] and in 12.32, wild-looking immigrants to Rome are thrown out onto the streets when they can't pay the rent.[40] In this quasi-Juvenalian, epic blast, Martial has us imagine Vacerra's hairy mother, 'huge' sister and ageing, red-headed wife lugging their obscene belongings from a basement flat like Furies emerging from the darkness of Hades (4–6). The red hair and stocky build of the women are meant to remind us of monstrous, awe-inspiring northern tribes, the kind depicted in Tacitus' *Agricola* and *Germania*. Martial's cruel derision marks another, poetic, conquest. At the same time, this poem signposts Rome's/epigram's ability both to reach out to the furthest borders of the empire, and to fold together spaces and cultures – not only by mixing barbarian and Roman, but by envisaging the integration even of mythic spaces (the penetration of the upper world by creatures of the underworld).

---

[38] Note that the verb *redire* is repeated five times in different contexts and with different implications within the space of ten poems (12.59.11, 12.60.10, 12.62.16, 12.67.2, 12.68.6).

[39] See also e.g. 7.30, where Caelia sleeps with men from all over the world in Rome, not one of them a born Roman.

[40] Martial often pictures aspiring provincials heading for Rome as poor losers, and poverty-stricken immigrants as statusless aliens. See e.g. 3.14 ('Starveling Tuccius left Spain to come to Rome. He was met with the story about the dole. Back he went from the Mulvian bridge'). In 3.4, Martial reports that he has himself been forced out of Rome by poverty, and is writing from Gaul. See also 4.5: 'An honest man and a pauper, true of tongue and heart, you're heading for Rome – what are you thinking of, Fabianus?' He won't be able to do any of the low-down dirty jobs that idealistic newcomers end up doing in Rome (a pimp, prostitute, reveller or actor): so what's he going to live on? Only rogues can make a living in Rome, and that's the message to would-be poet Sextus, too, in 3.38: Martial asks him 'What reason or prospect brings you to Rome, Sextus? What do you hope or look for from there?' He replies that he will plead cases more eloquently than Cicero and outdo all other rhetoricians in the fora. If that doesn't work, he'll write poetry, and be up there with Vergil. Martial replies, bursting his bubble, 'You're mad. All these people you see in frosty cloaks are Nasos and Vergils.' Naturally, we also get the 'opposite' scenario, the Roman who goes into voluntary exile full of hopes and dreams and is disappointed: see e.g. 7.64, where Cinnamus leaves Rome to dodge 'the Forum's grim laws' on being made a knight. But abroad, his skills are useless, and he'll be a depressed fugitive, forced to return to his old trade as a barber to make ends meet.

In 12.32, low-class barbarians are the new refugees, exiled in Rome itself, having mirrored (in a sense) the Trojans' 'original' journey to the shores of Italy, long-suffering and full of hope. They embody the funny, bitter dislocations and twists that come to define Book 12, and that cannot so easily be dismissed as the result of carefree or messy editing after Martial's death. Just as exile provides Ovid with a wealth of new creative opportunities, a new zone for the imagination in which he can innovate and also review/rewrite his life work as his own life nears its end, we might say that Martial's 'exilic' retreat to Spain is designed to amplify the world of epigram in a similar way, casting this poetry as *the* genre best able to enclose a kaleidoscope of perspectives about Roman identity and space in a new imperial age.

Indeed, the image of outside folded into inside, of being an exile in Rome itself, runs throughout Martial's corpus, recasting epigram's ability to collapse spaces and capture a big-small world. Seneca consoles his mother from exile in Corsica in the *Ad Helviam* by observing that Rome is a city full of exiles: she claims that being away from one's homeland 'is unbearable', but the city is bursting at the seams with people who have 'left behind the place where they were born to come to the greatest, even most beautiful city, but one which is not their own' (6.2–3). As Hinds suggests, Martial's allusions to the *Tristia* hint that Ovidian exile offers a model 'for the abject clientship and determinedly non-sublime art of the epigrammatist – who encounters *his* professed disadvantages without even leaving Rome'.[41] Fitzgerald argues that the arena of the Colosseum in *De Spectaculis* 4 and 5 already previews the sandy wastelands of exile that are soon to be the fate of this line-up of informers.[42] And in epigram 10.5, a poem I discussed in chapter 2, Martial's enemy will be exiled in the city itself, in the sense that he will be shunned by everyone, even beggars: *erret per urbem pontis exul et clivi, / interque raucos ultimus rogatores / oret caninas panis inprobi buccas* ('Let him wander through the city, exiled from bridge and slope, and end up last among the raw-voiced tramps, begging paltry scraps of bread fit only for the dogs,' 3–5). We've already seen how 10.58 imagines Martial himself as an epic refugee, after Aeneas, yet he is buffeted on the foreign seas of the city itself.

Whereas Rome, especially its crammed public places and dark, labyrinthine streets, can swallow up the harsh exterior world it represents,

[41] Hinds (2007).    [42] Fitzgerald (2007) 42.

empire no longer seems an unimaginably vast space, and distances are regularly compressed through epigram's magnifying lens:[43] when Domitian arrives back in Rome in 8.11, for example, the noise of the celebrations reaches the Rhine and 'terrifies' (*terruit*, 4) German tribes – 'the Sarmatic peoples, and the Hister and the Getae' (3).[44] The uproar is centred in the Circus Maximus, where nobody notices that the race has already begun after four false starts – the Circus, together with the amphitheatre arena, become symbolic focus points for epigram's miniaturisations, microcosms which can contain and represent spectators, as well as human and animal victims, from all over the globe. We have already seen (in chapter 3) how Martial evokes Ovid's model of the evolving universe in imagining the Colosseum as cosmos. Yet the scope of the arena to cage and even intensify alien forces is made emphatic at several points in the *Epigrams*, not just in the *De Spectaculis*. In 2.75, for example, a lion that mauls and kills a pair of slaves raking the arena displays 'a sudden return of savagery such that should not have existed on the hills of Libya' (3–4); in 8.53, one African lion's roar is as loud 'as that heard in Massylian wilds when the forest rages with countless lions' (1–2), while in 8.26 'the robber of Ganges . . . did not fear so many tigers in the East as your Rome, Germanicus, saw for the first time' (1–3). The compacting epicentre of the arena, as we've seen, also spills out to encompass the whole of Rome – as in 1.3, where Martial's book faces the rhinoceros noses of critics at a recital, or in 3.36, where the poet imagines the life of a low-ranking client as a gladiatorial boot camp, asking, 'don't you think I've earned my wooden sword (i.e. discharge) by now?' (10). The *Epigrams* specialise in this concertina-like effect, showing off again and again how this poetry can (make the world) distend and contract.

PAST PASTORAL

Martial's books are rooted in, and seek to express, a radical reconceptualisation of space. They do so against a backdrop of Roman literary endeavours,

---

[43] Compare again Ovid's exile poetry, where as Claassen discusses (1999, 187), the space between Tomis and Rome expands to a 'vast nothingness' (see *Tr.* 1.5.61–2): in Martial it is easily spanned, captured and condensed. Although distances can also expand: see e.g. 1.86, where Martial's neighbour in a block of flats is so close he could reach out and touch him with his hand, but he might as well be in Syene on the Nile, as Martial can't have dinner with him, can't see him or even hear him. The poem plays on the paradox of *prope* as *procul:* 'In all of Rome no one is so near to me and yet so far away' (10).

[44] Compare 7.7, where everyone's mind is so fixed on Domitian and his war in Germany that even the crowd in the Circus doesn't know which racehorse is running.

from Vergil to Statius, which reflect in subtle ways on Rome's origins, its place in the world, what it is to be 'Roman', and the relationship between centre and margin, urban and rural, in the imperial psyche. The genre of pastoral, always the most urbane of forms, synonymous with poetic cultivation itself, has a fascinating history in Latin, and is marked by its difficulty, its ability (as Gifford puts it) 'to both contain and appear to evade tensions and contradictions'.[45] Roman pastoral explores and deconstructs myths of freedom, conquest and the golden age, finding ever more complex permutations of the tense dialectic between town and country. The countryside is both 'home' and place of exile, both prime location for poetry or philosophy and a pre-artistic world that cannot stimulate or elevate, both retirement destination (for 'the future') and (so) the site for regressive nostalgia. It is a realm that, through Latin literature, is in continual (real and imaginary) flux – scarred by war, chopped up and relabelled by colonisation and land redistribution, modernised by the rich, stretched ever further into the distance by the machine of empire. So too the city, which appears as a growing beast, fixed centre and sprawling parasite, a multicolour paintbox for the artist and at the same time a morbid drain on all creative thought. In this brief summary, we have swung from the turmoil of tradition and modernism, cynicism and dreams that is Vergil's *Eclogues*, and the spiked rural fantasies of city-centred satire (Horace's *Satires* and *Epodes*, and Juvenal in particular), to the techno-pastoral of Calpurnius Siculus, where the countryside is the enemy of poetry, and the villa-lifestyles of Pliny's *Epistles* and Statius' *Silvae*, which see the countryside tamed and centralised for the leisured classes.[46] In Rome, the production of literature is intimately connected with thinking about *where* writing and the imagination are situated, where they come from, and where they belong.

Martial's poetics of paradox feeds hungrily on this tradition. Like Statius and his predecessors, he carves out his ambition by etching new perspectives on the evolving landscape of empire. As we've been seeing in this chapter, he is much inspired by the idea of exile as new terrain for contemplating poetry and/as Rome, and his provincial identity (like that of Statius, for whom Naples becomes an alternative Rome and epicentre[47]) is a tool for shifting, original visions of the world. Yet Martial, as with many things, takes the discourse of mobility that links the portable, fragmented epigram book with the diaspora and mixing of peoples that is so embedded in Roman ideas of origins and empire, and pushes it to its extreme. Just

---

[45] Gifford (1999) 11.    [46] See especially Newlands (2002, 119–53) on *Silvae* 1.3 and 2.2.
[47] See discussion in Newlands (2002) 163, 174, 284–5, 320.

as epigram can and does go where it likes, so Rome, in these poems, is an infinitely moveable concept. Look for example at poem 10.13, where Martial ponders whether to return to his native Spain and his dear friend Manius:

> Ducit ad auriferas quod me Salo Celtiber oras,
>     pendula quod patriae visere tecta libet,
> tu mihi simplicibus, Mani, dilectus ab annis
>     ex praetextata cultus amicitia,
> tu facis; in terris quo non est alter Hiberis
>     dulcior et vero dignus amore magis.
> tecum ego vel sicci Gaetula mapalia Poeni
>     et poteram Scythicas hospes amare casas.
> si tibi mens eadem, si nostri mutua cura est,
>     **in quocumque loco Roma duobus erit.**
>
>                                                    10.13

> If Celtiberian Salo lures me to gold-bearing shores, if
> I would love to see my home-town roofs perched high upon the hill,
> then you, Manius, dear to me from my years of innocence,
> whose friendship I cultivated in my boyhood gown,
> are the cause. In Iberia's land there is no sweeter man,
> none more worthy of my true love.
> With you I could lodge in the Gaetulian huts of sun-parched
> Carthage, or the cottages of Scythia, and love them.
> If you think the same, if these feelings of mine are mutual,
> any place will be Rome for the two of us.

Whereas in Vergil's first *Eclogue* Meliboeus, who is thrown out of his rural homestead to make room for veteran soldiers, sees himself and others like him being exiled to horrendous places like 'thirsty Africa and Scythia' (64–5), Martial is ready to love those distant (or not so distant) lands. This epigram makes the familiar connection between retirement to Spain and exile to exotic countries on the borders of empire, and plays with compressing and stretching distances. But it also erodes the very possibility of exile, as we know it, in epigram's world – a world which, as Fitzgerald puts it, 'has no centre'.[48] In an expanding empire, and in a world where epigram-as-Rome can go, and be, anywhere, Rome is an idea as much as a place. This is a crucial ramification of Martial's imperialistic vision of epigram as not just representing Rome, but *becoming* it. So, especially for soldiers stationed in the wilds of northern Britain, for officials working for

---

[48] Fitzgerald (2007) 198.

long periods in small towns in Gaul, Spain or Northern Africa, for Roman
emperors on campaign, or for Romanised 'foreigners', the *De Spectaculis*
is not just a souvenir from the games, it *is* the games, just as Book 11
*is* the Saturnalia of AD 96, and so on. Anywhere, 10.13 stresses, can be
Rome. While the *Epigrams* re-map space, in provocative and mischievous
ways, they also strive to transcend geography: again, we return to the
idea that these poems are constrained/inspired by their pure materiality,
their embeddedness in and dependence on context and occasion, yet at
the same time are much more than that – exercises in the imagination
that can change size or shape, and slip through the smallest gaps (in part,
ironically, *because* of their materiality, *because* of their corruptibility and
nothingness).

Yet one of the consequences of epigram's play with moveability (of
poetry, places and distances) is that, more than ever in Latin literature, we
tend to lose *any* real sense of the separability of town and country, centre
and margin. Strung throughout the corpus, we do find multiple traces of
the pastoral fantasy – the dream of a plot of land, the *otium* one can never
find in Rome (1.55), the comic cliché of the homely hearth, simple wife and
long nights of undisturbed sleep (2.90, 10.47), the country house as escape
(2.38, 4.64, 10.30) and ideal place for retirement (4.25, 10.44), the kudos-
rich achievement of owning property in the country (8.61, 9.97). Yet within
the crowded urban miscellany of an epigram book, there is no utopia, and
indeed no location, that can remain completely segregated and unpolluted.
Spisak reads *Epigrams* 10 as unified by a 'pastoral ideal', as a disillusioned
poet prepares to leave Rome for his home town of Bilbilis in Spain.[49] Yet
this is a limited reading which relies on marking off certain poems from
their neighbours and choosing to highlight certain points within those
poems in order to justify a sense of overall harmony. So the conventional
rural idylls offered in 10.30, 10.47 and 10.96, for example, are presented
as untouched by 10.94 (cf. 10.37.19), where Martial's unfertile garden at
Nomentum forces him to buy apples in a Roman market and pass them
off as home-grown country produce; by the ambivalence of 10.51, where
Faustinus has all the leisure he wants in his seaside villa, but is missing out
on Rome's famous theatres, baths and fora; by the opening poems (10.6
and 10.7) celebrating Trajan's return to Rome; by the tragedy of 10.26,
where centurion Varus dies before he can return to his beloved city; and
by 10.13, where as we've seen, Bilbilis, even Carthage, can become Rome.

---

[49] Spisak (2002), cf. Merli (2006), who sees a 'marked antithesis' between town and country in
Book 10.

What Spisak must preserve as a neat 'urban–rural contrast' is only *not* complicated and undercut if we are determined to extract discrete 'cycles' and not read the book as a whole.

As in Statius' 'villa poems' in the *Silvae*, in Martial we see the space between town and countryside narrowing,[50] yet the *Epigrams* exploit all the intricacies and paradoxes of Roman depictions of country versus town life to zigzag between and overlay spaces in an unprecedented way. More than ever, *rus* is part of the urban experience, while the clichés of tough city living are felt just as much in the countryside. The poet, together with his friends and enemies, deals with disappointments and frustrations (Book 12, *Pref.*), cramped and dark conditions (11.18, 11.34, 8.14), leaky roofs (7.36), problems with cash flow (1.85, 6.5). In Book 12, we've seen, Martial struggles to hold on to the *otium* he dreamed of, and is plagued by the boredom and hassle of provincial life. One of the longest descriptions of the pleasures of country living, in Bilbilis (1.49), is modelled on Horace's deadpan second *Epode,* where the encomium of rural pleasures is revealed to come from the mouth of usurer Alfius. The poems are written in the same unusual metre (a combination of iambic trimeters and dimeters), and as well as echoing the general features of landscape and lifestyle such as inviting waters, plentiful food and blissful sleep, Martial's picture of a winter hunt in the Spanish hills follows *Epod.* 2.29–36 closely. As Howell remarks of Horace's poem, 'the whole point of the joke is that the encomium itself is so convincingly expressed',[51] yet the point is also that it can never be so convincing the second time around. Notably, Martial's image of hare-hunting in lines 25–6 of 1.49 comes in a book famous for its 'cycle' of seven epigrams on the clever, teasing hare escaping the lion's jaws every time in the amphitheatre arena – in fact, 1.49 is framed by two of those poems, 1.48, and 1.51 (after the couplet at 1.50). As critics have suggested, Martial hints at the identification of epigram or epigrammatist with the hare, *lepus*, the tiny, delicate, naughty and ambitious animal[52] which 'plays' (*ludit*, 1.6.4) with the merciful lion-king,[53] and whose name is itself an epigrammatic slurring of the Catullan buzzword for clever neoterics, *lepōs* ('charm'), or *lepidus* ('witty', 'charming'). Yet in 1.49.23–6, bluntly, the hare is hunted down and run to death:

---

[50] See especially *Silv.* 4.3.     [51] Howell (1980) 213.

[52] It is addressed as *ambitiose lepus* at 1.51.2, described as *tenuis* at 1.51.6 and 1.22.4, *parvus* at 1.22.2, *improbus* at 1.48.7.

[53] E.g. Fitzgerald (2007) 83 sees the cycle as an 'allegory for the emperor's *clementia*'.

ibi inligatas mollibus dammas plagis
   mactabis et vernas apros
leporemque forti callidum rumpes equo –
   cervos relinques vilico.

There you will slaughter deers snared in
pliant nets, and native boars,
and run the cunning hare to death on a strong horse,
leaving the stags to the bailiff.

Not only, then, is the pastoral idyll in 1.49 tainted beyond redemption: Martial, like others before him, is also hinting that this kind of poetry cannot survive outside the dazzling and sophisticated arena that in 1.3 has already expanded to flood the whole of Rome. 1.49 reads as a surprise extension of the spectacular show that flashes through Book 1 and that serves as an overarching metaphor for the collection in the preface. Although it appears to take us far away, to let us indulge with its addressee Licinianus in a little nostalgic escapism, in fact it (also) draws us back to the city and squeezes spaces, right down to that ultimate epigrammatic microcosm, the Colosseum.

Do the *Epigrams* develop the pastoral genre, then, or do they mark the point at which pastoral is lost, and must be consigned to the past? Again, Martial's imperial expansionism is potentially double-edged. In (re-)inventing a poetic form which can dilate to envelop the entire globe, so that there is no space left that isn't Roman, or where epigram is not read, the notion of retreat (*recessus*) so core to Augustan and Neronian literature seems obsolete. When he has a *recessus* at Anxur, Martial moans at 10.58, there was time to cultivate the muses with Faustinus, yet now *nos maxima Roma terit*, 'mighty Rome grinds us down' (6), and 'life goes to waste in fruitless toil' (8). Can one really achieve *otium* in this poetry, and in this climate? And can that loss be recompensed by urban hyperstimulation? Is there anywhere left where one can truly be 'in exile'? As we saw in chapter 4 on the Saturnalia, conquest may well come at the expense of true freedom and space for the imagination. As Martial puts it at 8.55, as Rome has 'grown greater' with her emperor (*creverit et maior cum duce Roma suo*, 2), the city has stopped producing Vergils; yet let there be Maecenases, and 'your own countryside will give you a Vergil' (*Vergiliumque tibi vel rua rura dabunt*, 6). Similarly, Martial uses a ploughing metaphor to describe poetic production at 1.107.7–8. It is the countryside that spawns art, and artists.

Even the distinction between private and public space can be seen break-
ing down in the *Epigrams*: in 1.3, for example, which is modelled on Horace
*Epistles* 1.20, and the image of slave-like book escaping the safe confines of
his master's study for the excitement of the outside world, the *libellus* suffers
the same kind of harsh treatment inside as outside – in fact, any spearing it
gets from spiteful critics will be *better* than the cruel erasures of the poet's
pen. In making his verse fully public, and pushing out to the ends of the
earth, Martial must also sacrifice exclusivity, and expose himself to all the
harshness and complexity of a multicultural world. However, this hyper-
trophic poetry is bent on modernising through the reconceptualisation
of space, and sneakily imposes epigrammatic perspectives and restrictions
on *all* Romans. Martial would always rather be a Marsus than a Vergil
(8.55.24). Yet like Vergil in the *Aeneid*, his epic-scale oeuvre reaches out to
an audience of displaced people – travellers, foreigners and trail-blazers –
in search of ways to express new identities in a changed globe.

# *Epilogue*

### Ep. 1.35 *To a Censorious Critic*

So my verse offends you.
'No taste,' you say, 'no dig-
nity,' as though the classroom were my proper sphere.
My lines, Cornelius,
like husbands, have licence
to hone the pleasure point.
No stag-party ballad
goes to a psalm tune, your
Mardi-Gras whore would look
absurd frocked by Dior.
No; what I want in verse
is: scratch where you itch.
Then screw solemnity:
carnival's today. You'd
not castrate my poems,
I hope? Gelded Priá-
pus? There's obscenity!

Dudley Fitts (1903–68)

The American poet and critic Dudley Fitts, a leading voice in the early twentieth-century revitalisation of classics through translation, published this version of *Epigram* 1.35 in 1956, in an anthology called (count 'em) *Sixty Poems of Martial in Translation*.[1] His decision to translate 1.35 on its own, rather than, or with, 1.34, figures: like most of the other twentieth-century poets who have made Martial theirs, Fitts reminds us of how thrilling it has been to free Martial from his nineteenth-century closet, to put the *libertas* back into *liber* and to celebrate again this poet's 'unsentimental

---

[1] Fitts (1956) 95. In his introductory note on the text (ix), Fitts states that despite the fact that the 'majority' of Martial's poems are 'harmlessly topical', he sets out to draw upon the epigrams' 'acrid vein . . . making no apologies for slanting the evidence'.

treatment of sex and satiric punch'.[2] Modern English lends itself brilliantly
to poems like this, and even better to snappy, one-couplet epigrams like
*Ep.* 3.71, which Tony Harrison translates, under the title 'Twosum', 'Add
one and one together and make TWO: that boy's sore ass + your cock
killing you', or *Ep.* 6.36, which in Fiona Pitt-Kethley's post-feminist hands,
becomes, 'His tool was large and so was his nose. Papylus could smell
it whenever it rose.'[3] Reading 1.35 without 1.34, though, we skip over
all the guilt-tripping, perverse inconsistency that fuels Martial's books.
In this duo, we get a textbook flash or literal spelling out of Martial's
malicious matchmaking, the mating of poems, lines, words and images
which marks his anthropomorphic anthologising. In 1.34, as I discussed
in chapter 1, the poet takes on Cato's censorious pose (the Cato who is
invited to watch Book 1's stage show in the epistolary preface, as long as
he doesn't walk out in disgust), and tells exhibitionist prostitute Lesbia to
'learn some modesty' (*disce pudorem*, 7). Lesbia's naughty pleasure in being
watched in 1.34, together with Martial's role as over-strict pimp, and the
reminder that we too, like the awkwardly placed Cato, have been set up as
spectators of this risqué epigrammatic mime, slot into and jar against the
defiant willy-waving of 1.35, where Cornelius is the censor, and Martial the
priapic customer maintaining that epigram should no more be neutered
than Lesbia's talents veiled. Taken together, the two poems perform an
absurd contradiction, a chalk-and-cheese, water-and-wine combination
that this book, especially, flaunts. Yet they are also perfect partners: the
horny, voyeuristic poet in 1.35 is Lesbia's post-Catullan soulmate and ideal
customer in 1.34. The first poem's doors (and Lesbia's body) are open to
the interjection and metaphors of the second; 1.34 is the passive, elegiac
female to 1.35's iambic maleness, a row of castrated hexameters (after Ovid
*Amores* 1.1) threatening 1.35's wounded scazons. Even 1.34's *dura censura*
(9) is echoed in the paradoxically inflexible 'law' (*lex*, 10) of shameless
misrule in 1.35 – a wedding song without the words, indeed,[4] as well as
a prime example of how imperial carnival, like epigram, marries carefree
licence with bitter constraint. Martial's epigrams, 1.35 tells us, are husbands
and wives,[5] boys and girls, all itching for (inter-)action: therein lies your
pleasure, spectator-reader.

---

[2] I quote Sullivan and Boyle (1996) 305.
[3] From Tony Harrison, *U.S. Martial* (1981) and Fiona Pitt-Kethley, *The Literary Companion to Sex*
(1992). Both poems are collected in Sullivan and Boyle (1996), 364, 394.
[4] 1.35.6–7: *quid si me iubeas thalassionem / verbis dicere non thalassionis?* ('do you expect me to sing a
wedding song without using any wedding song words?')
[5] See 1.35.3–4: *sed hi libelli, / tamquam coniungibus suis mariti* . . . ('but these books are like husbands
with their wives . . .')

On every level, this book has shown, Martial puts on seductive display epigram's ambition to enact the sociality of urban life, to make Rome rise out of epigram's architecture and gestures. Throughout, I have been selling you a Martial we can't ignore, who never stops reminding us what we are missing even as he encourages haphazard editing and lazy reading. Martial must count as the most interesting commentator we have not only on the city of Rome in the first century AD, but also on what it means to be a poet in this new, advanced, multicultural world. So from where we stand now, does he look like an imperial triumph, an 'unexpected classic', as J. P. Sullivan names him in his 1991 monograph? Despite our looser, twenty-first-century morals, it's not hard to see why Martial might still cause offence, even though that's what we love about him. 'As though the classroom were my proper sphere . . .', he jokes. But can schoolteachers dole out 'straight' Catullus, or Ovid for that matter, if their pupils also get to read the *Epigrams* on the side, and not just in a heavily edited collection? In many ways, Martial does his best to ruin Latin literature as we know it, dumbing down, graffiti-ing over, in short *epigrammatising* everything from Vergil's *Aeneid* to Ovid's *Metamorphoses* and Horace's *Odes*. His polychromic collections (seek to) make favourites like Vergil's ten-poem *Eclogues*, Statius' *Silvae*, containing 5–9 poems a book, or (worst-case scenario, from epigram's standpoint) Horace's 1-poem, 1-book *Ars Poetica*, look impossibly turgid. And we know what Martial does with the epics: the giant, chaotic lump (*massa*) of Ovid's *Metamorphoses* gets parcelled into two lines at 14.192, and a miraculously *brevis membrana* (short bit of parchment) contains the whole of Vergil at 14.186. 'Screw solemnity', he says – is that a recipe for Classics today?

Through the *Epigrams,* which so often emphasise the role readers play in producing and perpetuating poetry, we confront the extent to which the study of ancient Rome is about examining and exercising fantasies about our Western past. We can't read Martial (at least, my point has been, we can't read him through, *perlegere*) without asking what we want Roman literature to be or stand for at the start of the third millennium, and what we reckon counts as 'good poetry', anyway, poetry worth remembering and fighting for – questions that a post-modern age dismissed and tried to forget altogether. At the same time, part of Martial's attraction is that he leaves us feeling powerless to answer such questions with any conviction. It's all here (and often difficult to separate out): the good, the bad, the in between, what leaves us cold, annoys us, or has us clamouring for more. As we have seen in the course of this book, the *Epigrams* come close to announcing the death of poetry and the imagination in post-Julio-Claudian, Flavian Rome: crucially, there is no domain of Ovidian exile in Martial – he plots empire as accessible, manageable and known, just like these mobile, modern poems; myth itself is downgraded and trumped in the microcosmic arena, and those frightening realms of imagined or half-glimpsed monsters have become cartoonish relics of the past. Martial frames epigram as the price literary culture pays for a successful empire, as a side-effect of ubiquitous 'Rome'. But in addition, I've tried to show, he creates a bright new empire of entertainment, and ingenious possibilities for metamorphosis, within epigram's tight, conservative borders. In Martial's endlessly clever play with paradox, we suspect, lies his most exciting offer of *liber*-ation.

# Bibliography

Adams, J. N. (1982) *The Roman Sexual Vocabulary*. London.

Ahl, F. (1984) 'The rider and the horse: politics and power in Roman poetry from Horace to Statius' *ANRW* II.32.1: 40–124.

Akbar Khan, H. (1967) 'Catullus 99 and the other kiss-poems' *Latomus* 26: 609–18.

Anderson, W. S. (1986) 'The theory and practice of poetic arrangement from Vergil to Ovid' in Fraistat (ed.) 44–65.

Austin, C. and Bastianini, G. (2002) *Posidippi Pellaei Quae Supersunt Omnia*. Milan.

Bakhtin, M. (1968) *Rabelais and his World*. Trans. H. Iswolsky. Cambridge, MA.

Barchiesi, A. (1997) *The Poet and the Prince. Ovid and Augustan Discourse*. Berkeley, Los Angeles and London.

 (2005a) 'The search for the perfect book: a PS to the New Posidippus' in Gutzwiller (ed.) 320–42.

 (2005b) 'Centre and periphery' in S. J. Harrison (ed.) *A Companion to Latin Literature*. Oxford. 394–405.

Bardon, J. (1791) *The Epitaph Writer*. Chester.

Barker, C. (2000) *Cultural Studies. Theory and Practice*. London.

Bartsch, S. (1994) *Actors in the Audience. Theatricality and Doublespeak from Nero to Hadrian*. Cambridge, MA.

Barwick, K. (1958) 'Zyklen bei Martial und in der kleinen Gedichten des Catull' *Philologus* 102: 284–318.

Batstone, W. (1998) 'Review of Swann's *Martial's Catullus. The Reception of an Epigrammatic Rival*' *CPh* 93: 286–9.

Beard, M. and Henderson, J. (2001) *Classical Art. From Greece to Rome*. Oxford.

Bernstein, M. (1992) *Bitter Carnival*. Princeton.

Best, E. E. jr. (1969) 'Martial's readers in the Roman world' *CJ* 64: 208–12.

Bing, P. (1988a) 'Theocritus' epigrams on the statues of ancient poets' *A&A* 34: 117–23.

 (1988b) *The Well-read Muse. Present and Past in Callimachus and the Hellenistic Poets*. Hypomnemata 90, Göttingen.

 (1998) 'Between literature and the monuments' in Harder *et al.* (eds.) 21–43.

Blümner, H. (1869) *Die gewerbliche Thätigkeit der Völker des klassischen Altertums*. Leipzig.

Bowra, M. (1938) *Early Greek Elegists*. Oxford.
Boyle, A. J. (ed.) (1988) *The Imperial Muse. To Juvenal through Ovid*. Berwick.
  (1995a) '*Martialis redivivus*. Evaluating the unexpected classic' *Ramus* 24: 82–101.
  (ed.) (1995b) *Roman Literature and Ideology. Ramus Essays for J. P. Sullivan*. Bendigo.
  (2003) 'Introduction' in Boyle and Dominik (eds.) 1–67.
Boyle, A. J. and Dominik, W. J. (eds.) (2003) *Flavian Rome. Culture, Image, Text*. Leiden and Boston.
Boyle, A. J. and Sullivan, J. P. (eds.) (1996) *Martial in English*. Harmondsworth.
Boym, S. (1991) *Death in Quotation Marks. Cultural Myths of the Modern Poet*. Cambridge, MA.
Bramble, J. C. (1982) 'Martial and Juvenal' in E. J. Kenney and W. Clausen (eds.) *The Cambridge History of Classical Literature*, vol. 2. Cambridge. 597–632.
Braund, S. M. (1996) 'The solitary feast – a contradiction in terms?' *BICS* 41: 37–52.
Bridge, R. T. and Lake, E. D. C. (1908) *Select Epigrams of Martial*. Oxford.
Brown, N. O. (1985) *Life against Death. The Psychoanalytic Reading of History*. Middletown, CT.
Bulloch, A. W. (1985) 'Hellenistic Poetry' in P. E. Easterling and B. M. W. Knox (eds.) *The Cambridge History of Classical Literature*, vol 1. Cambridge. 541–621.
Burnikel, W. (1980) *Untersuchungen zur Struktur des Witzepigramms bei Lukillius und Martial*. Wiesbaden.
Busch, S. (1999) *Versus balnearum. Die antike Dichtung über Büder und Baden im römisches Reich*. Stuttgart and Leipzig.
Butrica, J. L. (1983) 'Martial's little Livy (14.190)' *CB* 59: 9–11.
Byrne, S. N. (2001) 'Martial and three imitators: Luxorius, Godfrey of Winchester and Henry of Huntingdon' *CB* 77: 61–73.
Cairns, F. (1973) 'Catullus' *basia* poems (5, 7, 48)' *Mnemosyne* 26: 15–22.
Cameron, A. (1993) *The Greek Anthology from Meleager to Planudes*. Oxford.
  (1995) *Callimachus and his Critics*. Princeton.
Campbell, B. (1969) 'Martial's slain sow poems: an esthetic analysis' *C&M* 30: 347–62.
Carrington, A. G. (1960) *Aspects of Martial's Epigrams*. Windsor.
  (1972) 'Martial' in D. R. Dudley (ed.) *Neronians and Flavians. Silver Latin I*. London and Boston. 236–70.
Carson, A. (1999) *Economy of the Unlost. Reading Simonides of Keos with Paul Celan*. Princeton.
Casali, S. (2005) 'Il popolo dotto, il popolo corrotto. Ricezioni dell'*Ars* (Marziale, Giovenale, la seconda Sulpicia)' in L. Landolfi and P. Monella (eds.) Arte Perennat Amor. *Riflessioni sull'intertestualità ovidiana. L'*Ars Amatoria. Bologna. 13–55.
Cavallo, G., Fedeli, P. and Giordina, A. (eds.) (1991) *Lo spazio letterario di Roma antica*, vol. 3: *La ricezione del testo*. Rome.

Citroni, M. (1968) 'Motivi di polemica letteraria negli epigrammi di Marziale' *DArch* 2: 259–301.

(1969) 'La teoria lessinghiana dell'epigramma e le interpretazioni moderne di Marziale' *Maia* 21: 215–43.

(1975) *M. Valerii Martialis Epigrammaton Liber Primus.* Florence.

(1988) 'Publicazione e dediche dei libri in Marziale' *Maia* 40: 3–39.

(1989) 'Marziale e la letteratura per i Saturnali (poetica dell' intrattenimento e cronologia della publicazione dei libri)' *ICS* 14: 201–26.

Claassen, J. (1999) *Displaced Persons. The Literature of Exile from Cicero to Boethius.* London.

Clairmont, C. W. (1970) *Gravestone and Epigram. Greek Memorials from the Archaic and Classical Periods.* Mainz.

Coiro, A. B. (1988) *Robert Herrick's Hesperides and the Epigram Book Tradition.* Baltimore.

Coleman. K. (1996) 'The emperor Domitian and literature' *ANRW* 2.32.5, 3087–115.

(1998) 'Martial Book 8 and the politics of AD 93' *Proceedings of the Leeds International Seminar* 10: 337–57.

(2006) *M. Valerii Martialis Liber Spectaculorum.* Oxford.

Coleman, R. (1977) *Virgil, Eclogues.* Cambridge.

Colton, R. E. (1991) *Juvenal's Use of Martial's Epigrams.* Amsterdam.

Connors, C. (1994) 'Famous last words: authorship and death in the *Satyricon* and Neronian Rome' in J. Elsner and J. Masters (eds.) *Reflections of Nero.* London. 225–36.

(1998) *Petronius the Poet. Verse and Literary Tradition in the* Satyricon. Cambridge.

(2000) 'Imperial space and time: the literature of leisure' in O. Taplin (ed.) *Literature in the Roman World. A New Perspective.* Oxford. 208–34.

Crowther, N. B. (1979) 'Water and wine as symbols of inspiration' *Mnemosyne* 32: 1–11.

Cuomo, S. (2001) *Ancient Mathematics.* London.

Damon, C. (1992) 'Statius *Silvae* 4.9: *libertas Decembris?*' *ICS* 17: 301–8.

Darwall-Smith, K. (1996) *Emperors and Architecture. A Study of Flavian Rome.* Brussels.

Davies, P. J. E. (2000) *Death and the Emperor. Roman Funerary Monuments from Augustus to Marcus Aurelius.* Austin, TX.

Day, J. W. (1989) 'Rituals in stone: early Greek epigrams and monuments' *JHS* 109: 16–28.

De Man, P. (1979) 'Autobiography as de-facement' *Modern Language Notes* 95(5): 919–30.

(1985) 'Lyrical voice in contemporary theory: Riffaterre and Jauss' in C. Hošek and P. Parker (eds.) *Lyric Poetry. Beyond New Criticism.* New York. 55–72.

Derrida, J. (1978) *Writing and Difference.* Trans. A. Bass. London.

Devlin, D. D. (1980) *Wordsworth and the Poetry of Epitaphs.* London.

Dilke, O. A. W. (1987) *Mathematics and Measurement*. London.

Dinter, M. (2005) 'Epic and epigram: minor heroes in Virgil's *Aeneid*' *CQ* 55(1): 153–69.

Duff, J. W. (1929) *Martial, Realism and Sentiment in the Epigram*. Cambridge.

Dupont, F. (1999) *The Invention of Literature. From Greek Intoxication to the Latin Book*. Trans. J. Lloyd. Baltimore and London.

Duret, L. (1977) 'Martial et la deuxième *Épode* d'Horace: quelque reflection sur l'imitation' *REL* 55: 173ff.

Dyson, S. L. and Prior, R. E. (1995) 'Horace, Martial and Rome: two poetic outsiders read the ancient city' *Arethusa* 28: 245–63.

Edwards, C. (1996) *Writing Rome. Textual Approaches to the City*. Cambridge.

Evans, R. (2003) 'Containment and corruption: the discourse of Flavian empire' in Boyle and Dominik (eds.) 255–76.

Fagan, G. G. (1999) *Bathing in Public in the Roman World*. Michigan.

Fantuzzi, M. and Hunter, R. (eds.) (2004) *Tradition and Innovation in Hellenistic Poetry*. Cambridge.

Farrell, J. (1999) 'The Ovidian *corpus:* poetic body and poetic text' in P. Hardie, A. Barchiesi and S. Hinds (eds.) *Ovidian Transformations. Essays on the Metamorphoses and its Reception*. Cambridge Philological Society Supplement no. 23, Cambridge. 127–41.

Fearnley, H. (1998) 'Reading Martial's Rome'. Dissertation, University of Southern California.

(2003) 'Reading the imperial revolution: Martial *Epigrams* 10' in Boyle and Dominik (eds.) 613–36.

Feeney, D. (1986) 'History and revelation in Vergil's underworld' *PCPS* 32: 1–24.

(1999) '*Mea tempora*: patterning of time in the *Metamorphoses*' in P. Hardie, A. Barchiesi and S. Hinds (eds.) *Ovidian Transformations. Essays on the Metamorphoses and its Reception*. Cambridge Philological Society Supplement no. 23, Cambridge. 13–30.

Ferguson, J. (1963) 'Catullus and Martial' *Proceedings of the African Classical Association* 6: 3–15.

(1970) 'The epigrams of Callimachus' *G&R* 17: 64–80.

Fitts, D. (1956) *Sixty Poems of Martial in Translation*. New York.

Fitzgerald, W. (1995) *Catullan Provocations. Lyric Poetry and the Drama of Position*. Berkeley and Los Angeles.

(2007) *Martial and the World of Epigram*. Chicago.

Fletcher, G. B. A. (1983) 'On Martial' *Latomus* 42, 404–11.

Foucault, M. (1987) *Death and the Labyrinth. The World of Raymond Roussel*. London.

Foulou, A. (1996) 'La Mort et l'au-delà chez Properce' *REL* 74: 155–67.

Fowler, D. P. (1995) 'Martial and the Book' *Ramus* 24: 31–58.

(2000) *Roman Constructions. Readings in Post-Modern Latin*. Oxford.

Fraistat, N. (ed.) (1986) *Poems in their Place. The Intertextuality and Order of Poetic Collections*. Chapel Hill, NC, and London.

France, P. and Kidd, W. (2000) *Death and Memory*. Stirling.

Freudenberg, K. (2001) *Satires of Rome. Threatening Poses from Lucilius to Juvenal*. Cambridge.

(ed.) (2005) *The Cambridge Companion to Roman Satire*. Cambridge.

Friedländer, L. (1886) *M. Valerii Martialis epigrammaton libri*. Leipzig.

Friedländer, P. and Hoffleit, H. B. (1948) *Epigrammata. Greek Inscriptions in Verse from the Beginnings to the Persian Wars*. Berkeley.

Fusi, A. (2006) *M. Valerii Martialis Epigrammaton Liber Tertius*. Hildesheim.

Galán Vioque, G. (2002) *Martial, Book VII. A Commentary*. trans. J. J. Zoltowski. Leiden, Boston and Cologne.

Garber, F. (1988) 'Pastoral spaces' *Texan Studies in Literature and Language* 30: 431–60.

Garrison, D. H. (1978) *Mild Frenzy. A Reading of the Hellenistic Love Epigram*. Wiesbaden.

Garthwaite, J. (1990) 'Martial, Book 6, on Domitian's moral censorship' *Prudentia* 22: 13–22.

(1993) 'The panegyrics of Domitian in Martial Book 9' *Ramus* 22: 78–101.

(1998a) 'Patronage and poetic immortality in Martial, Book 9' *Mnemosyne* 51: 161–75.

(1998b) 'Putting a price on praise: Martial's debate with Domitian in Book 5' in Grewing (ed.) (1998a) 157–72.

(2001) 'Reevaluating epigrammatic cycles in Martial Book 2' *Ramus* 30(1): 46–55.

Geysson, J. W. (1999) 'Sending a book to the Palatine: Martial 1.70 and Ovid' *Mnemosyne* 52: 718–38.

Gifford, T. (1999) *Pastoral*. London.

Girard, R. (1977) *Violence and the Sacred*. Trans. P. Gregory. Baltimore, MD.

Gold, B. K. (ed.) (1982) *Literary and Artistic Patronage in Ancient Rome*. Austin, TX.

Gold, B. K. (2003) '*Accipe divitias et vatum maximus esto*: money, poetry, mendicancy and patronage in Martial' in Boyle and Dominik (eds.) 591–612.

Goldhill, S. (1994) 'The naïve and knowing eye' in S. Goldhill and R. Osborne (eds.) *Art and Text in Ancient Greek Culture*. Cambridge. 197–223.

Gow, A. S. F. and Page, D. L. (eds.) (1965) *The Greek Anthology. Hellenistic Epigram*, 2 vols. Cambridge.

Gowers, E. (1993) *The Loaded Table. Representations of Food in Latin Literature*. Oxford.

(2005) 'The restless companion: Horace, *Satires* 1 and 2' in Freudenberg (ed.) (2005) 48–61.

Gowing, A. M. (2005) *Empire and Memory. The Representation of the Roman Republic in Imperial Literature*. Cambridge.

Greenwood, M. A. P (1998a) 'Martial, gossip and the language of rumour' in Grewing (ed.) (1998a) 278–314.

(1998b) 'Talking to water: an epigram cycle in Martial Book 4 (4.18, 4.22, 4.63)' *RhM* 141: 367–72.

Grewing, F. (1996) 'Möglichkeiten und Grenzen des Vergleichs: Martials *Diadu-menos* und Catulls *Lesbia' Hermes* 124: 333–54.

(1997) *Martial Buch VI. Ein Kommentar.* Göttingen.

(ed.) (1998a) *Toto notus in orbe. Perspektiven der Martial-Interpretation.* Stuttgart.

(1998b) 'Etymologie und etymologische Wortspiele in den Epigrammen Martials' in Grewing (ed.) (1998a) 315–56.

(1999) '*Mundus inversus*: Fiction und Wirklichkeit in Martials Büchern XIII und XIV' *Prometheus* 25: 259–81.

Griffin, J. (1985) *Latin Poets and Roman Life.* London.

Griffin, M. (1976) *Seneca. A Philosopher in Politics.* Oxford.

Griffith, J. G. (1969) 'Juvenal, Statius, and the Flavian Establishment' *G&R* 16: 134–50.

Gunderson, E. (1996) 'The ideology of the arena' *ClAnt.* 15: 113–51.

(2003) 'The Flavian amphitheatre: all the world as stage' in Boyle and Dominik (eds.) 637–58.

Gutzwiller, K. J. (ed.) (1998) *Poetic Garlands. Hellenistic Epigram in Context.* Berkeley.

(ed.) (2005) *The New Posidippus. A Hellenistic Poetry Book.* Oxford.

Habinek, T. (1998) *The Politics of Latin Literature.* Princeton.

Hadley, P. (1991) *Epic to Epigram. An Anthology of Classical Verse.* London.

Hallett, J. P. (1996) '*Nec castrare velis meos libellos*: sexual and poetic *lusus* in Catullus, Martial and the Carmina Priapea' in C. Klodt (ed.) *Satura Lanx. Festschrift für W. A. Frenkel zum 70. Geburtstag.* Hildesheim. 321–44.

Hammond, M. (1972) *The City in the Ancient World.* Cambridge, MA.

Harcum, C. G. (1914) *Roman Cooks.* Baltimore.

Harder, M. A., Regtuit, R. F. and Wakker, G. C. (eds.) (1998) *Genre in Hellenistic Poetry.* Groningen.

Hardie, A. (1983) *Statius and the Silvae. Poets, Patrons and Epideixis in the Greco-Roman World.* London.

(2003) 'Poetry and politics at the games of Domitian' in Boyle and Dominik (eds.) 125–47.

Hardie, P. (1993) *The Epic Successors of Virgil. A Study in the Dynamics of a Tradition.* Cambridge.

(1999) 'Metamorphosis, metaphor and allegory in Latin epic' in M. Beissinger, J. Tylus and S. Wofford (eds.) *Epic Traditions in a Contemporary World. The Poetics of Community.* Berkeley, CA. 89–107.

(2002) *Ovid's Poetics of Illusion.* Cambridge.

Hellems, F. B. R. (1906) *The Epigram and its Greatest Master, Martial.* Colorado.

Helm, O. (1928) *Studien zu Martial.* Stuttgart.

Henderson, J. G. W. (1997) *Figuring out Roman Nobility. Juvenal's Eighth Satire.* Exeter.

(1998) *A Roman Life. Rutilius Gallicus on Paper and in Stone.* Exeter.

(1999a) *Writing Down Rome. Satire, Comedy, and Other Offences in Latin Poetry.* Oxford.

(1999b) 'Who's counting? Catullus by numbers' in Henderson (1999a) 69–92.

(2001) 'On Pliny on Martial on Pliny on Anon (*Epistles* 3.21 / *Epigrams* 10.19). *Ramus* 30: 56–87.

(2002) *Pliny's Statue. The Letters, Self-Portraiture, and Classical Art.* Exeter.

Hennig, J.-L. (2003) *Martial.* Paris.

Henriksén, C. (1998–9) *Martial Book IX. A Commentary*, vols. 1 and 2. Uppsala.

(1998) 'Martial und Statius' in Grewing (ed.) (1998a) 77–118.

(2006) 'Martial's modes of mourning. Sepulchral epitaphs in the *Epigrams*' in Nauta *et al.* (eds.) (2006) 249–367.

Herrman, L. (1962) 'Le "Livre des spectacles" de Martial' *Latomus* 21: 494–504.

Herrnstein Smith, B. (1978) *On the Margins of Discourse.* Chicago and London.

Hinds, S. (1998) *Allusion and Intertext. Dynamics of Appropriation in Roman Poetry.* Cambridge.

(1999) 'Do-it-yourself literary tradition: Statius, Martial and others' *MD* 39: 187–207.

(2007) 'Martial's Ovid/Ovid's Martial' JRS 97, 113–54.

Holzberg, N. (1988) *Martial.* Heidelberg.

(2002) *Martial und das antike Epigramm.* Darmstadt.

(2004–5) 'Martial, the book, and Ovid' *Hermathena* 177/8: 209–24.

Hope, V. M. (2000) 'Contempt and respect. The treatment of the corpse in ancient Rome' in Hope and Marshall (2000) 104–27.

Hope, V. M. and Marshall, E. (2000) *Death and Disease in the Ancient City.* London.

Howell, P. (1980) *A Commentary on Book One of the Epigrams of Martial.* London.

(1995) *Martial Epigrams V.* Warminster.

(1998) 'Martial's return to Spain' in Grewing (ed.) (1998a) 173–86.

Hudson, H. H. (1947) *The Epigram in the English Renaissance.* Princeton.

Humphreys, S. C. and King, H. (eds.) (1981) *Mortality and Immortality. The Anthropology and Archaeology of Death.* London.

Hutchinson, G. O. (1993) *Latin Literature from Seneca to Juvenal. A Critical Study.* Oxford.

Jackson, R. (1988) *Doctors and Diseases in the Roman Empire.* Norman, OK, and London.

Janan, M. (1994) *When the Lamp is Shattered. Desire and Narrative in Catullus.* Illinois.

Johnson, W. R. (2005) 'Small wonders: the poetics of Martial, Book fourteen' in W. Batstone and G. Tissol (eds.) *Defining Genre and Gender in Latin literature.* New York. 139–50.

Jones, F. L. (1935) 'Martial, the client' *CJ* 30: 355–61.

Jones, W. B. (1992) *The Emperor Domitian.* London.

Kay, N. M. (1985) *Martial Book XI.* London.

Kenney, E. J. (1964) 'Erotion again' *G&R* 11: 77–81.

(1982) 'Books and readers in the ancient world' in E. J. Kenney and W. Clausen (eds.) *The Cambridge History of Latin Literature*, vol 2. Cambridge. 3–32.

Kerenyi, C. (1962) *The Religion of the Greeks and the Romans.* Trans. C. Holme. London.

Knox, P. E. (1985) 'Wine, water and Callimachean poetics' *HSCP* 89: 107–19.
  (2006) 'Big names in Martial' *CQ* 101(3): 299–300.
Kübler-Ross, E. (1970) *On Death and Dying*. London.
Kurke, L. (1991) *The Traffic in Praise. Pindar and the Poetics of Social Economy*. Ithaca, NY.
Lattimore, R. (1962) *Themes in Greek and Latin Epitaphs*. Urbana, IL.
Laurens, P. (1965) 'Martial et l'épigramme grecque du 1er siècle ap. J.-C.' *REL* 43: 315–41.
  (1989) *L'Abeille dans l'ombre: célébration de l'épigramme de l'époque Alexandrine à la fin de la Renaissance*. Paris.
Leary, T. L. (1996) *The Apophoreta. Martial Book 14*. London.
  (1998) 'Martial's early Saturnalian verse' in Grewing (ed.) (1998a) 37–47.
  (2001) *The Xenia. Martial Book 13*. London.
Lehan, R. (1998) *The City in Literature. An Intellectual and Cultural History*. Berkeley and Los Angeles.
Lilja, S. (1972) *The Treatment of Odours in the Poetry of Antiquity*. Helsinki.
Lindsay, W. M. (1903) *M. Val. Martialis Epigrammata*. Oxford.
Lorenz, S. (2002) *Erotik und Panegyric. Martials epigrammatische Kaiser*. Classica Monacensia 23, Tübingen.
  (2004) 'Waterscape with black and white: epigrams, cycles and webs in Martial's *Epigrammaton liber quartus*' *AJPH* 125: 255–78.
Lowrie, M. (1997) *Horace's Narrative Odes*. Oxford.
Maguire, H. (1996) *Image and Imagination. The Byzantine Epigram as Evidence for Viewer Response*. Toronto.
Malamud, M. A. (1995) 'Happy birthday dead Lucan: (p)raising the dead in *Silvae* 2.7' in Boyle (ed.) (1995b) 169–98.
Malnati, T. P. (1987) 'Juvenal and Martial on social mobility' *CJ* 83: 133–41.
Manley, L. (1985) 'Proverbs, epigrams and urbanity in Renaissance London', *English Literary Renaissance* 15: 247–76.
Mendell, C. W. (1922) 'Martial and the satiric epigram' *CP* 17: 1–20.
Merli, E. (1993) 'Ordinamento degli epigrammi e strategie cortigiane negli esordi dei libri I–XII di Marziale' *Maia* 45: 229–56.
  (1998) 'Epigrammzyklen und "serielle Lektüre" in den Büchern Martials. Überlegungen und Beispiele' in Grewing (ed.) (1998a) 139–56.
  (2006) 'Identity and irony. Martial's tenth book, Horace, and the tradition of Roman satire' in Nauta *et al.* (eds.) (2006) 257–70.
Mills-Courts, K. (1990) *Poetry as Epitaph. Representation and Poetic Language*. Baton Rouge, LA, and London.
Mohler, S. L. (1927–8) 'Apophoreta' *CJ* 23: 248–57.
Moreau, P. (1978) '*Osculum, basium, savium*' *RPh* 52: 87–97.
Moretti, G. (1962) 'L'arena, Cesare e il mito: appunti sul *De Spectaculis* di Marziale' *Maia* 44: 55–63.
Morgan, L. (1997) '*Achilleae comae*: hair and heroism according to Domitian' *CQ* 47: 209–14.

Morris, I. (1992) *Death-Ritual and Social Structure in Classical Antiquity.* Cambridge.

Murray, O. and Tecusan, M. (1995) *In Vino Veritas.* Rome.

Nadeau, Y. (1984) 'Catullus' sparrow, Martial, Juvenal and Ovid' *Latomus* 43: 861–8.

Nagle, B. R. (1980) *The Poetics of Exile.* Brussels.

Nauta, R. R (2002) *Poetry for Patrons. Literary Communication in the Age of Domitian.* Leiden, Boston and Cologne.

Nauta, R. R., Van Dam, H.-J. and Smolenaars, J. J. L. (eds.) (2006) *Flavian Poetry.* Leiden and Boston.

Newlands, C. (2002) *Statius' Silvae and the Poetics of Empire.* New York.
   (1997) 'The role of the book in *Tristia* 3.1' *Ramus* 26: 57–79.

Newman, J. K. (1990) *Roman Catullus and the Modification of the Alexandrian Sensibility.* Hildesheim.

Newmyer, S. (1984) 'The triumph of art over nature. Martial and Statius on Flavian aesthetics' *Helios* 11(1): 1–7.

Nielsen, I. (1990) *Thermae et balnea. The Architecture and Cultural History of Roman Public Baths.* Aarhus.

Nisbet, G. (2003) *Greek Epigram in the Roman Empire. Martial's Forgotten Rivals.* Oxford.

Nisbet, R. G. M. and Rudd, N. (2004) *A Commentary on Horace: Odes Book III.* Oxford.

Nixon, P. (1927) *Martial and the Modern Epigram.* London, Calcutta and Sydney.

Ogilvie, R. M. (1970) *A Commentory on Livy Books 1–5*, 2nd edn. Oxford.

Pailler, J.-M. (1990) 'Le Poète, le prince e l'arène: à propos du "Livre des Spectacles" de Martial' in C. Domergue, C. Landes and J.-M. Pailler (eds.) *Spectacula*, vol. 1: *Gladiateurs et amphithéâtres.* Lattes, 179–83.

Panofsky, E. (1939) *Studies in Iconology.* New York and Oxford.

Pasoli, E. (1970–2) 'Cuochi, convitati, carta nella critica letteraria di Marziale' *MusCrit* 5–7: 188–93.

Paukstadt, R. (1876) *De Martiale Catulli Imitatore.* Dissertation, Halle.

Pavlovskis, Z. (1973) *Man in an Artificial Landscape.* Mnemosyne Suppl. 25. Leiden.

Pitcher, R. A. (1984) 'Flaccus, friend of Martial' *Latomus* 43: 414–23.
   (1998) 'Martial's debt to Ovid' in Grewing (ed.) (1998a), 59–76.

Plass, P. (1985) 'An aspect of epigrammatic wit in Martial and Tacitus' *Arethusa* 18: 187–210.

Poinar, G. O. (1992) *Life in Amber.* Stanford, CA.

Pomeroy, A. J. (1991) *The Appropriate Comment. Death Notices in the Ancient Historians.* Frankfurt, Bern, New York and Paris.

Pott, J. A. and Wright, F. A. (1925) *Martial. The Twelve Books of Epigrams.* London and New York.

Preston, K. (1920) 'Martial and formal literary criticism' *CPh* 15: 340–52.

Prinz, K. (1911) *Martial und die griechische Epigrammatik.* Vienna and Leipzig.

Prior, R. E. (1996) 'Going around hungry: topography and poetics in Martial 2.14' *AJPH* 117: 121–41.

Quinn, K. (1982) 'The poet and his audience in the Augustan age' *ANRW* 30.1: 75–180.

Richlin, A. (1981) 'The meaning of *irrumare* in Catullus and Martial' *CP* 76: 40–6.

(1992) *The Garden of Priapus. Sexuality and Aggression in Roman Humour*, rev. edn. Oxford and New York.

Rimell, V. (2002) *Petronius and the Anatomy of Fiction*. Cambridge.

(2007) 'The inward turn: writing, voice and the imperial author in Petronius' in V. Rimell (ed.) *Seeing Tongues, Hearing Scripts. Orality and Representation in the Ancient Novel*. Groningen. 61–85.

(forthcoming) 'Martial's *De Spectaculis* and the arena of Rome' in M. Gale and D. Scourfield (eds.) *Violence in Roman Literature*.

Roman, L. (2001) 'The representation of literary materiality in Martial's *Epigrams*' *JRS* 91: 113–45.

Russell, D. A. (2001) *Quintilian. The Orator's Education Books 1–2*. Cambridge, MA.

Salemme, C. (1976) *Marziale e la 'poetica' degli oggetti*. Naples.

Saller, R. P. (1983) 'Martial on patronage and literature' *CQ* 33(1): 246–57.

Santirocco, M. (1986) *Unity and Design in Horace's Odes*. Chapel Hill, NC.

Saylor, C. (1987) 'Funeral games: the significance of games in the *cena Trimalchionis*' *Latomus* 46: 593–602.

Scàndola, M. (1996) *Marco Valerio Marziale. Epigrammi*. Milan.

Scarborough, J. (1969–70) 'Romans and Physicians' *CJ* 65: 296–306.

Scherf, J. (1998) 'Zur Komposition von Martials Gedichtbüchern 1–12' in Grewing (ed.) (1998a) 119–38.

(2001) *Untersuchungen zur Buchgestaltung Martials*. Munich and Leipzig.

Schiesaro, A. (2003) *The Passions in Play. Thyestes and the Dynamics of Senecan Drama*. Cambridge.

Scodel, J. (1991) *The English Poetic Epitaph. Commemoration and Conflict from Johnson to Wordsworth*. Ithaca, NY, and London.

Scodel, R. (1992) 'Inscription, absence and memory: epic and early epitaph' *SIFC* 10: 57–76.

Segal, C. P. (1968) 'Catullus 5 and 7. A study in complementarities' *AJPH* 89: 284–301.

Selden, D. (1992) '*Caveat lector*. Catullus and the rhetoric of performance' in R. Hexter and D. Selden (eds.) *Innovations of Antiquity*. New York. 461–512.

Shackelton Bailey, D. R. (1993) *Martial Epigrams*. Cambridge, MA, and London.

Sharrock, A. (1994) *Seduction and Repetition in Ovid's Ars Amatoria II*. Oxford.

Sherwin-White, A. N. (1966) *The Letters of Pliny. A Historical and Social Commentary*. Oxford.

Siedschlag, E. (1977) *Zur Form von Martials Epigrammen*. Berlin.

Smith. B. H. (1968) *Poetic Closure. A Study of how Poems End*. Chicago.

Spaeth, J. W. (1929) 'Martial looks at his world' *CJ* 24: 361–73.

Spisak, A. L. (1994a) 'Martial 6.61: Callimachean poetics revalued' *TAPA* 124: 291–308.

(1994b) 'Martial's theatrum of power pornography' *SyllClass* 5: 79–89.

(1997) 'Martial's special relation with his reader' in C. Deroux (ed.) *Studies in Latin Literature and Roman History*, vol. 8. Brussels. 352–63.

(1998) 'Gift-giving in Martial' in Grewing (ed.) (1998a) 243–55.

(2002) 'The pastoral ideal in Martial book 10' *CW* 95: 127–41.

Sprenger, B. (1963) 'Zahlenmotive in der Epigrammatik und in verwandten Literaturgattungen alter und neuer Zeit'. Dissertation, Münster.

Stallybrass, P. and White, A. (1986) *The Politics and Poetics of Transgression*. Ithaca, NY.

Stambaugh, J. E. (1988) *The Ancient Roman City*. Baltimore.

Starr, R. J. (1987) 'The circulation of literary texts in the Roman world' *CQ* 37: 213–23.

Stroup, S. C. (2006) 'Invaluable collections: the illusion of poetic presence in Martial's *Xenia* and *Apophoreta*' in Nauta *et al.* (2006) 299–313.

Sullivan, J. P. (1982) *Essays on Roman Satire*. Princeton.

(1983) 'Themes and variations from Martial' *Helix* 18: 47–53.

(1988) 'Martial' in Boyle (ed.) (1988) 177–91.

(1991) *Martial. The Unexpected Classic*. Cambridge.

(1993a) *The Classical Heritage. Martial*. New York and London.

(1993b) 'Form opposed: elegy, epigram, satire' in A. J. Boyle (ed.) *Roman Epic*. London and New York. 143–61.

Swann, B. W. (1994) *Martial's Catullus. The Reception of an Epigrammatic Rival*. Hildesheim.

(1998) '*Sic scribit Catullus*. The importance of Catullus for Martial's *Epigrams*' in Grewing (ed.) (1998a) 48–58.

Szelest, H. (1974) 'Domitian and Martial' *Eos* 62: 105–14.

(1999) 'Ovid und Martial' in Schubert, W. (ed.) *Ovid. Werk und Wirkung. Festgabe für Michael von Albrecht zum 65. Geburtstag*. Frankfurt-am-Main, 861–4.

Tanner, R. G. (1986a) 'Levels of intent in Martial' *ANRW* II.32.4: 2624–77.

(1986b) 'Epic tradition and epigram in Statius' *ANRW* II.32.5: 3020–46.

Tarán, S. L. (1979) *The Art of Variation in the Hellenistic Epigram*. Leiden.

Thomas, R. F. (1998) 'Melodious tears: sepulchral epigram and generic mobility' in Harder, Regtuit and Wakker (eds.) 205–23.

Toynbee, J. M. C. (1971) *Death and Burial in the Roman World*. London.

Turner, V. (1969) *The Ritual Process. Structure and Anti-Structure*. Ithaca, NY.

Ullman, B. L. (1941) '*Apophoreta* in Petronius and Martial' *CP* 36: 346–55.

Valette-Cognac, E. (1997) *La Lecture à Rome*. Paris.

Van der Valk, H. L. M. (1957) 'On the edition of books in antiquity' *VChr* 11: 1–10.

Van Sickle, J. (1980) 'The book-roll and some conventions of the poetic book' *Arethusa* 13: 5–42.

(1981) 'Poetics of opening and closure in Meleager, Catullus and Gallus' *CW* 75: 65–75.

Vermeule, E. (1979) *Aspects of Death in Early Greek Art and Poetry*. Berkeley and Los Angeles.

Vernant, J. P. (1981) 'Death with two faces' trans. J. Lloyd, in S. C. Humphreys and H. King (eds.) *Mortality and Immortality. The Anthropology and Archaeology of Death*. London. 285–91.

Videau-Delibes, A. (1991) *Les Tristes d'Ovide et l'élégie romaine. Une poétique de la rupture*. Paris.

Walker, S. (1985) *Memorials to the Roman Dead*. London.

Wallace-Hadrill, A. (1989) *Patronage in Ancient Society*. London.

Walsh, G. B. (1991) 'Callimachean passages: the rhetoric of epitaph in epigram' *Arethusa* 24: 77–105.

Waters, K. H. (1963) 'The second dynasty of Rome' *Phoenix* 17(3): 198–218.

(1964) 'The character of Domitian' *Phoenix* 18(1): 49–77.

Watson, L. (1998) 'Martial 8.21, literary *lusus,* and imperial panegyric' *PLLS* 10: 337–57.

Watson, L. and Watson, P. A. (2003) *Martial. Select Epigrams*. Cambridge.

Watson, P. A. (1998) 'Ignorant Euctus. Wit and literary allusion in Martial 8.6' *Mnemosyne* 51: 30–40.

(2001) 'Martial's snake in amber: ekphrasis or poetic fantasy?' *Latomus* 60: 938–43.

Weber, F. P. (1914) *Aspects of Death and Correlated Aspects of Life in Art, Epigram and Poetry*. London.

Whaley, J. (ed.) (1981) *Mirrors of Mortality. Studies in the Social History of Death*. Rochester.

Whigham, P. (1985) *Martial. Letter to Juvenal and Other Poems*. London.

Whipple, T. K. (1925) *Martial and the English Epigram from Sir Thomas Wyatt to Ben Jonson*. California Publications in Modern Philology 10. Berkeley, CA.

White, P. (1974) 'The presentation and dedication of the *Silvae* and the *Epigrams*' *JRS* 64: 40–61.

(1975) 'The friends of Martial, Statius and Pliny and the dispersal of patronage' *HSCP* 79: 265–300.

(1978) '*Amicitia* and the profession of poetry in early imperial Rome' *JRS* 68: 74–92.

(1982) 'Positions for poets in early imperial Rome' in B. Gold (ed.) *Literary and Artistic Patronage in Ancient Rome*. Austin, TX. 50–66.

(1996) 'Martial and pre-publication texts' *EMC* 40 n.s. 15: 397–412.

Wickkiser, B. L. (1999) 'Famous last words: Putting Ovid's sphragis back into the *Metamorphoses*' *MD* 42: 113–42.

Williams, C. (2002a) 'Ovid, Martial and poetic immortality. Traces of *Amores* 1.15 in the epigrams' *Arethusa* 35: 417–33.

(2002b) '*Sit nequior omnibus libellis*: text, poet and reader in the epigrams of Martial' *Philologus* 146: 150–71.

(2004) *Martial Epigrams Book 2. A Commentary*. Oxford.

(2006) 'Identified quotations and literary models: the example of Martial 2.41' in Nauta *et al.* (eds.) (2006) 329–48.

Williams, G. D. (1994) *Banished Voices. Readings in Ovid's Exile Poetry.* Cambridge.

Wiseman, T. P. (1985) *Catullus and his World. A Reappraisal.* Cambridge.

Woolf, G. (1996) 'Monumental writing and the expansion of Roman society in the early Roman empire' *JRS* 86: 22–39.

Yegül, F. (1992) *Baths and Bathing in Classical Antiquity.* New York.

Zingerle, A. (1877) *Martial's Ovid-Studien.* Innsbruck.

# Index of Epigrams *discussed*

As most of the Epigrams are very short, where I have discussed only specific lines I have indexed them under the whole poem.

225

# Index of subjects

amber 82–6
anaphrodisiacs 151–5
*augere* 128
Augustus 20, 57, 62, 63, 75, 164, 167, 168,
    193
    as epigrammatist 167

beastification 60–3
*bis* 76–8
book
    the ideal 12
    personifications of 9, 25, 27, 30, 47, 130, 140,
        165, 166, 182, 208
    structure of 11–12, 22, 49–50, 138–9

Callimachean aesthetics 10, 26, 88, 94, 164,
    181
carnival (*see* Saturnalia)
    theories of 142, 143
carnivalesque reading 17, 25, 50, 207, 210
city, the
    modern concepts of 2, 20–4
Colosseum, the 9, 60, 62, 64–82, 89, 116–19, 185,
    199, 200, 205
contagion, 12, 14, 22–5, 51, 151–2, 175
copulating poems 208
counting (*see also* maths) 16
    and literature 98–9
    and names 99–100, 126–9
    and power 96–9
    and reading/writing epigram 102–3, 124–5,
        130, 139, 167, 177
    and reality 96, 103, 108
    and Roman identity 97–9
    and seduction 124, 131–9, 169–72, 174,
        177–8
counting down 103–11

*damnatio memoriae* 65, 71–2, 142, 143
dating (of *Epigrams* 12) 191–2

death
    and epigram 52–93, 209
    and exile 59, 74, 76, 78–80, 184
    life after 13, 53, 65–70, 82, 184
    and Martial's Rome 15
    and Neronian literature 56–7
    and representation 54
disease and health, 19–24
Domitian 24–5, 65–7, 71, 72, 74, 126–9, 142–3,
    147, 150, 152, 154–6, 166, 183–5, 188, 190,
    195, 200
drunkenness 34–40, 53, 88, 154

epigram, history of 6–7
epilogues/endings 68–70, 80–2, 91–3, 150
epitaphs and epitaphic rhetoric 51–93, 107
exile 8–9, 16, 28, 59, 74–6, 78–80, 89, 159, 165–8,
    182, 184–9, 201, 202, 205, 209

*fama* 59–65, 71, 76, 117, 183
fame culture 1–2, 42
fingers, uses of 30–2, 177–8
food, as metaphor for epigram 111, 145, 149
foreigners, as Romans 196, 198–9, 203
*furta* 11, 44, 48

geography, Roman interest in 188
girls, and birds 47
    as poems 36

hare, as figure for epigrammatist 204–5
hierarchy and social/poetic order 11, 22
hyperallusivity 11, 178

*interponere* 38, 45
intertextuality 13, 40–50, 165, 179
*iugulare* 34, 38

Julio-Claudian (vs. Flavian) dynasty 13, 14,
    117–22, 129

kissing 59, 131, 151, 163, 165, 169–80
  stinky 19, 24, 131–4, 173–5, 180, 197

*limina* 24–7

Maecenas, the absence of 9, 103, 164, 193, 205
Martial, as modern poet 1–3
  in translation 3, 207–8
masturbation 109–11
maths (*see also* counting) 94–138
metamorphosis 12, 49–50, 58, 83, 85, 89,
  92
microcosms 9, 62, 64, 89, 182, 200, 205
mixing, social/poetic 19–50
money 96–9, 111
monumentality 7, 15, 33, 51–93
myth, trumping of 60–3, 114, 210

Nerva 162–80, 190, 191, 193, 195
*nihil* 12, 105–11, 153
noses
  aggressive 65, 146
  smelling 146

one vs. many 112–22, 179
oneness 115–17, 179
Orpheus 62, 120
*otium* 9, 17, 142, 165, 203, 205
Ovid, after 2, 10

paradox, as defining Martial's aesthetic 10–11, 13,
  50, 52, 54, 64, 93, 112–14, 161, 201, 210
pastoral 17, 182, 200–6
phallic epigram 31, 47, 163, 164
plagiarism 9, 23, 27–8, 40–50
politics, Martial's 13–14, 114, 119, 141, 161, 164,
  168, 188
  of reading politics 13–14

readers, role of in Martial 3–4, 11, 27–8, 40, 49,
  51, 101–2, 139, 159
reciprocity, social 101–2, 105, 109
Rome, fantasies of 209
  and country/suburbs 185–6, 200–6
  as woman 196

Saturn 140, 143–4, 157
Saturnalia 5, 16, 35, 50, 82, 88, 101, 140–80, 197,
  205
slave, *libellus* as (*see also* book, personifications
  of) 9, 25, 27, 29, 30, 47, 63, 145
space
  in city 24–7, 29, 142, 152, 174, 180–1
  of empire/epigram 9, 16–17, 64, 94–5, 112,
    181–206
  and poetic mobility 182–9, 201, 203
  post-modern perspectives on 20
Spain, Martial's return to 79–80, 186–7, 190–9,
  202–3
(non-)spectacle, epigram as 28, 30–2, 49, 140
stars, soaring to the 60–5

*tangere* 11, 23, 28–32
teaching Martial 209
threes and twos 126–30
*tota urbs/totus orbis* 25
Trajan 190–3, 195
*turba* 11, 12, 21, 23, 46, 51, 159

*ulcus* 172–4

*variatio* 6, 12, 15, 20, 35, 40, 49, 50, 76
violence, of amphitheatre 60–5, 89, 119–21, 198

water 15, 83–9
wetness 87–9
wine, and water 33–40

Lightning Source UK Ltd.
Milton Keynes UK
UKHW022305040619
343897UK00006B/13/P